This book is to be returned on or before
the last date stamped below

THE UNIVERSITY OF EXETER

EXETER HOUSES 1400—1700

D. PORTMAN

Frontispiece. Nos. 225-226 High Street, built as a pair probably in 1567, with No. 227, of mid-seventeenth century date, beyond them

EXETER HOUSES

1400 — 1700

by

D. PORTMAN, M.A., B.LITT. (OXON), PH.D. (EXON)

728·
0942

UNIVERSITY OF EXETER

1966

ACKNOWLEDGMENTS

I am very much indebted to the many people who kindly allowed me to enter, and often to measure, their homes and business premises. Without their willing co-operation this survey could not have been made. I have benefited from the advice of Professor Frank Barlow, and I am particularly grateful to Mr. A. W. Everett, F.S.A., who has freely placed his remarkable knowledge of local architecture and topography at my disposal. As one who has been a citizen of Exeter for over seventy years, he has been invaluable in supplying information about buildings which have disappeared or have been altered in his lifetime. I must also thank for their help the Exeter City Librarian, Mr. N. S. E. Pugsley, and the staff of the City Library and of the muniment room; Mrs. A. M. Erskine, Exeter Cathedral Archivist; Mr. L. J. Lloyd, Librarian of the University of Exeter; Miss J. Sinar, former Devon County Archivist; and Dr. R. C. Blackie, Curator of the Royal Albert Memorial Museum, Exeter. For the use of certain plans I am obliged to Mr. A. W. Everett, Exeter School Historical Society, and Messrs. Clutton and Drew, Surveyors. I must express my gratitude to my wife for her patient and generous assistance.

Finally, I wish to record my grateful thanks to the Council of Management of the Marc Fitch Fund for a generous grant in aid of the publication of this book.

PUBLISHER'S NOTE

Since this book was completed, some houses
mentioned in the text have been demolished

Printed for the University by The Devonshire Press, Torquay

CONTENTS

ILLUSTRATIONS
    Frontispiece: Nos. 225–226 High Street
    List of plates
      Plates 1–39
    List of figures
      Figures i–xx
    MAP OF EXETER showing buildings referred to in the text

ABBREVIATIONS

ECM	Exeter City Muniments
D & C	Muniments of the Dean and Chapter of Exeter Cathedral
DRO	Devon Record Office
TDA	*Transactions of the Devonshire Association for the Advancement of Science, Literature and Art*
DCNQ	*Devon and Cornwall Notes and Queries*
Dn.	Description

LIST OF ILLUSTRATIONS

Plates

LIST OF ILLUSTRATIONS

Figures

INTRODUCTION

Between 1400 and 1700 Exeter was the provincial capital of the south-western peninsula, and one of the principal cities of England. Its position as the county town of Devon, together with the presence of the Cathedral, made it a regional centre for both secular and ecclesiastical administration and a hub of social life, while its geographical location at the meeting point of inland communications with sea-routes to the Continent put it at the very heart of the economic activity of a large, rich hinterland. Exeter's commercial prosperity, based largely on the cloth trade, reached its peak in the early eighteenth century, but during the greater part of our period it nevertheless consistently ranked fourth to sixth in wealth among provincial cities; in the 1520's, for example, only Norwich, Bristol, Newcastle and Coventry ranked above it, in that order.[1] This success was achieved by a population which probably amounted to just under three thousand people at the beginning of the fifteenth century, and which still numbered no more than fifteen or sixteen thousand in 1700.[2] But it was a society in which grave inequalities existed. Civic power and most of the wealth were concentrated in the hands of a small upper class, consisting mainly of merchants, who represented only about six per cent of the total population; the 'middle class' added up to no more than twenty per cent, while the large majority of the citizens lived in dire poverty.[3]

By 1400 the pattern of Exeter's physical development was well established. The medieval stone walls, over a mile and a half in length and raised on the lines of the original Roman defences, enclosed an area of just under ninety-three acres, taking in the whole of the gravel-topped hill on which the city stood and sweeping down to the west towards the river below. But though they defined the city so that, in Hooker's words, ' It is not altogether fowre square but declinethe somewhat towards a rowndenes ',[4] they did not confine it. Already by the twelfth century the cutting of leats, or watercourses, in the river marshes outside the West Gate had led to the creation of Exe Island, and with the use of the new water power to drive the city's fulling and corn mills a

---

[1] W. G. Hoskins, ' English Provincial Towns in the Early Sixteenth Century ', *Trans. Royal Hist. Soc.*, 5th Series, VI (1956), 4.

[2] Estimates of population figures before the first Census of 1801 are usually highly debatable, and these represent a reasonable compromise between various assessments (see R. Pickard, *Population and Epidemics of Exeter in Pre-Census Times* (1947); W. G. Hoskins, ' The Population of Exeter ', *DCNQ*, XX (1938-39), 242-247; W. J. Harte, ' Some data for assessing the population of Exeter at the end of the Seventeenth Century ', *ibid.*, 210-214). St. Thomas, the large parish directly across the river, was economically closely associated with Exeter but did not come under the city's jurisdiction. According to an official return it contained 1,705 inhabitants in 1695 (*Exeter in the Seventeenth Century: Tax and Rate Assessments 1602-1699*, ed. W. G. Hoskins, Devon & Cornwall Record Society, New Series, II (1957), xvi).

[3] Wallace T. MacCaffrey, *Exeter, 1540-1640* (1958), 249.

[4] John Hooker, *The Description of the Citie of Excester*, ed. W. J. Harte, J. W. Schopp and H. Tapley-Soper, Devon & Cornwall Record Society, II (1919), 30. Hooker was Chamberlain of the city from 1555 to 1600.

flourishing industrial quarter had grown up on the reclaimed land. Further
suburbs were also developing outside the other gates at an early date, particularly to the east in the St. Sidwell's area, which housed a high proportion of the
working class, and by the 1520's a quarter of the citizens were living outside the
walls.[1] Later on, in the seventeenth century when Exeter was expanding rapidly,
it was these same areas which assimilated the bulk of the increasing population.

If Exeter encroached on the surrounding countryside this was because, in a
sense, the countryside had already invaded the city which, like so many of its
contemporaries, was remarkable for the amount of open space left within the
walls. Hooker's well-known map of 1587 gives us some idea of how extensive
this was.[2] The Cathedral, the castle and Bedford House, with their respective
precincts, dominated the eastern half of the city, while the south-western quarter
near the Snayle Tower was taken up largely by Friernhay, with its racks for
drying the partly finished cloths, and by the grounds of the then dissolved St.
Nicholas Priory. In addition there were many large gardens and orchards
scattered about. Altogether about one third of the enclosed area was open
space and remained so throughout the whole of the period, for it was not until
the late eighteenth century that the built-up intramural sectors began to be
appreciably extended.

The houses in the suburbs, set among a patchwork of gardens, closes and
orchards, lined the main approaches to the city and formed no set pattern.
But the arrangement within the walls was much more formal, dictated as it was
by a street plan which, for convenience's sake, tended towards the gridiron
type. Thoroughfares lay roughly parallel with or at right angles to each other,
and were further connected by a maze of narrow alleys. In this restricted
setting only the town houses of the aristocracy and of ecclesiastical dignitaries
could command sufficient space to spread themselves, as they did in the Close
(fig. iii). Elsewhere the townspeople, from the merchants downwards, who
lived in the main streets were forced to accommodate themselves on narrow,
rectangular sites, though wider ones were often to be found in some of the
back streets, where the pressure on space was less severe. At worst sites might
be large enough to contain only the house itself, but the more fortunate
inhabitants had a tenement strip long enough to take a private garden at the
rear, though in the central areas these have long since been sacrificed (figs.
i–iii). The plan of Exeter represented a particular response to a particular
set of topographical, economic and social circumstances, and the success of this
can be judged by the fact that most of the old property boundaries remained
substantially unchanged until the Second World War.

---

[1] MacCaffrey, 13.

[2] This is the earliest known printed map of Exeter. It exists in two states, with certain minor differences
between them. The first version is crudely coloured and is now in the British Museum; the second,
uncoloured, is kept in the Guildhall, Exeter. See K. M. Constable, ' The Early Printed Maps of
Exeter 1587-1724 ', *TDA*, LXIV (1932).

PART I — 1400 - 1550

HOUSE PLANS

It is now impossible to give anything like a complete account of domestic architecture and home life in Exeter between 1400 and 1550: too much has disappeared. But a fair proportion of physical evidence still survives from the fifteenth century, particularly in the Close, and there is a good selection of documentary material—largely in the form of leases, surveys, accounts, maps and drawings deposited in the Cathedral and city archives—which in fact goes back to well before 1300. Altogether the sources are sufficient to indicate many of the major features during the period.

Of course, nothing now remains of the homes of the labouring poor, who made up what was by far the greatest part of the city's population at that time. Their dwellings, though of a constant design, must have had a very short life, for they consisted almost certainly of one-roomed huts constructed of cob or elementary timber-framing, with thatched roofs. They were to be found particularly in the extramural areas of St. Sidwell's and Exe Island.

RECTANGULAR HOUSE   Among the more substantial dwellings there was one type which also persisted throughout the entire period. This was of rectangular plan, standing at right-angles to the street and presenting its gable to it. It was two or three storeys high with one large room or two small ones on each floor, and in a minority of cases there was also a cellar below. The chimney-stack was placed in a rear or side wall, and the stairs were in a rear corner. This type found its simplest expression in the ground floor shop with a solar or living-room above, an arrangement for which no physical evidence now exists, though it is recorded in many early deeds, and was clearly established in Exeter long before 1300. For example, a deed of 1262 records a solar over a shop in North Street,[1] and in the late 1270's there were two shops with solars within the city near the West Gate.[2] For centuries buildings like these were a common sight in the main streets, where they were often to be found clustered in sizeable groups. Thus a lease of 1372 describes three shops with living-rooms above in North Street and mentions that there were more shops on both sides,[3] while in the early fifteenth century one property in Guinea Street contained, in addition to a number of deep cellars, seven shops with seven solars above them.[4]

The medieval shop was generally a workplace rather than a store, and took up no more space than was required by the hand-craftsman. It was usually open at the front on the ground floor, and a common feature was the stall or ' bulk ' which stood before it for the display of goods. This began as a remov-

[1] D & C, Deed 166.   [2] D & C, Deed 277a.   [3] ECM, 51/1/2/5a.   [4] D & C, Deed 216.

able piece of furniture but over the years it developed, in a vast number of cases, into a permanent encroachment on what was often already a narrow street.[1] Above the stall a pentice flung the rainwater clear and wooden shutters gave protection when the premises were not in use (pls. 7 and 8). By modern standards shop sizes were very small, and frequently two shops standing side by side shared one solar above; this would be occupied by one of the shopkeepers whilst the other lived elsewhere. No doubt it was a shop of this type, one of a pair, which stood in the High Street in 1336 occupying an area of only five feet by four; but another standing near Broadgate in 1338 must have extended across the whole width of the site, though even this example measured no more than ten feet by six.[2] Similar conditions prevailed after 1400.

Shops as small as these clearly left enough space behind them for another room to be accommodated on the ground floor, and this was the original arrangement of three Exeter houses of rectangular plan which have survived from the latter part of the fifteenth century. They are basically a development of the simple shop and solar type. The most striking of these, No. 16 Edmund Street (pl. 4, fig. x, dn. 15), situated on a corner just outside the West Gate,[3] is three storeys high and has a ground floor area of little more than 10 ft. by 14 ft., but the rather plain arcading and the fireplace there suggest that the space was once occupied by a shop and a kitchen, with stairs or a stair ladder in the south-west corner. Above these was the hall or solar (the living-room), and the second floor was divided into two chambers; in addition there was a cockloft in the roof-space. In fifteenth century terms this was the house of a man of some substance, as were Nos. 11–12 West Street (pl. 5, dn. 33), the other two buildings, which were erected nearby at much the same date.[4] No. 11, also a three-storeyed corner house but a larger one, once had a plan that was almost identical with that at No. 16 Edmund Street. The ground floor was originally taken up by a small shop with a large kitchen behind; there was a first floor hall (having independent access by a side door to Stepcote Hill) and probably two chambers, as there are now, on the top floor. There was a fireplace in the rear wall on each floor, with a staircase in the north rear corner. No. 12 is only about 10 ft. 4 ins. wide internally and is unusual in rising to a height of four storeys. It has been very much altered but it, too, probably had a shop and kitchen on the ground floor, with a hall and chambers above.

It seems that a considerable number of dwellings similar to these three were put up in that quarter of the city at the end of the fifteenth century. The

---

[1]In the 1440's there was a serious dispute between the city and cathedral authorities (see *Letters and Papers of John Shillingford Mayor of Exeter 1447-50*, ed. S. A. Moore, Camden Society (1871), p. 85). The latter were accused of encroaching on High Street by putting up five stalls, extending 60 feet in length by 3 feet in breadth, before the recently erected New Inn. They were guilty of a similar offence in Bullhill Street, i.e. the middle part of South Street. For sixteenth century regulations concerning stalls see Hooker, *Description of the Citie of Excester*, III, 935-936.

[2]W. G. Hoskins, *Two Thousand Years in Exeter* (1960), 45.

[3]This building was removed to the corner opposite St. Mary Steps Church in December 1961.

[4]William Wilford, who made his will in 1413, lived in a house in St. Petrock's which consisted of only a hall, a chamber, a kitchen, a pantry and a buttery. Yet he was a rich merchant who was seven times mayor and represented the city in four parliaments (Hoskins, *Two Thousand Years*, 39-40).

houses which once stood by the Water Gate (pl. 6) were apparently almost identical with No. 16 Edmund Street. Others of rectangular plan were erected beside it in Frog Street,[1] and those in the old Butcher Row were of the same type. Exeter's butchers had already been gathering for generations at the head of Smythen Street (fig. i) when in 1499–1500 the city authorities put up as a municipal enterprise the shops shown in pls. 7 and 8. Nineteen were erected in the first instance and a twentieth was added some time later.[2] It seems that they were almost completely demolished between 1831, when the engraving (pl. 7) first appeared, and 1850 (White's *Directory* of that year does not include a Butcher Row), but the scanty remains of two or three of the buildings are still *in situ* on the north side of Smythen Street. They go back about 21 ft. from the roadway and one section is about 25 ft. wide. This must represent the width of the pairs of buildings presenting their gables to the street in the illustrations, so each shop was about 12 ft. across. Those in the other type of structure shown here, that having its roof parallel with the street (pl. 7), were of much the same size. The dwellings in the Butcher Row were of three storeys, and they probably followed the standard plan of the rectangular house by having one or two rooms on each floor. However, the only direct light thrown on the internal arrangements comes from the probate inventory of a butcher, living in the Butcher Row, who died in 1590.[3] His house contained a hall, a chamber over the hall, a middle chamber, a back chamber and a kitchen. Possibly he had his shop with the kitchen behind on the ground floor, his hall and middle chamber above, with the chamber over the hall and the back chamber on the top floor. Below all these there was a cellar.

The cellar featured in many medieval Exeter houses, even the small ones, and it is frequently recorded in early documents. For example, a good number of deeds dating from the thirteenth to the fifteenth century refer to rectangular houses consisting of a cellar with the shop and/or solar above. It is clear, however, that in many, perhaps most, of these cases the cellar followed a standard medieval practice in being only half below ground, so that the floor above it was raised three feet or so above the street level. The entrance to the cellar, which was sometimes graced by a porch, was by a flight of stone steps descending from the street, and it might have another entrance at the rear; the cellar of a corner house might have entrances from both streets. Another external flight of steps, rising from the street, would give access to the living-room overhead. Generally speaking this type of cellar was associated with a vaulted stone ceiling which rendered it fireproof, but it seems that this feature was not common in Exeter. There is no physical evidence of such a ceiling in any surviving domestic building, and the only one recorded as having had 'groined, vaulted undercrofts' is No. 65 High Street.[4]

Probably the most common form of cellar roof consisted simply of wooden

[1] They are no longer there, but they are shown in a drawing, dated 1851, in the City Library.
[2] Note by W. G. Hoskins, *DCNQ*, XXVI (1954-55), 109.
[3] ECM, Orphans' Court Inventory 42.
[4] Harbottle Reed, ' Demolition of Ancient Buildings of Exeter during the last Half Century ', *TDA*, LXIII (1931), 280. The site is occupied by a branch of the National Provincial Bank and the undercrofts were destroyed when that part of High Street was widened in 1905.

(fig. viii, dn. 8), was also originally a quadrangular house. Here the main hall, now the Law Library, stood at right-angles to the street and at some distance from it, with the private solar range, represented today by an early eighteenth century brick house, lying to the north. The kitchen and other domestic offices were contained in the range fronting the street, and it seems that this was not an uncommon arrangment in medieval Exeter. For example, a deed of 1397–8 refers to the postern next to a kitchen which faced Waterbeer Street,[1] and the kitchen of the Vicars Choral lay to the north of their hall alongside South Street. Furthermore, the original service block (now much altered) at the Deanery (dn. 14) is the nearest part of that building to the Close, and in fact almost abuts it. Space was more freely available about the Cathedral, for yet another quadrangular house still survives in part at No. 7 The Close, now occupied by the Devon and Exeter Institution. A plan of 1764 (fig. ix) shows the building very much as it must have been in the fifteenth century, with the hall lying in the centre of the complex between two court-yards. The two-storeyed front section possibly contained an extension of the private apartments, at least on the first floor, for it communicated directly with the main block by means of a narrow strip of building running along the east side of the forecourt. The great hall, with its imposing entrance porch leading to the screens passage, had cellars or an undercroft at its east end, and the solar was presumably above these. At the other end were the domestic offices, which extended into the rear wing facing the garden; in fact, the kitchen was situated there (that in the front block in 1764 must have been a subsequent arrangement), and was connected to the hall by a continuation of the screens passage. The stables lay at the far end of the site, with direct access to Egypt Lane.

ROOFS

A good number of early roof-trusses, all of fifteenth century date, still remain in Exeter. Most of them are more or less visible or accessible, and they can be divided into several distinctive types. The surviving evidence does not neces-sarily reflect either the individual popularity of these or the full range of choice available during the period, but it does show the quality of the work being done at that time, and also the kinds of house with which various trusses were associated.

SINGLE HAMMER-BEAM   This type is now represented only by the example at the Law Library in the Close (fig. vi, dn. 8), which was erected c. 1450 in what was then the main hall of an imposing quadrangular house. The superb quality of the work makes it exceptional and it may well have been unique in the city, for the hammer-beam roof is not an indigenous West Country type,

---

[1]D & C, Deed 272.

though there is another (now mutilated) of very similar construction at Cadhay, twelve miles away near Ottery St. Mary.[1]

WAGON ROOF   This consists of closely set trussed rafters with curving ribs that are virtually arch-braces describing a rough semi-circle between wall-plate and collar-beam level.   During the fifteenth century it featured in the larger houses where it might be set over a ground floor hall open to the roof, or over a smaller chamber on an upper floor.   The type still survives over the first floor chapel at No. 10 The Close, and also above what was once a principal first floor chamber (an intermediate floor has since been inserted) in the house at the rear of the Devon and Exeter Institution nearby; but in both cases these are concealed by a decorated plaster ceiling applied at a later date.   However other, visible, examples, identical with those that would be found in a private house, remain in buildings which are not strictly domestic, namely at the Tuckers' Hall in Fore Street (erected in 1471) and at the Annuellars' Hall in the Close, both of which also have an inserted floor in what was once a ground floor open hall.   Moulded ribs with carved wooden bosses at the intersections divide the coved ceilings into rectangular panels.   At the Annuellars' Hall these have been plastered over but at the Tuckers' Hall they have been left open, and it may be that both styles were current in fifteenth century Exeter.

ARCH-BRACED ROOF   It seems that this was by far the most popular type of construction used in the larger houses in the fifteenth century, and it can be further divided into two or more sub-types.   The most ornate and certainly the most imposing of these is represented by the roofs still *in situ* over the hall and solar at Bowhill (fig. v), which was erected *c*. 1450; at the Guildhall (between 1468 and 1470); and at the Deanery in the Close, which was probably the latest of them.   These clearly constitute a distinct stylistic group, and one, furthermore, that is closely related to the hammer-beam roof at the Law Library (fig. vi).   The two most important common features are the decorated intermediate ribs between the principal trusses and, in particular, the coved ceiling above collar-beam level, which seems to have been the distinctive mark of a highly skilled school of carpenters which flourished in and around Exeter during the second half of the fifteenth century.[2]

For the many who could not afford workmanship of this quality there was always the plainer type of arch-braced roof, which was also exposed to view from below.   This was introduced as early as 1388, when the hall of the Vicars Choral was erected in South Street, and later, in the fifteenth century, it was used again in a religious institution, over the great guest hall at St. Nicholas Priory, where an intermediate member forming the apex of the arch helps to support the sharply cambered collars.

But the plain arch-braced roof was particularly associated with domestic

[1]There is a drawing of this in *Arch. Journ.*, CXIV (1957), 161. The earlier single hammer-beam roof, erected in the 1390's, which once stood at Dartington Hall, near Totnes, was simpler than that at the Law Library and was not coved above collar-beam level (Anthony Emery, ' Dartington Hall, Devonshire ', *Arch. Journ.*, CXV (1958), 196).

[2]Cf. Cadhay, near Ottery St. Mary, Devon.

architecture. A range of fifteenth century buildings 134 ft. long by 23 ft. 6 ins. wide, which stood in Bear Street before the war, was roofed entirely by this method,[1] as was the so-called Norman House in Preston Street (dn. 26). At the same time it was being employed in most of the houses along the northern side of the Close. The original roof, now inaccessible, which still remains above the front part of No. 6 is in all likelihood of arch-braced construction,[2] and that over No. 9a, formerly the east wing of the quadrangular complex containing the Law Library, certainly is; so is that over the first floor in the north wing of No. 10, and that above the range fronting the Close at No. 11. There is another example further afield, in the west range at Bowhill, though in this case the bays were divided by an intermediate vertical rib, under the influence of the two ornate roofs in the house. Finally, it is possibly significant that the plain arch-braced roof is found in both of the houses with a central hall, Nos. 36 and 38 North Street (fig. xii), erected c. 1500. It is a form of construction that goes well over an open hall, and also over an upper room, and it may well be that the arch-braced roof was an inevitable corollary of this type of house-plan.

Both the ornate and the plain arch-braced roof often, though not inevitably, included wind-braces supporting the lowest, or the two lowest, sets of purlins. In the case of the ornate type these were either entirely straight (Guildhall) or straight with a curved lower end (Bowhill, cf. Law Library), but those in the plain roof were curved, e.g. in the guest hall of St. Nicholas Priory and at No. 36 North Street. In the former example, however, the pairs of wind-braces in both rows form pointed arches, whereas at No. 36 those in the upper row are inverted. Finally, judging from the surviving evidence, a ridge-tree was usually an essential feature of the plain arch-braced roof, but it is lacking in that over No. 9 The Close, the front range of the original quadrangular house. This latter form of construction was possibly used in other buildings at that time, and it may perhaps be tentatively classified as a further sub-type.

CURVED POST This type, employed throughout the period, was clearly illustrated in a building which until the war stood in Egypt Lane (pl. 9), behind the houses on the north side of the Close. Collar-braced principal rafters were halved at the apex, with two pairs of purlins and a ridge-tree passing through them, but the posts were the most striking feature of the arrangement, for they were let into the underside of the principals and were curved at the head to meet them.[3] The design was a good, economical one. In those large houses or parts of houses where no particular display was called for, it enabled reasonably wide spans to be bridged without the use of arch-braces. Furthermore, it was adaptable. In the building at Egypt Lane it

---

[1]Note by A. W. Everett, *DCNQ*, XX (1938-39), 131-132.

[2]It was revealed for a short time some years ago.

[3]According to an agreement of 1478 a malthouse, to be erected near Wynard's almshouses, was to have stone sleeper walls 2 feet high supporting a further 10 feet of mud walling and also the bases of three couples (L. F. Salzman, *Building in England down to 1540* (1952), 540-541). Salzman describes the couples as 'crucks', but there is no evidence of cruck building in Exeter, and it is more likely that they were trusses of the curved post type.

was used over a large, first floor room, but by a simple shortening of the post the truss could be made to accommodate a cockloft, as at No. 166 Fore Street (fig. xi). In other respects, however, this latter case is not strictly identical with the earlier example, for the collar is not cambered, and the three pairs of purlins and the ridge-tree are let into the top side of the principals instead of passing through them.

A modified version of this type of construction was employed when Nos. 1–2 Catherine Street (fig. vii) were erected *c.* 1450, and it enabled a fairly spacious top floor to be accommodated half in the roof of a small house. In this instance the purlins and the ridge-tree were passed through the principals, but because of the small span there was no collar-beam. The greatest divergence, however, came at the head of the post, where the curving part was represented by a separate member. This method was no doubt used in other small dwellings at that time, and it appears that, fifty years later, at least some of those in the Butcher Row had trusses of similar construction. The pair of houses in the centre of pl. 7 had their top floor contained half in the roof, which in all probability was of the curved post type.

TRUSSED RAFTER WITH TIE-BEAM   The roof-trusses previously considered are all of the open type, that is, they were not normally hidden above a flat ceiling. But in the period before 1550 a great many houses, particularly the smaller ones, did have a flat ceiling over the top floor and often contained a cockloft in the triangular roof space above this. Houses of this type were common near the West Gate and in Frog Street at the end of the fifteenth century, and a number of nineteenth century drawings now deposited in the City Library show that these were predominantly of three storeys with cocklofts. Today the only survivors from that period—and they also happen to be in that quarter of the city—are No. 16 Edmund Street and Nos. 11–12 West Street, the original roofs of which are either missing or inaccessible. Nevertheless it is possible to reconstruct, to a large extent, the type of truss that was used in buildings such as these. Clearly there were trussed principal rafters, and the presence of a flat ceiling with a cockloft above presupposes a tie-beam; but there was no collar-beam, for that would have impeded movement and furthermore it was structurally unnecessary. There were purlins (a photograph of No. 16 Edmund Street, taken probably before 1900 when the original gable was *in situ*, shows the butt-ends of three pairs) and almost certainly a ridge-tree. In fact the type of roof-truss used in buildings of this kind all over the city was in all likelihood similar to the later example which still survives at No. 46 High Street (fig. xiii).

INTERIORS

Even the best houses during the period must have been cold and draughty, and all were no doubt sparsely furnished. Many of the timber-framed dwellings, like No. 16 Edmund Street and No. 12 West Street, were also cramped, and in the smaller homes it was necessary to make the fullest possible use of available space. Rooms might serve two or more purposes—living, cooking, sleeping and so on. Most were used in some degree for sleeping and it was not unusual for the principal bedroom to be found on the ground floor.[1] Nevertheless interiors, at least in the larger houses, were often impressive. Those dominated by the great hall took pride of place, but others lacking this feature might have the ceiling of the principal ground floor room divided into rect-angular panels by heavily moulded beams or ribs. Examples of these, all probably of late fifteenth century date, still remain at the White Hart in South Street, where the beams bear a hollow-roll-fillet-ogee-fillet-hollow moulding; in the hall at No. 10 The Close, where the ribs have bosses at the intersections; and at No. 38 Holloway Street, where moulded joists are placed between the beams. Wainscotting and partitioning of oak, elm, poplar and Baltic wood imported from Riga were used when No. 229 High Street was rebuilt in 1394–5,[2] and even smaller houses might have an internal stud-and-panel partition on the ground floor (Nos. 1–2 Catherine Street).

DOORWAYS   It seems that in the better type of timber-framed building these were of simple design, consisting of a plainly chamfered frame enclosing a low-arched head.   An example of this type is still *in situ* at No. 11 West Street, and there was an identical arrangement, with both internal and external doorways, at No. 16 Edmund Street. In the best stone houses the doorway with two-centred arch was popular, and this might be plainly chamfered externally (e.g. remains at corner of South Street and Bear Lane), simply moulded (No. 19 Waterbeer Street) or heavily moulded (Bowhill); single or double doors might be used with these, often with a drawbar behind. The most imposing doorways, however, were those with the four-centred arch, usually associated with double doors. This type was accompanied by decorative treatment of the spandrels, perhaps incorporating heraldic designs, and the arch itself might be enriched with formal floral motifs (e.g. gateway to Law Library).

WINDOWS   The surviving physical evidence, which is all of fifteenth century date, shows that there was considerable variety in the construction of windows in Exeter at that time—in style, size and the materials used. This applies particularly to the stone-framed, square-headed window, which was always placed at the outer face of the wall, with an internal splay of varying width. At its simplest it consisted of a single light up to about 18 ins. wide, with a plain external chamfer (e.g. No. 9 The Close, the former No. 173 Fore Street); a wider aperture resulted in two lights with a central mullion of rectangular section (No. 9 The Close). When it was more elaborately treated the single-light window might have a cinquefoil head (No. 10 The Close), and perhaps a square label in addition (Bowhill). The open halls of the period, with

[1]There is evidence of this in Izacke's account of a certain John Cove, living beside the river, who in a storm had the end of his house washed away by the rising water. His servants, in a chamber over him, were drowned, but he and his wife, who were sleeping in a low room, were carried away in bed and managed to reach the bank (Richard Izacke, *Remarkable Antiquities of the City of Exeter* (1681), 119).

[2]Mrs. A. M. Erskine and D. Portman, ' The History of an Exeter Tenement (229 High Street) ', *TDA*, XCII (1960), 146.

relatively closely set roof-trusses, usually demanded high, square-headed windows which were not too wide. Those at No. 10 The Close are of one or two tall, narrow lights, the latter having a central mullion with external hollow moulding. At Bowhill, however, the two-light hall windows are divided by a transom, with cinquefoiled heads above and below; the external square labels terminate in human heads. But not all windows were narrow. Those in the central halls at Nos. 36 and 38 North Street, on the first floor at No. 166 Fore Street, and on the ground floor at No. 38 Holloway Street, were originally three or four lights in width. Generally speaking windows were of the square-headed type and rather secular in style, but the private chapel found in certain houses in the Close was given windows identical with those used in current church architecture, like that at No. 10 The Close with its two-centred arch and Perpendicular tracery. A small minority of windows projected from the wall. For example, the house occupied by Thomas Elyot, Comptroller of the Royal Customs in the ports of Exeter and Dartmouth at the end of the fifteenth century, was a stone structure with a great three-storeyed bay window fronting the Close, having five forward facing lights and a splayed light on each side.[1] It seems that this building also had an oriel window in the same wall, for in 1500 Elyot was given permission by the Dean and Chapter to insert two stone corbels extending two feet towards the Close, and to raise a window upon them.[2]

Windows with wooden frames were square-headed, usually small and containing only one to three lights. At their plainest they were simply rectangular openings, but in the better houses they, too, were given decorative treatment. No. 11 West Street, for example, has a window of two lights with cinquefoil heads; at No. 16 Edmund Street nearby the single-light and two-light windows also have cinquefoil heads, but with quatrefoil or cusped tracery above; two single-light windows at No. 10 The Close have moulded jambs and a low, triangular head with carved spandrels.

Glass was rare in the fifteenth century and usually too expensive to be widely employed in domestic architecture. Even in the hall at Bowhill it was used, in the form of small leaded panes, only in the upper lights. Wooden shutters were hung in the lower ones, and this was the universal device for keeping out the elements. Intruders were deterred by iron grilles in the windows of those who could afford them (e.g. Nos. 9 and 10 The Close, No. 36 North Street). This state of affairs continued beyond 1500 but by the middle of the sixteenth century stone had been ousted by timber-framing, and the stone-framed window was succeeded almost entirely by its wooden counterpart.

FIREPLACES   During the period the larger houses, belonging to leading merchants and church dignitaries, had fireplaces in all or most of the main rooms —in the hall, kitchen, parlour and principal chamber. This was also the case in houses of middling importance, like those in the Butcher Row for example, but as these had fewer rooms altogether, there might be only one or two fireplaces in a dwelling, and No. 11 West Street was exceptional in having one on all three floors.

[1]This window is now incorporated, in an altered condition, in the Bishop's Palace.
[2]D & C, Deed 372.

Fireplaces were commonly plain but massive in construction, having moulded stone jambs and enormous lintels, with relieving arches above; the lintels, however, were occasionally of wood, as in the room, probably the parlour, at No. 166 Fore Street (fig. xi). The mouldings, in keeping with the general style, were simple. For example, a surviving fireplace (*c.* 1500) on the second floor of No. 11 West Street has an ogee moulding, those at No. 36 North Street (*c.* 1500) are broadly similar with semi-pyramidal stops, that above the hall at No. 10 The Close (second half of the fifteenth century) has a chamfer-fillet-roll moulding. Some of the fireplaces were a little more ambitiously designed. That standing in the open hall at No. 36 North Street is 6 ft. wide and quite high in proportion, with a stone hood corbelled out above it, and may perhaps be taken as typical of the best that one would find in a prosperous merchant's house *c.* 1500.[1] But those erected in the finest houses during the fifteenth century achieved a decorative magnificence that was not to be surpassed for another hundred years or more, and the stone fireplace which stands in the hall of the Deanery—it was originally taken from the Precentor's house—is a good example of these. It has splayed, panelled jambs and a lintel covered with cusped tracery and bearing heraldic shields. Engaged columns terminate in small crocketed pinnacles embracing an embattled parapet of stiff flowers in the Perpendicular style.[2] But perhaps the most impressive fireplaces of all at that time were those in the kitchens of these large houses. They were simply fashioned but of enormous dimensions, ten feet and more across and, together with their ovens, they might take up almost the whole side of a room (fig. iv). The late fifteenth century example still *in situ* at No. 11 The Close has an arch consisting of a double row of voussoirs, like those in the kitchen fireplaces at St. Nicholas Priory, and a great tapering chimney. A flue leads into this from the oven on the right, carrying off the smoke when the oven was being fired for baking. This was not a common feature, but the arrangement was repeated in the detached rear kitchen at No. 38 North Street, which was erected at much the same time.

STAIRS   Between 1400 and 1550 a high proportion, possibly the majority, of houses in the city having upper floors no doubt gained access to them by means of a ladder or an open flight of steep stairs; these were probably similar to the solid oak steps which once led to the cockloft of Nos. 70–71 High Street, erected in the early sixteenth century.[3] Even houses like Nos. 1–2 Catherine Street (fig. vii) and No. 16 Edmund Street (fig. x), though occupied by persons of some importance, hardly had sufficient space on the ground floor to permit a more ambitious arrangement. In the larger houses, however, the newel stair

---

[1]Fireplaces of similar style, but somewhat earlier in date, still remain at No. 68 South Street and at the White Hart Hotel nearby (both examples are on the ground floor and are mutilated). A first floor solar fireplace, formerly part of No. 18 Smythen Street (the building is now missing), can still be seen in the side wall of No. 17.

[2]A similar large, ornate fireplace in the Perpendicular style, also with splayed jambs, still survives in the old Annuellars' Hall behind No. 5 The Close. There was another one in the hall of the Vicars Choral in South Street (see Ethel Lega-Weekes, *Some Studies in the Topography of the Cathedral Close, Exeter* (1915), illustration facing 53).

[3]Reed, 'Demolition of Ancient Buildings of Exeter', 280.

with wooden or stone steps was the common type, rising from one of the principal rooms and often half recessed into the thickness of the wall, though that which once opened off the north end of the hall at Bowhill was contained in a projection. It might be placed in a corner, like that at No. 8 Milk Street (fig. x) and like another fourteenth century example, 7 ft. 6 ins. across, still standing for the most part at the junction of South Street and Bear Lane, but it was also frequently to be found in a side wall. This was the arrangement at No. 166 Fore Street (fig. xi) and formerly at No. 173 nearby.[1] There are surviving examples in the south wing of the old Annuellars' Hall in the Close.

SANITATION There is evidence that this was accepted as a public responsibility at an early date. Already in the twelfth century, and possibly well before that, a stream, recorded unequivocally as the Shitbrook, was being used as a receptacle for the human refuse of the city. It flowed well outside the walls, along the falling ground to the south-east, and after skirting Holy Trinity parish for several hundred yards, entered the Exe at a point some distance below the quay. At a much later date, but before 1467, common latrines were provided by the city authorities over one of the mill-leats on Exe Island, and it seems that ' a long vaulted room, commonly called the Pixey or Fairy House ' on the old Exe Bridge was used for a similar purpose.[2]

It was as well that some public provision was made—though the dependence on naturally running water outside the walls resulted in the common ' necessaries ' being strategically ill-placed—for the vast majority of the citizens in the fifteenth century were left to their own devices. Judging from the surviving physical evidence it was by no means universal for even those living in the better class houses to have their own domestic sanitary arrangements. Possibly, apart from the added expense, which could be considerable, many people were deterred by the sheer difficulty of accommodating a ' garderobe,' as it was called, in what was often a small if substantial dwelling on a restricted site. In Exeter the garderobe was enclosed in a thick stone wall, at the side or rear of the building, though it appears that some were at least partly of timbered construction.[3] A door opened on to the tiny apartment, which contained a wooden seat placed over a shaft that led to the cess-pit below, and it was the clearing of this which usually presented the most serious problem. For example, the garderobe of the fourteenth century house which formerly stood in Milk Street (fig. x) had to be cleared from the street itself, and at Nos. 1–2 Catherine Street (fig. vii) the situation was more complicated. There the garderobes on the ground and first floors were cleared from the cellars below—indeed the small, cramped cellar at No. 2 was constructed solely for this purpose—and as access to these was only by internal stairladders, the operation must have been a distinctly unpleasant one, for workmen and occupants alike.

[1] See photographs of No. 173 (in National Buildings Record) taken after it was damaged in the air raid of 1942.
[2] Hoskins, *Two Thousand Years*, 47.
[3] See D & C, 5151, a roll dated 1379–80 and containing a list of rents and expenses relating to Cathedral property in the city and suburbs. In connection with repairs to David Glasier's house 12 boards costing 3s. were bought for a latrine. See also App. p. 92.

In the year 1463 the sum of 4d. was paid for 'cleaning the common gumphus' of certain Vicars Choral property, possibly Nos. 1–2 Catherine Street.[1] This strange term probably derives from the old dialect word 'gumph', meaning a bad smell, and it emphasises a further serious disadvantage of medieval sanitation. Despite this it seems to have been the long-standing custom in Exeter not to place the garderobe in one of the less frequented parts of the house, but to have it opening directly off the main living-room, either the hall or the solar. On the marriage of their daughter in 1345 Nicholas Holeman, an Exeter mason, and his wife had granted to their son-in-law 'half the solar with a certain latrine (*cloaca*) in the same, which is situated beyond the high table of the hall in our house' in South Street.[2] The garderobe at No. 8 Milk Street stood in a corner of the hall, though it was at least ventilated by a small slit window, but those at Nos. 1–2 Catherine Street did not even have access to fresh air.

The houses in Catherine Street were exceptional in having two garderobes, a feature which may be explained by the fact that the buildings possibly served as small blocks of one-roomed 'flats' for resident priests. An earlier stone house erected nearby in 1404 or soon after, also contained two latrines in the upper rooms,[3] but generally one was considered sufficient. By 1500, however, the practice of erecting garderobes was apparently declining. Neither No. 36 nor No. 38 North Street, both houses of importance, seem to have had one. By 1550, with the growth of an overwhelmingly timber-framed tradition of building and the disappearance of the thick, medieval-type stone wall, the practice had probably died out altogether, with occasional exceptions.

WATER SUPPLY For those who could not get water for themselves there were waterbearers, travelling about the city probably with a handcart or with buckets suspended from a yoke, who would bring it to them. It is likely that Waterbeer Street, recorded as early as 1253, took its name from these—the street of the waterbearers—and the occupation persisted in the city until *c.* 1800.[4] There were also public wells or 'tye-pits', as the deep ones were called, but these eventually proved inadequate to satisfy the needs of a growing population, and more sophisticated methods had to be introduced. By the early thirteenth century water from a spring, well outside the walls in the parish of St. Sidwell's, was being conveyed by means of an underground passage to the Cathedral Close, and in 1226 a third of this was granted to St. Nicholas Priory. In 1346 the Dean and Chapter were making piped water available to the city as well, but in the early fifteenth century the citizens constructed a separate underground passage bringing piped water from St. Sidwell's, down High Street, to a conduit erected in 1441 at the junction of High Street, North Street and South Street.[5]

[1]D & C, VC/22229 m. 2.

[2]Hoskins, *Two Thousand Years*, 46.

[3]See D & C, 5550, fol. 95, a note or abstract of a mason's agreement to build the house. It is reproduced in Salzman, *Building in England*, 477-478.

[4]Thomas Shapter, *The History of the Cholera in Exeter in 1832* (1849), 76-78.

[5]See Aileen Fox, ' The Underground Conduits in Exeter, Exposed During Reconstruction in 1950 ', *TDA*, LXXXIII (1951), 172-178.

The public supply was thus assured, but a fair proportion of people in the better houses were individually well catered for. According to Hooker, in the late sixteenth century water was being piped to sundry canons' houses from the conduit in the Close (shown as a round-topped building in pl. 16), and had been for some time.[1] Meanwhile other householders, lay and clerical, had their own private wells, which were common in a city built upon gravel soils lying over the harder rocks, and which were also very conveniently placed. The majority were to be found in the courtyard, as at No. 10 The Close and No. 166 Fore Street, for example, or in the garden behind the house. But a good number were situated in the cellar, at a point much nearer the water table, which was generally about ten feet below ground level.[2] Nearly all of these have since been filled in, but examples still remain *in situ* at No. 17 Cathedral Yard and at No. 4 The Close, and there are signs of others at No. 16 Cathedral Yard and No. 47 High Street.

BUILDING MATERIALS

COB   This material was made up of a mixture of stiff clay and chopped straw, with the occasional addition of cow-hair. It was then mounted on a dry stone footing, and is virtually impossible to date without the help of associated features; but, so far as is known, none survives in the city from the period before 1550. However, there is evidence of cob building in Devon as early as the thirteenth century,[3] and the material was certainly being used in Exeter by the fifteenth. Because of its cheapness and availability it must have been employed to a great extent in the construction of homes for the labouring poor, and also for the outbuildings of many of the better houses. In fact, in 1478, a malthouse, principally of cob, was constructed by Wynard's almshouses just outside the South Gate. It measured 20 ft. by 14 ft. and was of two storeys; it had sleeper walls two feet high ' of lyme and stone ', and a further ten feet of ' mudwalle ' was raised on these.[4] In all probability substantial houses within the city walls were being erected in cob at that time, and it may well be that the two-storeyed fifteenth century building which formerly stood in Egypt Lane (pl. 9) was representative of these. The walls were largely remade with modern brick, but sections of cob, which was perhaps the original material, still remained.

TIMBER-FRAMING   This method of construction was that most widely employed between 1400 and 1550, for it was comparatively cheap and it was suitable for use in a broad range of buildings, from the home of a poor labourer to that of a prosperous merchant. Few examples of timber-framed buildings survive from

[1]Hooker, *Description of the Citie of Excester*, II, 39.
[2]Hoskins, *Two Thousand Years*, 4. A new well that was dug in Rock Lane (i.e. Coombe Street) in 1670 was 35 feet deep and commonly bore 25 feet of water (Richard Izacke, *Remarkable Antiquities*, 174).
[3]W. G. Hoskins, *Devon* (1954), 268.
[4]Salzman, *Building in England*, 540. There is some cob walling, of uncertain date, in the cellar of No. 2 Catherine Street.

the period, but altogether there is sufficient evidence to indicate some of the major characteristics of the style.

Timber-framed houses were usually small, and before 1550 they were rarely higher than three storeys with cocklofts. They commonly oversailed on the upper floors, by as much as two feet in some places; at No. 16 Edmund Street (pl. 4, fig x, dn. 15), for example, the first floor projects by 1 ft. 11½ins. and the second by about 1 ft. 8 ins. This same building is constructed on massive lines, and considering its small size the timbers used are of huge proportions. The ground floor cross-beam is 13 ins. square in section, the post supporting it measures 12 ins. x 8 ins., the corner post is 13 ins. x 11 ins., and the joists above are 7½ ins. x 6½ ins. The structure is stiffened by pairs of curving braces on the upper floors, which are notable for the fine dragon-beam construction essential to a corner house oversailing on two sides (cf. No. 11 West Street). Other dwellings were erected beside No. 16, in Frog Street, at much the same time, and they were also of three storeys with cocklofts.[1] They were exceptional in projecting only at first floor level, but they, too, were massively constructed, as were their contemporaries outside the Water Gate (pl. 6).[2] However, this was clearly not a universal feature of fifteenth century timber-framing in Exeter. The houses in the Butcher Row were somewhat lighter in construction, and Nos. 11–12 West Street are similar in this respect. But these last two buildings are also stiffened by curved braces—though they have fewer than No. 16 Edmund Street—and it is probable that this feature was fairly general at that time.

Even in the heavily built houses the vertical studs were not closely set, and generally they might be between one and two feet apart. One way in which the spaces were filled is illustrated at No. 16 Edmund Street, where the studs have holes bored into their sides at intervals of seven to nine inches. Cross-rods were fitted into these, and a lattice-work of twigs or wooden slips was woven through them. This was then covered with a mud plaster which, it appears from contemporary building accounts, consisted of wet earth or clay stiffened with chopped straw or, less frequently, with dung.

Judging by the available evidence the style of timber-framing in the city during the period was commonly characterized by its soundness and straight-forward workmanship rather than by its decorative extravagance. Internally beams might be plainly chamfered (No. 16 Edmund Street) with raised hollow stops (No. 36 North Street); externally a corner post, with its triple head supporting an upper floor oversailing on two sides, might again be only simply chamfered, with a moulded base (No. 16 Edmund Street, No. 11 West Street). Of course, there are the finely carved windows at No. 16, and a timber-framed dwelling of late medieval date which once stood on the corner of High Street and North Street had at its angle the figure of St. Peter treading on paganism.[3] But it is likely that the carpenter's highest skills were reserved for the superb

[1]Drawing, dated 1851, in Exeter City Library.

[2]No. 199 High Street (altered in 1904) once had overlooking the courtyard a massive timber-framed wall of fifteenth century date, containing cusp-headed window lights (Reed, ' Demolition of Ancient Buildings of Exeter ', 277 and illustration on 278).

[3]It still survives and is attached to the present building on the site.

roofs in the great stone houses, and in some of the civic and ecclesiastical buildings. The era of splendid timber-framed houses did not begin until the middle of the sixteenth century.

Those who built substantial houses of timber could not altogether avoid stone, and they were forced to include a stone wall, usually that at the rear, to accommodate the fireplaces and the garderobe, if there was one (e.g. No. 16 Edmund Street, Nos. 11–12 West Street, Nos. 1–2 Catherine Street). Other dwellings were virtual hybrids in having side walls of stone, often gracefully corbelled forward on the upper floors, with front, rear and internal walls of timber-framing. This arrangement was found in the smaller buildings like those in the Butcher Row—as the remains in Smythen Street show—and also in larger ones like No. 166 Fore Street (fig. xi) and Nos. 36 and 38 North Street.[1] In the latter side walls of stone were probably necessary to withstand the thrust of the arch-braced roof, but generally, apart from their structural significance, the walls were of tremendous importance in preventing the spreading of fire in a city that was terribly susceptible to this danger. In other cases timber-framing was incorporated in what was predominantly a stone building. As early as the fourteenth century stone houses in Exeter might have a timber-framed facade (No. 8 Milk Street), and this arrangement was repeated in the fifteenth century at No. 9 The Close (pl. 2), though here the timbering was restricted to the oversailing first floor. Other combinations at the time might be more bizarre, like that at the so-called Norman House, for example, a stone structure where only a gable-end was timber-framed.[2]

STONE If timber was the most popular building material, stone was the most important, and houses might almost be graded by the amount that they contained. The very best were constructed entirely of the more expensive material or, like No. 9 The Close, included only a small amount of timber-framing. There was much more stone than timber in great merchant houses like No. 166 Fore Street and Nos. 36 and 38 North Street.

Between 1400 and 1550 a fairly wide variety of building stones were used in the city, most of them local in origin. One of the exceptions was Beer stone, which was brought from twenty miles away to the east, and which had to be transported by sea to Topsham and then by packhorse or by cart to Exeter, so that the cost of carrying it was twice as great as the cost of the stone itself.[3] But this fine, white calcareous sandstone was superior to any other variety near the city, for these were unsuitable for any really detailed work. Consequently in the best houses Beer stone was often used for the dressings of the principal windows and doorways, and it may be seen at its best in the carved, four-centred archway beside No. 9 The Close. Salcombe stone, taken from the greensand quarries a few miles to the west of Beer, was employed in the same specialized way. It was yellowish in colour and similar to Beer stone in consistency, but it was not used to the same extent.

Harder volcanic trap rock was popular during the period, and this basaltic

---

[1]There is also evidence of this in the surviving fifteenth century wall at No. 68 South Street.
[2]Photograph in National Buildings Record.
[3]Hoskins, *Devon*, 260.

material was easily available at quarries in the neighbourhood of Exeter—at Raddon near Thorverton, at Silverton, and at Pocombe, just west of the city. A good proportion of Raddon stone was employed in the rebuilding in 1394–5 of a house formerly on the site of No. 229 High Street. Altogether 143 feet at 4d. a foot and 668 feet at 3d. were purchased and this amounted, with carriage, to £12 11s.[1] However, the most convenient sources of volcanic trap were located only just beyond the city walls, in Northernhay, where there were quarries on both sides of the Longbrook valley which had formerly supplied materials for the Roman defences and for the Norman Rougemont Castle. Trap rock, of a reddish or purplish colour, often with white veins, can still be seen in quantity at Bowhill. It served as a general walling material but some varieties were good enough for the chamfered or simply moulded surrounds of doors and windows, and for plain fireplaces.

Whipton stone, a fine-grained sandstone from another nearby source, had been taken for the Cathedral before 1350, and in 1394–5, when the house mentioned above was being rebuilt at No. 229 High Street, 3,917 stones costing £18 0s. 9d. were purchased from Whipton quarry, far exceeding the amount of Raddon stone being used in the same dwelling.[2] The New Inn in High Street, put up in the 1440's, had in the cellar a well lined with ' red sandstone ',[3] and this probably came from Whipton. However, by far the most popular stone employed for general purposes throughout the period was the red breccia, or ' Heavitree conglomerate ', drawn principally from the Wonford quarry, which was first worked c. 1390 in the adjoining parish of Heavitree. There was another source across the river at Exminster, and no doubt many small quarries were opened up for a time in and about Exeter. The St. Thomas area and the lower part of the city were possibly served by sources in the Alphington neighbourhood. The breccia commonly used consists of compacted angular fragments, a mixture of sedimentary and igneous material, suitable for walling and, like the trap rock, for simply treated fireplaces and door and window surrounds. Its popularity is fairly accurately reflected in the physical evidence that survives today. For example, the fifteenth century stone houses in the Close; the former merchant houses at Nos. 36 and 38 North Street; the stone party walls in the Butcher Row, No. 16 Edmund Street and Nos. 11–12 West Street, are all entirely or principally of the conglomerate variety.

OTHER MATERIALS AND COSTS   The stonework, cob or structural timber-framing constituted the bulk of a house, but a variety of other materials might be involved in its construction. These are noted in detail in a number of scattered building and repair accounts (App., p. 92) which relate to various properties belonging to the Dean and Chapter, and give a lively if limited picture of building operations during the period. Most of the accounts are concerned with incidental repairs, but there is one important exception which deals completely with the erection in 1394–5 of a large town house with shops at No. 229 High Street, and shows not only the kind but the quantity of the

[1] Erskine and Portman, ' History of an Exeter Tenement ', 145.
[2] *Ibid.*
[3] R. Dymond, ' The Old Inns and Taverns of Exeter ', *TDA*, XII (1880), 402.

materials used.[1] Altogether 49,000 roofing slates, at 2s. 5d. a thousand, were required; these cost 30s. 7½d. to transport, and they were probably brought from the slate quarries in the Kingsbridge area, almost forty miles away to the south-west.[2] There were also 73 ' crestys ' or ridge-tiles, valued at 9s. 6d., and one of these, carrying the figure of St. Paul, was apparently placed at the apex of the gable overlooking the street. Probably corresponding figures occupied this position on other houses at that time, and the custom may have persisted unbroken until the seventeenth century, for a similar practice was being followed then. Two other large items were 1,800 loads of sand and 313 quarters of lime, costing £4 10s. and £12 13s. 1d. respectively, and from Branscombe there came 26 loads, valued at 4s. in all, of the fine white gypsum known as plaster of Paris. Among other materials purchased there were laths for roofing and plastering, 11,950 of them at 4½d. to 6d. a hundred; 25,350 lathnails at 15d. or 16d. a thousand; 20,000 plank nails at 6d. a thousand; 6,000 pins at 1½d. or 2d. a thousand; and 3,000 ' hachnayls ' for the doors. Doors were often two or more planks thick, and the hachnayls were the long, large-headed nails used for holding the planks together by clinching; at 3s. 9d. or 4s. 2d. a thousand, they were far more expensive than any of the other varieties. There were also lead and solder for the gutters, and a selection of iron fittings. Bolts and window bars, together with hooks and ' twystys ' for fastenings, cost £4 5s. 6d., and locks accounted for a further 6s. 10d. They were placed, complete with rings and mounting plates, on the doors of the hall, the cellar and the two shops fronting the street.

The other accounts add little to this picture, and as they are concerned with incidental repairs they supply no information about overall building costs. Indeed these are very difficult to discover, and we can obtain only a general idea from the few details that are available. In 1478 the mason Willyam Glydon was paid £8 for building by Wynard's almshouses the malthouse referred to previously. It measured 20 ft. by 14 ft. and was of two storeys, with a roof incorporating three trusses. Stone sleeper walls two feet high were surmounted by a further ten feet of cob. There were doors, windows and a ' stare ', but it seems that the timber was supplied free.[3] Prices must have risen considerably in the fifteenth century, for over seventy years earlier, in 1404, another mason was paid £6 6s. 8d. for constructing a much more important building, a stone house to the north of St. Martin's church. It was of two storeys, apparently, with a gable at each end. There were at least two rooms on the upper floor, which also contained two fireplaces and two latrines; and altogether there were two doors and four windows.[4]

In very general terms, then, during the greater part of the period at least,

---

[1]See Erskine and Portman, ' History of an Exeter Tenement ', for an analysis of this document. For accounts dealing with incidental repairs see D & C, 5151, 5154, 5192, 5193.

[2]Valuable quarries for blue roofing-slates were recorded at Charleton, two miles south-east of Kingsbridge, in 1439, and examples of blue slate have been excavated in medieval contexts at Polsloe Priory, a mile or so from Exeter (E. M. Jope and G. C. Dunning, ' The Use of Blue Slate for Roofing in Medieval England ', Antiquaries Journ., XXXIV (1954), 215-216).

[3]Salzman, Building in England, 540-541.

[4]Ibid., 477-478.

who died leaving orphans, too young to govern their own affairs, the custody of whom was granted to the Chamber of the city by a Charter of 1561. The collection has its limitations, the most significant one being that the majority of the citizens, those too poor to aspire to the status of freeman of the city, are not represented in it. In addition to this some of the inventories are obscure or incomplete, but the great mass of them present, often at tremendous length and in miscroscopic detail, a true picture of the manner in which many of the people of Exeter lived in the sixteenth and seventeenth centuries, from the craftsman and small tradesman to the most prosperous merchant and civic dignitary. Item by item the pieces of furniture and household equipment are named, and as in the written record we follow the appraisers about the house,[1] we can observe the function of each room and its importance in the domestic scheme. Moreover, in many cases it is possible to work out the positions of the rooms and so reconstruct, to a great extent, the plan of a house that no longer exists.

HOUSE PLANS

For this later period there is again no surviving physical evidence of the type of dwelling occupied by the labouring class, which constituted well over half of the city's population. Those buildings which still stand today must have been among the best of their kind, and the contemporary labourer's house in the sixteenth and seventeenth centuries would have had a comparatively short life, perhaps only a few decades. It no doubt continued to be a mean structure with walls of cob or crude timber-framing and a thatched roof; until *c.* 1600 it consisted in all likelihood of a single living-cum-cooking-cum-sleeping room, though a second room sharing these functions might sometimes be created by subdivision. Among the inventories only that of the joiner, Richard Hedgland (App., p. 98), can give us some idea of the living conditions of so many of his fellow citizens who were too poor to merit such a document.

Among the larger dwellings for which physical evidence still survives the quadrangular house, which had never been common in the earlier period, was by 1550 no longer a current design. In fact those houses erected after this date were, it seems, mainly confined to a narrow range of types which fell into two broad categories, namely, buildings which lay at right-angles to the street and presented their gables to it, and those which lay along the street with their roofs running parallel to it. They can be separately distinguished as follows.

A1   This type, which presented its gable to the street, was essentially only one room deep from front to back, usually being no more than about 20 ft. long. Sometimes, however, the one room might be subdivided into two small ones. The chimney-stack, when there was one, was in a side wall, and the staircase or stairladder was probably situated in one of the rear corners. Such a building

---

[1] It is not always easy to do this, for they often wandered around the building in a most haphazard way.

might be as low as one storey, a labourer's dwelling perhaps, or as high as four. In fact Nos. 3–5 Cathedral Yard (dn. 3), which date from the second half of the sixteenth century, are of four storeys with cellar, though there have been so many subsequent alterations to these structures that it is impossible to state definitely where the stack and stairs were, or if there was a side through-entry on the ground floor. Nos. 34–35 North Street, both timber-framed and contemporary with Nos. 3–5 Cathedral Yard, were originally also of four storeys (No. 34 is now reduced to two), and though No. 35 is only 12 ft. wide it still retains its through-entry, a full 5 ft. across, on the south side (pl. 10). This type must have been fairly common throughout the whole of the period, and in fact a late example survived until it was demolished in the summer of 1959. This was No. 178a Cowick Street, built c. 1700 (dn. 12).

A2 An important type that developed in the second half of the sixteenth century also presented its gable to the street. This structure, however, was two rooms deep from front to rear, and an inevitable feature was the side through-entry on the ground floor. In the sixteenth and early seventeenth century fireplaces were often situated in the side wall opposite the entry, but in the later seventeenth century they were more commonly housed in a central stack placed between the front and rear rooms. However, the framed staircase, which was becoming a general feature in such dwellings as these from the mid-sixteenth century on, always lay between the front and rear rooms. The entry was an integral part of the scheme. In addition to the doors at both ends there were further doors along its length, opening on to the two ground floor rooms, though there would probably be direct intercommunication between the rooms as well. Often a third door opened immediately on to the stairs, and this might be the only means of access to them at ground level.

Surviving sixteenth century examples of the type are Nos. 2–4 The Close (pl. 19, fig. xvi, dn. 6), Nos. 225–226 High Street (*front.*, dn. 22) and probably Nos. 46–47 High Street (pl. 11, fig. xiii, dn. 21). No. 18 North Street (dn. 27), a building of three storeys with cocklofts and dating from c. 1600, is a particularly good specimen and illustrates very well the measures that were taken when the required number of rooms could not be accommodated in a single block.[1] In such cases a second block was erected a few yards behind the first, so forming an almost completely enclosed courtyard, and often one or two galleries afforded direct access between the blocks at upper floor levels. At No. 18 the rear block was originally also three storeys high and the two galleries are still *in situ* (pl. 24). Although the rear block might also be two rooms deep and have its own staircase or stairladders, it seems, from the inventories and the example of No. 18 North Street, that it was unlikely to have a through-entry as well. The inventories do not distinguish two separate entries, and the rear block at No. 18 does not appear to have had one. The type illustrated in the front block persisted strongly throughout the seventeenth century. No. 227 High Street (*front.*, dn. 23), built c. 1650, once had a through-entry with a staircase opening off it, and its less imposing contemporary, No. 40 Alphington Street

---

[1] The rear part of the building was destroyed in the air raid of 1942, but the original layout is clear. Houses of similar type also survive at Totnes, in Fore Street (e.g. Nos. 52 and 66).

(dn. 1), still retains its original entry, central stack and staircase. Many of the houses erected outside the South Gate after the Civil War, replacing those destroyed in the defence of the city, also conform to this plan. In 1700 it was still popular and kept all the essential features, as is shown by the classic example of No. 182 Cowick Street (fig. xix).

A3 In most respects this is similar to A2. It presents its gable to the street and is also two rooms deep on each floor. The staircase lies between them, and the fireplaces are accommodated either in a side wall or in a central stack beside the stairs. This type also usually housed any sizeable number of extra rooms in a separate rear block, which was often connected by a gallery or galleries to the main dwelling.

The one thing that it lacked was the side through-entry and the convenience that this afforded, for to reach the rear court or garden from the street it was necessary to go through both ground floor rooms. The governing factor in this arrangement seems to have been the width of the building. For example No. 45 High Street (pl. 11, fig. xiii, dn. 20), which is less than 9 ft. wide, is too narrow to take a side entry, for this would mean that the ground floor rooms would be no more than 6 ft. across. On the other hand its contemporary, No. 67 South Street (pl. 28, fig. xviii, dn. 31), which was also erected c. 1600, is so wide that there is room for two central stacks, but they are placed against the walls and so prevent the insertion of a side entry.

This type seems to have run contemporaneously with A2. We have seen that it was established by 1600, but it was probably introduced at the beginning of the period, for it appears that Nos. 41–42 High Street (pl. 13, fig. xiv, dn. 19), built in 1564, had no ground floor entry. There could hardly have been one running alongside the outer wall, for that contained at least one fireplace, and the stairs are wrongly positioned in relation to an entry lying against the inner wall. Almost one hundred and fifty years later the arrangement was still in favour, as is shown by the example of No. 4 Cowick Street (pl. 38, fig. xx, dn. 11), dating from c. 1700. This building, with chimney-stack and staircase placed against opposite side walls, clearly never had an entry. However, despite the persistence of this type, it is probable that, because of its comparative inconvenience, it was not as popular as A2.

Hooker's map of 1587 shows that at that time the type of dwelling presenting its gable to the street predominated in the main thoroughfares of the city. This is hardly unexpected and indeed it must always have been the case, for it was in such areas that the pressures on building land and the commercial attractions of a shop frontage were physically expressed in the typically long, narrow shapes of the tenement strips. In some of the lesser streets, however, and in parts of the extramural suburbs, the decreased pressures resulted in a different picture. Sites there were often shorter and wider, and the spiky profile of a long series of consecutive gables was relieved or replaced entirely by the calmer horizontal lines of roofs running parallel with the street.

The map gives us a good idea of the distribution of the latter type. However, it is most important that the document should not be taken too literally where the great majority of the buildings are concerned, for in some respects it seeks to convey an impression rather than reality. For example, it clearly does not depict every house in the city, and even those shown are, to a large extent, conventionally represented. In particular, doors, windows and chimney-stacks are set out as regularly as in a child's drawing, and can bear only an accidental relationship to the original. In these circumstances the very fact that there is variation in the angles at which the buildings stand to the streets suggests that, in this matter at least, the map is more truly representative. Though the picture it portrays is no doubt exaggerated and oversimplified it can be accepted with a fair degree of confidence.

Bearing these considerations in mind we see that in 1587 it was not uncommon for one or even both sides of a street in Exeter to be given up to the form of construction involving the parallel roof. Paul Street, the west end of Corry Lane (now Gandy Street), Preston Street, Rack Lane and North Street particularly stand out on the map. There are also odd groups on Exe Island and outside the East Gate; and in the more rural parish of St. David's, beyond the North Gate, the type is quite pre-eminent. Even allowing for exaggeration we can be sure that the proportion of such buildings in the city at that time was, though far less than half the total, nevertheless quite a high one.

A great many of the houses shown on Hooker's map must have been erected before 1550, and it is likely that the type having its roof parallel with the street went back to at least 1500, for examples of this are shown in the illustration of the Butcher Row (pl. 7). Of course these may represent a rebuilding but, on the other hand, they may have been part of the original scheme. That the type persisted after 1587 there is no doubt, for there is physical evidence of this. Besides, the same basic conditions regarding the dimensions of the site continued to apply. And yet it seems that there were changes, and that the dwelling lying parallel with the street was often replaced by one which presented its gable to it, probably because the latter type had a plan that was less rigid, and it was also more easily extended when there was a shortage of accommodation. North Street provides an instance of this development, for according to Hooker's map the houses on the west side were almost all of the parallel roof type, and yet, when that part of the street was largely rebuilt at the end of the sixteenth century, the new structures presented their gables to the roadway (pls. 23 and 24).

It appears, therefore, that the house with the parallel roof was a declining type, certainly from c. 1600 onwards, but even then the number of these buildings was large enough to imply the existence of several different plans. However, only two have survived to be recorded, and these are described below.

B1 This type had its roof parallel with the street, and it was only one room deep from front to back, and one room wide on the ground floor. It had a side through-entry with a door to the ground floor room opening off it, and the stack was contained in the side wall opposite or perhaps, less commonly, in the rear wall. The staircase or stairladder was probably situated in one of the rear corners. Only one building of this kind, No. 15 Frog Street (pl. 18, fig. x, dn .17), dating from the second half of the sixteenth century and occupying a short, wide site, remained to be surveyed, and this has since been demolished (in the summer of 1961). It was only two storeys high, but there were no doubt other, higher buildings with a similar ground plan.

B2 This type also had a parallel roof but though, like No. 15 Frog Street, it was only one room deep from front to rear it was in other respects a bigger building, being two rooms wide on the ground floor. This might necessitate such a plan as that of the Tudor House on Exe Island (pl. 31, dn. 32), a structure of four storeys which has a central doorway with a passage leading from this, between the two ground floor rooms, to the stairs placed against the rear wall. An alternative to this arrangement might be the substitution for the passage of a central through-entry, of the type suggested in a lease of 1661. This describes a tenement on the south side of Guinea Street, in the parish of St. Mary Major, as having an entry with a shop on each side on the ground floor, three chambers and a closet on the first floor, and three chambers and a cockloft on the second floor.[1] In a case like this the stairs would probably be situated in a rear corner in one of the ground floor rooms. The chimney-stack or stacks would be housed, as in the dwelling with the passage, in the side walls or, less commonly, in the rear wall.

Although the two categories A and B covered the vast majority of houses in the city, there was a further type of construction that can be classed separately from them.

C This was essentially a compromise between A and B, for the structure consisted of a parallel roof, with a transverse gable at one end presented to the street and running from front to rear of the building. If the amount of available evidence is anything like a direct reflection of its popularity then this arrangement was never common in the sixteenth and seventeenth centuries. This is understandable for it required a broad site, and these were relatively few, and furthermore it presented more structural problems than were encountered in the more popular kinds of dwelling. There is an engraving in the City Library collection of a building of this type, a late sixteenth century house in Catherine Street.[2] It was of two storeys and had a central front entrance, though it is not possible to say if the passage went right through to a rear door. It was in all likelihood one room deep from front to back on the ground floor, and there was a room on either side of the passage, so in plan it was similar to B2. On the first floor there were probably two rooms beneath the transverse gable, and it seems that there was a chimney-stack in the side wall at that end of the house. No. 7 Cowick Street, dating from the early part of the seventeenth century, is constructed on much the same principle, but the ground floor has been altered to such an extent that it is impossible to make out the original plan. In this case, however, the part beneath the parallel roof is of two storeys whilst the transverse section has additional cocklofts, and the stack is centrally placed.[3]

Of the remaining houses in the city only three have enough in common to be

---

[1] D & C, 6006/2/2.
[2] A note pencilled on the illustration says that the building was destroyed in 1865 or 1866.
[3] Mr. A. W. Everett informs me that No. 8 was originally of similar construction.

regarded, and this loosely, as a separate group. In many ways they are quite distinct from the other dwellings that have been considered. The first of the three, Bampfylde House, was erected some time in the 1590's as the town house of the Poltimore family.[1] It was a building of two storeys with cellar and cock-lofts, and stood on the corner of Bedford Street and Bampfylde Street, just within the East Gate, until it was demolished as a result of enemy bombing in the Second World War. The other two structures, Old Matford House and Cowick Barton (fig. xvii, dns. 30 and 10), both date from c. 1600 and were once out in the country beyond the city limits. In fact Old Matford House was the country residence of Sir George Smyth, three times mayor and the richest merchant of his day in Exeter, while the term 'barton' (farmstead) clearly points to some agricultural pursuit at Cowick. Today, however, both proper-ties lie within the city boundary, and because of this they have been included in this survey.

The outstanding feature common to all three is their plan, which consists essentially of a main block with a cross-wing at both ends, one containing the domestic offices, the other an extension of the living quarters accommodated in the middle part of the house. Each building, however, is a separate variation on this broad theme, and Bampfylde House is perhaps the simplest of these. Its plan was that of the conventional E–type, but lacking the middle bar usually supplied by the projecting central porch. It did in fact have an open porch, with a very small room above it, in the internal angle formed by the main block and the north wing, but the fact that this partly obscured a window shows that it was a later addition. However, the original entrance, a less imposing one, was in that position and it opened, perhaps by way of a screens passage, on to the ground floor hall in the main block, with the domestic offices to the north. The hall (with a cellar below) had a large fireplace in the middle of the rear wall, and the principal staircase rose in a corner to the rooms above.

The plan of Old Matford House is also of the E-type with the middle bar missing, but though it has a porch this is not placed in either of the internal angles. A reason for this is that the orientation of Old Matford is diametrically opposite to that of Bampfylde House and the main entrance, instead of opening on to the small courtyard enclosed on three sides, is placed in the back of the long bar of the 'E', and leads to a screens passage with the hall on one side and the staircase on the other. In some ways Cowick Barton is the most con-ventional of the three, with its central porch projecting into the courtyard and the two staircases rising in the corner of each wing. But the shape of the 'E' is very much modified. Each wing is joined to the main part of the building only at one corner, and both are virtually separate blocks in their own right.

ROOM NAMES AND FUNCTIONS

Much has been said in the preceding pages about the number of rooms to be found on each floor in the different types of dwelling, about the positions of some of them and the ways in which they were related to such features as the

[1] R. Dymond, 'Bampfylde House, Exeter', Arch. Journ., XXXI (1874), 100.

entrance, the through-entry, the staircase and the chimney-stack. So far, however, few rooms have been specifically named, and only the most general comment has been made about the functions which they fulfilled. But in fact Exeter houses during the period 1550–1700 possessed between them a wide range of different kinds of room, serving a variety of purposes that were not always reflected in the name given. Both the expected and the unexpected details are amply illustrated in the Orphans' Court inventories, and the following accounts have been based almost completely upon these documents.

HALL   This was the main living room and, generally speaking, was the most important room in the house; in fact, in the poorer dwellings it was often the only one. It was usually situated on the ground floor, and if there was more than one room at that level the hall was much more likely to be at the rear of the building than at the front. In many cases, however, it was to be found at first floor level and here, if it did not occupy the whole floor, it was more commonly placed at the front of the house, and was often known as the forehall. Some of the larger dwellings, those containing over ten rooms and ranging from three to five storeys in height, had two halls, one on the ground floor and one on the first floor, and these are severally described in the inventories as the hall and the low hall, the forehall and the hall, and the upper hall and the hall. A soapboiler's inventory, dated 1605, describes a house which had both a forehall and a lower hall, and yet consisted altogether of no more than about five rooms accommodated in only two storeys.[1] In the vast majority of homes the hall was the eating room, particularly when it was on the ground floor, though the first floor hall occasionally fulfilled this function. In a good many cases, and not only in the smallest houses, the hall served additionally as a kitchen and the cooking was done there. Furthermore, in a significant number of inventories both the ground floor and first floor types of hall are shown containing a bed, so they were clearly used as an extra sleeping room, though this was a subsidiary function.

In the three buildings of the cross-winged variety the hall was always on the ground floor in the main part of the house, either taking up all of the available space or, as at Cowick Barton, sharing it with another room.

CHAMBER   This ranked second to the hall in importance and in the poorest dwellings, originally consisting of only one room open to the roof, it was the first addition to be contrived, either by dividing the ground floor area or by boarding over part of the general living space. The latter arrangement is described as the children's chamber in the inventory of Hugh Bydwell, a shoe-maker of St. Mary Steps parish, whose house in 1591 had only a shop and a hall on the ground floor.[2] In the middle and large-sized buildings, however, there were usually several chambers, so it far outnumbered any of the other rooms.

The chamber was primarily a sleeping room, though it often had a secondary storage function. It seems from the inventories that even in the larger dwellings

[1]ECM, Inventory 90.   [2]ECM, Inventory 44.

it was very occasionally to be found at ground level, but its usual place was on one of the upper floors. The most important chamber in a house which might boast several was the great chamber, the principal bedroom where the master and mistress slept, though it is usually given no distinguishing name in the inventories. The most common position for this room was at the front of the building on the first floor, but if the forehall happened to be placed there then the great chamber would often be set directly above it. It was the practice for servants, apprentices and the like to live in, and their sleeping quarters, frequently denoted by the terms ' men's chamber ' and ' maids' chamber ', were in most cases near or at the top of the house. The word chamber was sometimes used in certain room names which referred directly to a particular function or product, for example, starching chamber, (di)stilling chamber, wool chamber and milk chamber.

KITCHEN   This was the third commonest room in the house. As one would expect it served primarily as the cooking place, but in an age when home-brewed ale was the staple drink of many it was also used very often for brewing. The kitchen was almost inevitably on the ground floor and at the rear of the house, but it is clear from the inventories that in a good number of the larger dwellings, those having about eight rooms or more, it was frequently placed just across the courtyard. In this position it might be first of a series of rooms in a one-storey structure extending down the site, or it might be contained in a second block of several storeys, as at No. 18 North Street, for example (pl. 24, dn. 27).

In a very few houses, it seems, the kitchen was not on the ground floor. A six-roomed merchant's house in 1609 had a higher kitchen, which was apparently on the first floor at the rear, though there were also cooking implements in the low parlour beneath.[1] An inventory dated 1572, almost forty years earlier, describes a dwelling of seven rooms with a higher kitchen and a lower kitchen, but in this case the upper room was used, at that time at least, as sleeping accommodation.[2] There is evidence to suggest that, in one or two places, food was prepared below ground level. A description of part of No. 229 High Street, rebuilt by Sir George Smyth in 1584 and demolished in 1930, refers to ' the traces of an extensive kitchen, with a huge fireplace ' in the basement.[3] This is an unusual arrangement, associated rather with the Georgian and Victorian terrace house, but it seems to be confirmed by one of the inventories. That of a clockmaker, dated 1628, clearly assigns his cooking implements and pewterware to the cellar.[4]

A house containing a lower and a higher kitchen has already been referred to. A handful of the inventories describe other dwellings with two kitchens, for example the kitchen and the inner kitchen, or the kitchen and the backer kitchen. In fact the arrangement persisted into the last quarter of the seventeenth century, for two kitchens are mentioned in a terrier of 1679–80 relating

[1]ECM, Inventory 101.   [2]ECM, Inventory 22.

[3]W. Cotton and H. Woollcombe, *Gleanings from the Municipal and Cathedral Records relative to the history of the City of Exeter* (1877), 119.

[4]ECM, Inventory 175.

to the vicarage of St. Thomas, newly built after the Civil War.[1] However, although in these cases the term kitchen was applied to both rooms, only one was generally used for cooking and the other served as a brewhouse.[2]

PARLOUR   In some respects this room was similar to the hall, for it could also be found on either the ground or the first floor, though it was usually at the rear of the building.   There might well be a parlour in dwellings of only two storeys, but it was more commonly associated with those of three storeys and above.   It seems to have embraced a number of functions.   It might be used as a general withdrawing room, and in a good number of homes the family also ate there.   In the inventories it is recorded fairly often as containing a bed, and it clearly fulfilled a marked secondary function as a sleeping room.   In some of the larger houses there were occasionally two parlours, usually one on the ground floor and one on the floor above, but this feature was not as common as the possession of two halls.   An inn might have three or four parlours, all or most of them serving as sleeping accommodation.

CELLAR   The cellar is recorded in about one-fifth of the Orphans' Court inventories, but the surviving physical evidence suggests a far higher proportion than this, one which could be put at over fifty per cent.   However, it appears from this same evidence that there was a decline in the popularity of the cellar, and that it was less likely to be included in a building erected after 1650 than in one put up before that date.   The cellar was usually to be found in the larger dwellings, those with ten or more other rooms, but it occurred in some with as little as five other rooms, and one of the inventories just quoted, that describing a clockmaker's house in 1628, lists only a cellar, a hall chamber (most probably a hall), an upper chamber over the hall and a workroom.[3]

It seems that the cellar was always below ground level, and was usually placed at the front of the building where there was often direct access to the street outside. A merchant might well have two, with a back cellar lying behind the fore cellar and opening off it, an arrangement which still persists at No. 47 High Street (fig. xiii).   Or there might be one cellar beneath the main block at the front, and another separate one beneath the rear block or lesser outbuildings across the courtyard.   A few of the houses had more than two.

The cellar was generally used as a storage place, and served as a warehouse for many merchants and tradesmen—or it might contain just a few odd pieces of lumber.   Fuel was sometimes kept there and it was a popular repository for barrels of beer and wine.   Finally, as we have seen, there are also some signs that in rare cases it was used as a kitchen.

[1]DRO, E/GT (Terriers).

[2]The general practice of having two kitchens came later, and was widespread throughout much of the country in the nineteenth and early twentieth centuries particularly. The main kitchen was on the ground floor at the rear of the house and was the cooking, and often the eating, place. The back kitchen, or scullery, was contained in an extension or a detached structure behind it. This usually had a large sink for the preparation of vegetables and a copper for washing clothes.

[3]ECM, Inventory 175.

COCKLOFT   This was the term employed to describe the room or rooms at the top of the house, and either partly or wholly contained within the roof. They were used for storage and/or sleeping accommodation. A haberdasher's inventory of 1592 refers to the higher and lower cockloft, but that probably means that the top floor of this large dwelling, which contained well over a dozen rooms, was not all on one level, and not that one cockoft was on the floor below the other.[1]

Another, though less common, name for the space at the top of the building was simply the loft, and the term garret was occasionally employed. This occurs in a merchant vintner's inventory dating from 1594–5,[2] and in a lease of 1608–9 relating to a house near the Guildhall.[3] The word has the flavour of a later period for us, but surprisingly it does not appear in any of the subsequent inventories. Of course, if these top floor rooms were not too cramped then they might well be referred to as chambers. In fact the word chamber could be used for even a confined roof space, like that created when a single storey dwelling was partially lofted over (see under CHAMBER above), so to some extent the terms cockloft/loft/garret and chamber were synonymous.

SHOP AND WAREHOUSE   The word shop in the inventories has three separate meanings. It might refer to the room where goods were sold, or to the room where articles were made or, as in the terms wool shop and cloth shop, to the place where raw materials or finished products were stored. It was not uncommon for one room to share two of these functions. But the shop was primarily regarded as a place of sale, and as such it was situated almost inevitably at the front of the building on the ground floor. Where the business was a small one, or where the craftsman did not require a great deal of space, then it might also serve as a workshop. Otherwise the latter would be accommodated in the room behind, or on the ground floor of a building across the courtyard. When used for storage the shop might be in any of these three places, though this function would usually be subsidiary to those of selling and working. However, in some cases the shop as a storage place could also be found on the first floor, and there are references, in a few of the inventories, to the upper shop and the lower shop, which clearly make this distinction.

The warehouse, which was used solely for storing goods, can be closely identified with the shop in its third function as a storage place. In fact, if only a small warehouse was required, the room directly behind or above the sales shop might be used for this purpose. However, if a great deal of space was needed then the warehouse was more likely to be situated across the courtyard behind the main dwelling, running down one side of the tenement towards the end of the site. There it would occupy the space above a workshop and/or other outbuildings or, if the business was an extensive one, it would be a large, separate building in its own right. On the other hand, a merchant was not bound to store all of his goods on the site partly occupied by his house. Some of the inventories mention goods stored down at the quay, and at other, rented, warehouses—and cellars too—elsewhere in the city.

[1] ECM, Inventory 51.   [2] ECM, Inventory 57.   [3] ECM, D1/13/8.

BUTTERY OR SPENCE   The terms buttery and spence,[1] interchangeable in sixteenth and seventeenth century Exeter (though buttery was the more popular of the two), usually referred to a room, which was occasionally known as the drinkhouse. However, they were also often used to describe a cupboard contrived by partitioning off a corner or end of a room. Most houses did not possess a buttery, a good number had only one, but some had two, consisting either of separate rooms or of one room and a cupboard. This latter pair might come together in a confusing manner, which is exemplified by an innholder's inventory of 1620 that lists a spence in the buttery.[2]

In the middle ages the buttery (the room) was the place where provisions, particularly drink, were kept, but by the time the inventories came to be made it fulfilled a more general function, at least in the houses under discussion here. Food and drink were often stored there, but so were all kinds of household utensils—tableware in the form of trenchers and tankards, cooking implements, breadmaking and brewing equipment, all might find their way into the buttery. Of course, when it took the form of a cupboard it accommodated only the smaller utensils. As one would expect, the buttery was principally associated with the kitchen or hall, either opening off or being contained within them, but in some dwellings it might be associated with the parlour.

GALLERY   By far the most common form of gallery was that spanning a courtyard and linking together at upper floor level two sizeable blocks of building, one lying directly behind the other on a narrow site. It might consist merely of an open passageway, but it was more likely to be enclosed and it is clear from the inventories that it was sometimes large enough to constitute a room in its own right. When this was the case it would often contain furniture of a general nature—chests, a side table, a few chairs—and have no specific function. Occasionally, however, it had one or even two beds, and served as an additional sleeping room (App., p. 100). A second type of gallery, an open one running across the front of the building, is still to be seen at No. 227 High Street (front., fig. xiv), but this was essentially a vantage point and must have been very rare in Exeter houses before 1700. There is no evidence that the earlier internal gallery in houses with a central open hall (Nos. 36 and 38 North Street) persisted after 1550.

About one-eighth of the inventories record a gallery. It was usually associated with a large building having ten or more rooms, but there are two instances of a gallery in houses with only five other rooms. However, the smallest dwelling mentioned is that of Henry Drake, a chandler in the parish of St. Mary Major. His inventory, dated the 16 February 1629, lists, in addition to the gallery containing a great chest, a parlour, fore chamber, back chamber, hall and shop —five rooms in all.[3] Though it was usual to have only one gallery (of the first type) a small proportion of the buildings had two, one being placed directly above the other like the pair surviving at No. 18 North Street (pl. 24).

---

[1]The buttery was originally the room where drink was stored (from Old French ' boterie', later ' bouteillerie ' = the place where the bottles or the flasks are kept). The spence (from O.F. ' despense ') was the place where both food and drink were stored, and from which they were ' dispensed '.

[2]ECM, Inventory 136.   [3]ECM, Inventory 179.

DINING CHAMBER   This term occurs in nine or so of the inventories ranging in date from a possible 1590 to 1675 (App., p. 119),[1] the main concentration being within the period 1620–30. In one document dated 1629 the expression dining room is used. Two of the buildings described were inns, and the remainder were merchants' houses, usually containing over a dozen rooms. It seems that the dining chamber was, to a large extent, synonymous with the hall or the parlour (one or both of them is missing in some of the inventories), and it might be found on either the ground or the first floors in one of the positions normally occupied by these rooms. One example, dating from 1630, was also used for sleeping purposes, and this emphasises the similarity between them. On the other hand a merchant's house in 1612 had a dining chamber over the kitchen, in the rear block across the courtyard. In this case, and in two others, the dining chamber was additional to the hall and parlour, and this suggests a slight tendency towards specialization of function in the seventeenth century merchant's house. Eating was considered by some people to be worth a separate room with a distinctive name.

MISCELLANEOUS   The study and countinghouse, like the buttery, might be rooms in their own right, or they might be subdivisions of a room created by the erection of wooden partitioning. It was fairly common to find one or the other, and occasionally both, in the house of a merchant or well-to-do tradesman (a merchant's inventory of 1577 also lists a spying house beside the little study).[2] But they were by no means always at ground level in close association with the business premises; they were often situated on one of the upper floors. In some cases there might be two countinghouses or two studies, in different parts of the building (App., p. 119-120).

The Orphans' Court inventories contain references to a variety of other rooms, such as the larder and washhouse, but more particularly to those associated with home-baking and brewing, which were important features of the domestic economy in many homes, notwithstanding the proximity of the local tradesmen. The bakehouse occurs fairly often, the pastryhouse more rarely. Another room that is sometimes mentioned is the boltinghouse or buntinghouse, where the flour was sifted. So far as drink is concerned the brewhouse is listed with some frequency, though brewing was often carried out in the kitchen. The alehouse is also alluded to a very few times, but it might be either a place where drink was made or where it was stored, so to some extent it was cognate with the buttery. The ' Syder howse ' is included in an inventory of 1607, describing a tailor's dwelling in St. Mary Arches parish.[3] These rooms were all situated on the ground floor, occasionally at the rear of the main building, but more usually within the secondary complex across the courtyard. However, the distinctions between them were not always as clear cut as the names imply. Sometimes the name bore little or no relation to the

[1] Inventory 195, that of the merchant William Newcombe, is undated, but in the Collection it is tentatively ascribed to 1590.

[2] ECM, Inventory 27. The spying house was probably a room from which an eye could be kept on the shop.

[3] ECM, Inventory 95. Apparently he made cider as a side-line.

function, and there was a tendency to use the rooms partly or wholly for general storage purposes.

SOME 'TYPICAL' HOUSES

We have seen that there was considerable variation in the internal arrangements of Exeter houses in the late sixteenth and seventeenth centuries. Functions were not always clearly defined and directly allocated, and a room, the hall for example, might well be found on the ground floor at the rear in one building and on the first floor at the front in another, a few doors away down the street. Similarly one householder might have his kitchen in the main dwelling, while his neighbour's wife had to cross the courtyard to do her cooking. Nevertheless, a broad pattern is discernible in the deployment of room functions, and it is possible to put forward examples of the houses occupied by different classes of citizens, though this necessarily involves oversimplification and some distortion of the true picture.

The lot of those at the bottom of the social scale has already been described. They could usually afford only a mean, one-roomed dwelling where the whole family cooked, ate, slept and stored any goods it might possess; though in some cases—and it is impossible to estimate how many—an extra room would be contrived by subdivision or by partial lofting over. The class of small craftsmen and tradesmen above these was most likely to occupy a house of two storeys, like that of a baker of Trinity parish who died in 1564. Behind his shop on the ground floor lay the kitchen and bakehouse, and above these were his hall and chamber.[1] The more substantial members of this group might add a cockloft, but when the house was raised to three storeys it was likely to shelter the lesser merchants and manufacturers, and the professional men. These would have further chambers at the top of the building, and they might introduce a parlour or a buttery on one of the lower floors. There would sometimes be a cellar as well, and there was always the possibility of another room or two across the courtyard—a kitchen or a brewhouse or a workplace.

However, it was in the houses of four and five storeys, those containing from ten to sometimes nearly twenty rooms and often extending to a second block across the courtyard, that the greatest diversity occurred. These were inhabited by the wealthy merchants and manufacturers who comprised the civic elite and in whose hands the government of Exeter largely rested. Certain features were more or less constant. For example, such buildings nearly always had a cellar, often more than one, and the rooms on and above the second floor usually consisted almost entirely of chambers and cocklofts. Below these, however, the hall and parlour might be situated on either the ground or the first floor, or there might be one on each; the kitchen could be on either side of the courtyard; and these rooms would often be further interspersed with butteries, countinghouses and studies. A sales shop was an almost invariable feature at the front of the dwelling on the ground floor, but there might also

[1]ECM, Inventory 3. Houses of much the same type are briefly described in certain late seventeenth century surveys (App., pp. 117-118, 122-123).

be a workshop and a storage shop, a warehouse and additional domestic offices to be fitted in, usually across the courtyard from the main building. Any remaining space behind these might be taken up by a small garden and/or a stable, provided there was ready access to a back street. The house of a leading citizen could be a complex organism.

BEDFORD HOUSE

However, the dwelling of even the grandest merchant, like Sir George Smyth or William Spicer (App., p. 101), paled beside Bedford House. Until the Dissolution this was the house of the Dominicans or Black Friars, but it was acquired in 1539 by John, Lord Russell, who quickly converted it into a town house for the Bedford family. At a later stage in its history it witnessed the birth of Princess Henrietta in 1644, when Charles I's Queen was sheltering in Exeter during the Civil War. It was afterwards converted into tenements, and was finally demolished in 1773 to make way for yet another ducal enterprise, the Georgian minor masterpiece of Bedford Circus. This in its turn was gutted by enemy bombs in the last war, and the site is now occupied by the new buildings of Bedford Street.

Fortunately the edifice in which the Russells installed themselves is not entirely lost to us, for its external appearance is roughly recorded in Hooker's two plans of the Close, one of which is reproduced as pl. 16.[1] Moreover, the survey of what was then an empty and somewhat dilapidated structure, made in 1594 within a few years of the plan,[2] gives a good deal of information about the interior of the building. Hooker's perspective view shows the house behind the Cathedral, set in extensive grounds running from the city wall to some sort of lodge fronting what is now Chapel Street. Together these two symbols of ecclesiastical and secular power dominated that quarter of Exeter.

The structure of Bedford House was marked by three parallel gables and, judging by the windows shown in the drawing, it was only two storeys high; but in fact these are conventional representations, and the survey suggests a height of three storeys with garrets in the roof above. At the back a high, curving wall enclosed what must have been the garden, overlooked by a number of rooms, including the great chamber and the drawing chamber, and directly accessible from the gentlewomen's chamber. At the front was an imposing entrance facing the 'great Greene Courte', but the customary round-headed opening included in the plan hardly does justice to what the survey describes as 'the great Poarch', containing a barred and bolted gate with a hammer to knock at it. The word 'great' occurs again and again throughout the document, emphasising that we are far from the homely world of the Orphans' Court inventories.

The main building apparently conformed in great measure to the standard pattern of the sub-medieval large house. The great hall or dining room took

---

[1]Hooker, *Description of the Citie of Excester*, II, facing 61. This is a view from South Street. The other view, from High Street, is in the Cathedral Library (D & C, 3520), and is reproduced in *An Original MS. of John Hooker, Chamberlain of the City of Exeter, 1555*, ed. H. E. Reynolds (undated), 16.

[2]The survey is transcribed in *DCNQ*, XVII (1932-33), 17-30.

up much of the ground floor, and we can follow the surveyor as he passed through the screens at one end, across the passage, and round the multifarious domestic offices on the other side, the pantry, the buttery, the kitchens and so on. In one corner of the hall, at the opposite end from the screens, the stairs rose to the great chamber on the first floor, the principal private room of the Bedfords—the living room, for there was a bed in his lordship's own chamber. From the great chamber a door opened on to a gallery, which is not mentioned until much later in the survey. It seems to have been a modest version of the long gallery incorporated in many large Elizabethan houses, a place to saunter in, quite unlike those in the homes of the merchants along the nearby High Street. It had a good number of windows, at least six, it overlooked the great court and also had a door giving on to the garden.

There were other retiring and sleeping facilities on this first floor, a drawing chamber, dressing rooms for Lord Russell and his wife, a bedroom for the gentlewomen and perhaps one or two for guests. The servingmaids' chamber was also on the same level, but those of the servingmen, four lodgings in all, were on the floor above, on the left of the stairs rising from the great chamber to the garret. In fact, there seems to have been a confusion of subsidiary chambers and garrets at the top of the house, and it may be that the main structure was not of a uniform height throughout, a feature which would not necessarily be shown on Hooker's simplified drawing. Possibly part of the building was of three storeys with garrets, and the remainder one floor lower.

It seems from the survey that the nursery chambers, the evidence house (where documents were stored), the audience chamber and a number of other rooms were grouped together in that part of the structure nearest to a range of single-storeyed outbuildings which contained the fishhouse, washhouse, bolting-house, slaughterhouse and stables. This range may be that shown in Hooker's plan, running off along the far side of the great court. In this case the building crossing it at the end furthest from the house would be of two storeys containing the middle porch, which would then look over the other wall-enclosed court extending to the entrance-lodge. However, this supposition is made doubtful by the fact that the gallery, whilst clearly opening off the great chamber, was apparently closely associated with the middle porch (though it may have been entered out of place in the survey). But the siting of the armoury house also presents difficulties. It opened on to both the great court and the garden (or a garden), yet it was near the middle porch, so suggesting that the latter feature was part of the main structure.

INTERIORS AND FURNISHINGS

A true impression of Exeter interiors between 1550 and the latter part of the seventeenth century can be gained only by looking in detail at the many probate inventories.[1] Generally speaking, however, the differences between the various homes reflected in these were, as one might expect, frequently differences of degree rather than of kind. The more modest dwellings were plainly, often

[1] See Appendix for a representative selection.

sparsely, furnished, but they were far from being devoid of all comfort. Even the joiner, Richard Hedgland (App., p. 98), with an estate valued at less than £4, had a good bed in his single room. As one rises higher in the social scale one finds more furniture recorded, and a greater variety of it, including pieces bought for appearance as well as for utility, until, arriving at the most substantial households in the city, one ultimately detects an element of luxury.

At the head of local society the merchants lived in considerable ease, relieved by frequent touches of extravagance. A variety of coffers and chests, cupboards, joined stools, chairs and tables, some of them elaborately carved or imported from the Continent, filled their main rooms, contrasting with the gleam of brass, tin, pewter and silver plate. This last item was of particular significance. Merchant fortunes were usually tied up in commercial ventures or in goods on hand, and might even consist largely of debts owing to them, with no absolute certainty of recovery. In the absence of banks silver plate was a sound liquid asset, and probably the only convenient one apart from any ready money that a merchant might care to keep in the house.[1] Consequently it often figured prominently in his total estate—Alderman Thomas Martyn in 1620 left plate and jewels worth over £158[2]—and even middling citizens would have one or two pieces to set against a rainy day.

Comfort was provided by cushions, rugs, table carpets and tapestries, often heavily embroidered, and there might be curtains at the windows.[3] Sometimes there was a musical instrument, usually of the keyboard type, in addition to all this, but William Spicer (App., p. 101), with an organ in the parlour, and a pair of virginals in the forehall and in the chamber above, was exceptional. Books, too, were a fairly common possession, though they tended to be few in number and limited in range, being mostly of a religious and legal nature, with the Bible understandably predominating. But here again there were exceptions. The son of the Alderman Thomas Martyn mentioned above had books worth nearly £15 in a study in his father's house, and some forty years earlier, in 1578, the merchant Henry James died leaving a private library of about sixty volumes.[4] James seems to have had unusually wide intellectual interests for an Exeter merchant, for his books included English and Latin Bibles, a Greek dictionary, ancient classics by writers like Horace, Terence and Lucan, a number of unidentified French works, four singing books and others in his native tongue.

Sleeping facilities varied a great deal. In the principal chamber the high standing bedstead might be carved or gilded, or it might have a painted canopy, and it would certainly have curtains, which were a common feature. This type of bed was often accompanied by a low truckle or trundlebed on wheels which was pushed underneath it when not in use. Occasionally, too, one comes across a reference to a field bed, similar to our modern camp bed, in a

---

[1]MacCaffrey, *Exeter, 1540–1640*, 266.   [2]ECM, Inventory 132.

[3]Window curtains are recorded in just under one-tenth of the inventories, usually those of merchants and manufacturers, though not necessarily the wealthiest of these. The possession of window curtains seems to have been more a matter of personal taste than general custom, and even then they were commonly found in only one or two principal rooms.

[4]ECM, Inventory 29.

lesser chamber. The best bedding—pillows, bolsters and so on—was filled with feathers, the second best with flock, and there are one or two instances of a dust bed, which was presumably filled with chaff and used by the servants. In all cases blankets, rugs and coverlets provided the necessary warmth.

Linen for the bed, and for the table too, has a prominent place in the invent-ories of all kinds of people and indicates, perhaps more clearly than any other possession, a general concern for comfort and cleanliness. Thus in 1577 the napery, as it was called, of one merchant was valued at over £31,[1] whilst that of yeoman John Fawell amounted to nearly a tenth of his total estate (App., p. 101). Wearing apparel is another major item, and the finery of a merchant and alderman could be worth many hundreds of pounds in modern terms, with his scarlet gown of office (William Spicer's was valued at £16 in 1604) taking pride of place.

Candlelight was the only artificial means of illumination, and candlesticks of tin or latten (a brass-like alloy) together with an occasional lantern, are recorded in nearly all of the documents. The tin basin and ewer for washing purposes also make a frequent appearance—food was freely handled at the dining table—and in a widow's hall in 1571 was supplemented by ' a sesterne (a cistern) of led to washe hands to '.[2] Rainwater or river water might be used for general cleaning purposes, and in fact in 1695, after an abortive attempt just sixty years earlier, water from the Exe was successfully conveyed through wooden pipes to those householders who agreed to pay the set rate.[3] Water for cooking and brewing was obtained from private wells, by those lucky enough to have one in the cellar or behind the main dwelling; from several common wells; or from the public conduit at the principal cross-roads in the centre of the city. The waterbearers were a final source of supply, and it seems that a certain John Coomes and his wife followed this trade, for in the 1630's they were recorded as delivering water to the merchant John Hayne for 1s. 6d. quarterly.[4]

Weapons and armour—the odd corselet, bow and arrows, sword, dagger or firearm—were likely to be found in any of the rooms, and it was not uncommon for a tradesman's stock to be distributed about the house. In 1592 Thomas Grenewode, a very wealthy haberdasher, had a good proportion of his mer-chandise stored on the top floors of his dwelling, as well as in the shop below,[5] and William Spicer (App., p. 103) had one hundred and thirteen reams of white ' pott paper ', valued at £22 12s., in his lavishly furnished forehall. But perhaps the animals constitute the most disconcerting element. These are mentioned quite frequently in a wide range of inventories. Poultry and pigs were the most popular, and were kept in the courtyard or the garden when any considerable number were involved (a brewer on Exe Island had sixteen pigs in his court in 1586).[6] However, it is clear that live animals were kept inside a good proportion of Exeter houses, for a capon coop or a cage for poultry, and more rarely a coney or rabbit hutch, are often recorded in the kitchen or in an ancillary room. Perhaps the animals were put there temporarily

[1]ECM, Inventory 27.   [2]ECM, Inventory 19.
[3]George Oliver, *The History of the City of Exeter* (1861), 149.
[4]T. N. Brushfield, ' The Financial Diary of a Citizen of Exeter, 1631-43', *TDA*, XXXIII (1901), 211.
[5]ECM, Inventory 51.   [6]ECM, Inventory 35.

whilst waiting to go into the pot. Other examples of the practice are less ambiguous and certainly more surprising. The dyer Stephen Austyn had two pigs in his house in 1641 (App., p. 116), and though he was exceptional in this respect he was not alone.

Features such as these, however, remained relatively constant. Others were more subject to change and need to be discussed in greater detail.

CEILINGS The majority of ceilings in Exeter down to c. 1650 must have been quite simply treated, with the natural wood of the beams and joists left exposed and the interstices plastered and whitened. Beams in the principal rooms of some of the better houses might be heavily moulded, like that on the first floor of No. 41 High Street (fig. xiv), but the surviving physical evidence suggests that in most cases they were more plainly treated and bore only simple chamfers and stops. However, we know from the painted chevrons and running tendrils on part of a ceiling at No. 1 Catherine Street (pl. 20) that, during the latter part of the sixteenth century at least, it was a practice to apply coloured decoration to the woodwork, though it is impossible to gauge the extent of this activity.

One thing we can be sure of, for there is ample proof, is that the decorated plaster ceiling, hiding the beams and joists, featured in the great majority of the leading houses from very early in the period right through to 1700 and beyond, and the continued existence of several of these in the city today (there must be hundreds in the county as a whole) indicates that they were usually very expertly laid.[1] One method of construction, described by Crocker[2] and declining to follow the continental fashion of working in plaster of Paris, was to spread upon a base of stout oak laths a half-inch thick layer of coarse material made up of clayey earth, a little lime and a large amount of animal hair. Over this was placed a further skin three-sixteenths of an inch thick, of fine slaked lime and hair, on which the plaster ornamentation was worked. Another method, which was possibly used at the end of the seventeenth century, is shown in part of a ceiling preserved at the local museum. In this case rushes, kept in position by oak slips, are used as a base for the earthen layer.

The moulded plaster ceiling was introduced into this country by Italian craftsmen in the second quarter of the sixteenth century, but the new tradition did not establish itself in Exeter for at least another two decades. The early examples were noted for their slender, hand-run, single ribs, based at first on timber prototypes, which curved and intersected in a variety of geometrical shapes. Ornamentation at this period consisted mainly of floral sprays at the terminals, bosses at the intersections, badges, fleurs-de-lys and Tudor roses, all cast in moulds and then applied. Exeter's earliest surviving ceilings, those at St. Nicholas Priory and No. 7 The Close (dn. 7), dating from c. 1580, contain many of these motifs, and that on the top floor of No. 7 is a particularly fine piece of work. It is laid on a wagon roof and the rib design, though a

---

[1]Those still remaining in Exeter are discussed in the text. For a more comprehensive and detailed study of the subject see Kathleen and Cecil French, 'Devonshire Plasterwork', *TDA*, LXXXIX (1957), 124-144.

[2]Crocker, *Old Exeter*, in the introduction (pages not numbered) to drawings of plaster ceilings.

relatively simple one based on a square, is relieved by a profusion of extravagantly large floral sprays, with the whole composition centring on a great
moulded pendant.

The ceiling on the first floor of No. 67 South Street, which can be ascribed
to *c.* 1600, is a curious one. At a time when the general trend was towards
more and more robust detail, the craftsman responsible for this example
decided on simplicity and severity. A wide moulded beam merging into a
cornice divides the ceiling into two unequal halves (fig. xviii), and in each of the
eight corners thus formed a single, large flower is placed. There is a different
one in every case, with the rose, daffodil and vine still immediately recognisable.[1]

However, that half of a very elaborate ceiling which remains in what was
once the first floor hall or great chamber of No. 38 North Street (pl. 22), is an
excellent illustration of the Jacobean style. The panels are filled with lavishly
extended floral designs, and a variety of birds and beasts dominate the frieze.
This extravagance is repeated in a later ceiling at No. 144 Fore Street (*c.* 1640),
with its naturalistic delineation of fruit, tendrils and similar motifs, and its
fauna ranging from a snail and a butterfly to an elephant. But in fact the
process before 1650 went beyond even this. A further development was to
mark out the panels with two parallel ribs instead of only one, and the final
stage was to enrich the narrow space between these, usually with a running
vine pattern. No examples of these subsequent phases survive in Exeter, but
fortunately a few from Bampfylde House and former merchants' houses in
Fore Street were recorded before they finally disappeared (pl. 26).[2]

After 1650 the houses of the middling citizens had plain plaster ceilings with
perhaps a moulded cornice, but in the grander homes the ceilings of the
principal rooms continued to be highly ornamented. The style, however,
changed drastically under the sustained influence of the Renaissance. The
complex, interlacing, geometrical patterns of the earlier periods were succeeded
by simpler arrangements comprising separately disposed circles, ovals and
rectangles. But a great deal of ornamentation was generally retained; ribs
became even broader, fresh motifs like the classical acanthus and the laurel
were introduced, and the detail stood out in far greater relief. A fine example
from the latter part of the seventeenth century, and typical of others laid in
Exeter homes at that time, still remains *in situ* at the Custom House (pl. 36).
It was for this and other work there that £35 was paid out to John Abbott
(pl. 37) in 1680–1.[3] The rectangular design has had to be sacrificed in one
awkward corner, but the other features are regular enough—the acanthus

---

[1] *Ibid.*, Pl. XXXIX.   [2] Crocker, *Old Exeter.*

[3] For the ceiling, begun in 1689, of the Apollo Room at the New Inn the plasterer Thomas Lane
was paid £50. The inn was the principal one in the city, and the Apollo Room was 32½ ft. long by
23½ ft. wide by 17 ft. high (Dymond, ' Old Inns and Taverns of Exeter ', 402). The cost of the ceiling
was equivalent to, or greater than, that of many a house erected in Exeter at that time. A number of
deeds dating from the 1640's to 1700 relate to the building of houses, mostly outside the city walls,
though no details of the structures are given. The sums recorded range from £20 to £300, but the
majority are concentrated around £100, and this can probably be taken as the average price of a
plain, medium sized, timber-framed house, say one of three storeys with about six rooms, in the second
half of the seventeenth century.

leaves around the outer edge, the inner border enriched with running tendrils, the crossed wreaths of oakleaves and thistles, the oval centre-piece, and so on. A ceiling of a different design, but equally impressive, survives from the old Half Moon Hotel, which used to stand on the corner of High Street and Bedford Street.[1] It dates from c. 1700 and consists of a coved cornice, a frieze and an oval ceiling centre, heavily decorated with bold, free-standing flowers, fruit and leaves. On the cornice these take the form of festoons, accompanied by hanging draperies. Houses beyond as well as within the city limits were up with the times, and at Bellair (c. 1700) a two-storeyed mansion now part of Exeter but once out in the country along the Topsham road, some fine ceiling decoration in a somewhat lighter style is still to be seen.

WALLS The great majority of the citizens represented in the inventories attempted, in varying degrees, to bring colour and warmth to the walls of their main living and sleeping rooms. They achieved their object either by fixing ‘ seeling ’, i.e. wainscot, to them, or by hanging up large, coloured cloths. The panelled woodwork with its dull, homely glow and often bearing a linen-fold design, was clearly a valued possession during the first half of the period. It is recorded in the documents together with the other movable goods, and a tenant would be prepared to take it with him from house to house. Even Richard Hedgland had a piece of wainscot, probably with benches fixed to it and valued at 3s., in his only room (App., p. 98), while at the other end of the scale his near contemporary, the merchant William Spicer, had sixty-eight yards of it running around the whole of his parlour (App., p. 102). It was worth £6 16s., more than Hedgland's entire estate. Some of Crocker's draw-ings of interiors in Bampfylde House and No. 229 High Street (pl. 21) show how impressive such panelling could be at its best. It covered the walls from floor to ceiling, and was surmounted by a carved, wooden frieze bearing animal heads, running floral patterns and strapwork.[2] Often, too, it was divided into bays by fluted pilasters with curious Ionic capitals and extravagantly carved pedestals, and a modest example of this type of work is still to be seen on the first floor of No. 1 The Close.

The hangings, which were sometimes placed in wooden frames, varied a good deal in quality and in the materials used. William Hurst, a leading merchant and a mayor of the city who died in 1568, refers in his will to ‘ my hangings of Tapestry in the hall ’,[3] while in the chamber over Spicer's forehall there were some of green kersey (a coarse woollen cloth) valued at £1 10s. But the commonest material was probably canvas. There were two methods of treatment. The hanging was either stained a particular colour, or some ‘ story ’, usually drawn from the Bible or from mythology, was painted upon it. Thus Alderman William Chappell's inventory, made in 1579, records the hangings of canvas portraying the story of Joseph in the great chamber over the

---

[1]Preserved in the Royal Albert Memorial Museum, Exeter.

[2]Sections of three similar wooden friezes—7½ ins., 9 ins. and 11½ ins. deep—are preserved in the Royal Albert Memorial Museum, Exeter. They are also of late sixteenth century date, and they were formerly at Nos. 170-171 Fore Street.

[3]*Guide to St. Nicholas Priory, Exeter*, revised by Joyce Youings (1960), 17.

hall,[1] and in the same year his fellow alderman, William Tryvet, had ' a litle paynted cloth of the prodigall sone' (worth only 2d., however) in a chamber over the parlour.[2] It was not uncommon for wainscot and stained or painted cloths to be in the same room, where they might be placed on different walls. But another arrangement prevailed in the hall of a merchant of St. Martin's parish in the 1570's.[3] There the old hangings of red and green say (a fine serge-like material) with a border of painted cloth were suspended above the wainscot, which covered only the lower part of the wall.

In the course of the first half of the seventeenth century the practice of putting up stained and painted cloths gradually ceased. During the same period references to wainscot become rarer in the inventories. However, the implication is not that this, too, was discarded but that, like glass, it became commoner. It grew to be no longer regarded as a movable fixture, and so was not recorded in the documents. Though there is no adequate evidence of its development, Exeter wainscot of the later seventeenth century almost certainly followed traditional lines. The small panels of the earlier woodwork, rarely more than 1 ft. 6 ins. high by 1 ft. 0 ins. wide, grew larger, and more pronounced mouldings were used. By the end of the century the number of panels was drastically reduced, and these were very formally disposed around the room. Framed by bolection moulding and surmounted by a cornice, a series of very large, single panels was set above a low dado rail, with squat ones of the same width below this. After the often fussy detail of the Elizabethan and Jacobean seeling, the effect was one of restful dignity.

It has been pointed out that the panelled woodwork and the hangings served to retain warmth within the rooms, but other ways of relieving the wall surfaces were more purely decorative in effect. In all likelihood some of the most eminent citizens had one or two of their main rooms partly, perhaps completely, decked out with wall paintings similar to those which, for example, still survive at the Golden Cross Hotel and at No. 3 Cornmarket, Oxford.[4] In the latter building a whole wall is covered with a coloured trellis pattern of interlacing geometrical forms enclosing sprays of fruit and flowers, and dating from some time between 1560 and 1580. In the Golden Cross there are two further styles of ornament. The first of these, applied c. 1595, is marked by bird, fruit and flower motifs, and occasional grotesques, with classical arabesques beginning to degenerate into scrollwork and foliage. The colours used are low in tone—brown, green, orange-red and pinky-red, all with black outline. The other work is much earlier—it was executed c. 1550—an example of vigorous Italianate decoration in black and white, incorporating fantastic pilasters surrounded by arabesques, masks, putti and grotesques. In fact, though it is a superior piece of work, it seems to bear a fairly close resemblance to the only secular wall paintings still surviving in Exeter, those in the guest hall of St. Nicholas Priory. These designs, also in black and white, are placed in the reveals of the west windows and in a frieze running round the room, and they originally extended over a much larger area. They were probably

[1]ECM, Inventory 28a.   [2]ECM, Inventory 28b.   [3]ECM, Inventory 27.
[4]See W. A. Pantin and E. Clive Rouse, ' The Golden Cross, Oxford ', *Oxoniensia*, XX (1955), 46-89.

introduced in the third quarter of the sixteenth century, when the western range of the priory was lavishly converted into a private residence.

In the former priory guest room opening off the hall is another type of wall decoration, a plaster design including a Tudor rose and further floral motifs. At Old Matford House (dn. 30) fleurs-de-lys and the repeated coat of arms of its builder, Sir George Smyth, still remain in the first floor great chamber.[1] This kind of ornamentation must have been fairly common in the better homes down to *c.* 1650, especially in those upper rooms where the ceilings were coved and there was ample space above cornice level on the end walls.

The last method of decoration is the one that is most familiar to us today, namely the hanging of pictures and the occasional map upon the walls. It seems that the pictures, like the painted cloths, often portrayed mythological subjects, at least during the early part of the period, and a touch of the curious is provided by a painter's inventory of 1618,[2] which records four earthen pictures, probably his own work, in the chamber within the hall. The practice of having a few pictures in the principal room was established among the merchants well before 1600, and it spread in the course of the seventeenth century. No doubt portraits became increasingly popular, for around 1680 John Abbott, the plasterer, who lived in an obscure North Devon village and not in the high society of the county capital, saw fit to have his painted (pl. 37).

DOORS   Throughout the period the poorer type of door was a plain, boarded one, but those in the better rooms of the more prosperous citizens generally matched the wall-panelling. Thus before 1600 they would be made up of small panels, perhaps with a linenfold design on some of them, and these grew larger in the course of the seventeenth century.[3] Occasionally they were associated on the inside of the room with a portal, a small entrance lobby made of wainscot which helped to keep out draughts. An outer door, however, would be more robustly constructed and might have iron studs on the face. The wood used was commonly oak, though a sixteenth century iron-studded door preserved in the local museum is made of deal. Iron latches, rings, bolts and locks were fitted, as necessary. Small door-frames in 1600 might be simply chamfered with raised, hollow stops (e.g. No. 67 South Street), but the larger ones were of a more impressive appearance, with roll or double-roll moulded surrounds ending in ' urn ' stops (Old Matford House, No. 18 North Street). This last building also has door-frames inserted a hundred years or so later, and the treatment of these is far more architectural. The moulded surrounds are flat and wide, and they are surmounted by an overdoor with a bold profile.

In the late sixteenth and early seventeenth centuries a number of huge, elaborately detailed street doors, with square or round heads, were hung in the city, and though the few surviving today do not belong to houses erected during

[1] In both wings on the same floor the lower parts of certain roof-trusses, which protrude through the ceiling, bear fluted plasterwork or plaster figures.

[2] ECM, Inventory 129.

[3] Two internal doors from the former No. 229 High Street (erected in the mid-1580's) are preserved in the Royal Albert Memorial Museum, Exeter. One is 3ft. wide and contains nine panels, the other is 2 ft. 3 ins. wide and has six panels, the top two bearing a linenfold design.

the period 1550–1700, they are perhaps typical of others that were (pl. 27). Examples can still be seen at the Guildhall (*c.* 1593) and at No. 10 The Close (between 1597 and 1621).[1] The heavy ornamentation was bolted to one or two thicknesses of planking, and the whole construction was so ponderous that a smaller wicket-gate for everyday use had to be let into the centre. The style persisted until at least 1654, when the gate which formerly stood opposite St. Sidwell's Church was installed (No. 2 in Crocker's drawing). Where the aperture was smaller lighter double doors might be used, like those made in 1593 for the round-headed entrance of the old High School in Musgrave Alley.[2] They have the same bold decoration as the others but are only about five feet wide overall, and this type was more likely to be employed in domestic architecture.

FIREPLACES Implements connected with the fireplace are very common in the inventories. The kitchen nearly always contains a variety of brass pots and pans, cauldrons and dishes, iron spits, bars and hooks for cooking over the open fire. In the living room there is usually a pair of dogs or andirons (the more expensive type being tipped with brass), and perhaps in the better homes a fire pick or poker, a fire pan, a pair of tongs, bellows, a shovel, and sometimes a brush to complete the set. Very occasionally a cage for burning coal in is mentioned, and it is surprising that it does not appear more frequently in the documents, for though wood was the most popular fuel, coal was used in an increasing number of Exeter homes from at least the 1570's onwards.

It may well be, however, that the poorest homes had no proper fireplaces at all, and it seems that some of the more imposing houses were without them, too. In Nos. 45–47 High Street, for example, all of the present fireplaces are later insertions and there are no signs of original stacks, though these would have been in the centre of the buildings and not easily disposed of.[3] Moreover, some of the inventories (e.g. App., pp. 94, 96) do not list any fire-irons in the main rooms, only in the kitchen which was often across the courtyard and so not a part of the main structure. In such cases braziers may have been used, though none of these are mentioned in the inventories, and they would have gravely increased the danger of fire breaking out. But even in the more conventional dwellings of well-to-do citizens it was customary, in the early part of the period, to have fireplaces in only one or two of the principal rooms. From the late sixteenth century onwards, however, the number steadily increased until in 1700 a typical medium-sized house might have a fireplace in every room (fig. xx).[4]

The fireplaces of the middling tradesmen and craftsmen remained much the

[1]The arms of Dr. William Cotton, Bishop of Exeter 1597-1621, are above the gateway.

[2]Now in the Royal Albert Memorial Museum, Exeter.

[3]Nos. 34-35 North Street similarly contain no evidence of these. Both buildings were probably once four storeys high but they extend only about 20 ft. from front to rear.

[4]But such dwellings were still occupied only by the more prosperous citizens; the great majority of people had only one or two fireplaces. The Exeter hearth tax assessment of 1671 shows that in that year 19% of the houses had 3-5 hearths, and 8½% had 6-9 hearths; 2½% (including inns) had 10 or more (W. G. Hoskins, *Industry, Trade and People in Exeter, 1688-1800*, History of Exeter Research Group, Monograph No. 6 (1935), 118-119).

same throughout the period. They usually had stone jambs and wooden lintels, both chamfered and stopped. In the larger dwellings the kitchen fireplaces, frequently with ovens opening off them, were simply bigger versions of these, but in principal rooms from the late sixteenth century onwards the fireplace was intended as the focal point of what was often a lavish interior design, and great pains were taken to make it look as striking as possible. That in the hall at Cowick Barton, with its outer frame of an embattled stone cornice resting on engaged columns (dn. 10), was modest compared with dozens of others that were being installed in many merchants' houses in the last years of Elizabeth's reign and in the early decades of the seventeenth century, often bearing the date of their insertion. They were very elaborate indeed, and that which stood in the principal room of Sir George Smyth's town house, No. 229 High Street (pl. 21), a building containing several other superb examples, was typical of them and must have been one of the finest in Exeter at that time.[1] This fantastically carved chimney-piece incorporated most of the current decorative motifs—the fluted pilasters, the cartouches, the strapwork, the coat of arms (in this case that of Elizabeth, but often a personal one), the grotesques, the floral and foliated designs, the frieze—and the whole composition rose to a height of 10 ft. 6 ins. As in the previous example the wooden overmantel was generally an integral part of the scheme, but it was sometimes omitted. When this occurred it was a common practice to substitute for it a decorated plaster cartouche or tablet, like those which still remain at Cowick Barton in the hall, the parlour, and in the chamber over the kitchen. Or it might be a carved wooden panel in the style of that now kept in the city's museum. This is a seventeenth century bas-relief, measuring 4 ft. 6 ins. by 2 ft. 0 ins., and representing the Judgement of Paris. It was formerly in No. 195 High Street.

In the course of the seventeenth century Jacobean extravagance was succeeded by the calmer lines of the Palladian style, with its reduction in detail and its more restrained proportions, though the chimney-piece still often rose to the ceiling. An alternative arrangement, more truly English in character and introduced at the close of the period, was to frame the fireplace with a plain bolection moulding (e.g. No. 18 North Street), and place one or two large wooden panels above it.

WINDOWS   In the first half of the period the homes of the humblest citizens were entirely lacking in windows as we know them. The openings which admitted light to their dwellings were almost certainly covered with a lattice-work of interwoven twigs or oak slips affording some sort of privacy, and wooden shutters, or ' leaves ', kept out the worst of the weather when necessary. Both of these devices—though better wrought—were employed in the more substantial houses (they are mentioned in the Bedford House survey, for example), but from the latter part of the sixteenth century onwards the use of glass spread rapidly. For a long time it was to be obtained only in small pieces known as ' quarrels ', and these were mounted between strips of lead,

---

[1] A number of old fireplaces are illustrated in Crocker, *Old Exeter*,

which were tied to iron casements or to vertical iron bars of diagonal section set in the wooden framework of the window. Some of the casements could be made to open, and might then be furnished with curiously wrought iron handles. The arrangement still survives at No. 67 South Street. The quarrels were themselves set either vertically or diagonally, often in elaborate patterns similar to those in the façade of No. 227 High Street (though these are not original but late nineteenth century restorations). However, we can be sure that at least some of the merchants had windows of this type. We do know that in the grander homes it was a practice to insert painted armorials in the windows of an important room. There were six coats of arms, possibly brought in from the house at Poltimore, in the upper panes of the hall window at Bampfylde House,[1] and the custom was still in evidence a century later, for *c.* 1700 the arms of the Bankes family, worked in stained glass, were installed at No. 171 Fore Street.[2]

The glass in its lead mounting was easily transportable, and it was clearly valued sufficiently to be included among the movable goods until the early seventeenth century. It is catalogued in a fair proportion of the inventories, but that of Richard Sweete, a merchant and a Receiver of the city who died in 1591, records the details more methodically than most.[3]

'The glasse in the windowes

Inprimis in the fore Chamber a windowe of nyne lightes glased, in the parlor one windowe glased of vj lightes transide (?transomed), in the halle one windowe of vj lightes glased, In the gallery one windowe of one lighte glased, in the chamber ouer the parlor a transide windowe of vj lights glased, in the kitchen a windowe of vij lights halfe glased, in the forechamber ouer the kitchinge a windowe of vij lights, in the studie a windowe of iiij lightes glased, in the highest forechamber a windowe of iiij lightes, in the butterie a windowe of one lighte glased, all which glasse amountethe vnto Clviij foote.'

It was valued at 52s. 8d.

Sweete's windows, however, were comparatively modest; the largest consisted of only nine lights. He must have been exceptional among those who attained to his eminence, for a striking feature of the Exeter merchant's house from the 1560's to the middle of the seventeenth century was the great expanse of its windows. Often the most important one, that at the front on the first floor serving the hall or principal chamber, extended across the whole width of the building. That at No. 67 South Street is sixteen lights from end to end (pl. 28). At Nos. 225–226 High Street (*front.*), very early examples erected in 1567, the windows extend the width of the façade on both the first and second floors, and this pattern was repeated forty years later at Nos. 78–79 Fore Street (pl. 30). Around 1650 at No. 227 High Street (*front.*) a window was originally built across the whole of the third floor frontage as well, behind the open gallery[4], and in the same dwelling, at the rear on the first floor, an impressive

[1]*DCNQ*, VI, Pt. 1 (1910-11), 225 and illustration facing.
[2]C. Worth, *The History of the Suburbs of Exeter* (1892), 16.
[3]ECM, Inventory 49. Punctuation marks have been inserted.
[4]But cf. the narrower No. 46 High Street (*c.* 1550), which had a window of eight lights extending the width of the top floor.

window may have taken up the entire width. One certainly did so at No. 72 High Street, a house erected *c.* 1600 and altered in 1905.[1]

The bay window was a common feature to beyond 1650. Those windows on the top floors, usually smaller and consisting of only five lights or so, were very often of this type, and a characteristic of the great, wide window was an imposing central bay (pl. 28). Indeed there was a danger of these projections becoming too imposing, for the consent of the Mayor and Aldermen, or of the Chamberlain, had to be obtained before a bay window oversailing the street could be built.[2] In fact, one Roberte Hunte exceeded a limit of sixteen inches when, in 1563, he added a bay window to his house near the Shambles, and for his sins he had to bear the complete destruction of his work.[3] However, the bay usually figured only in the façade, and No. 18 North Street was exceptional in having one on two floors at the rear (pl. 24). Another type of window which established itself early in the period was the gabled dormer. It is recorded in Hooker's map of 1587—when it must have been in existence for some years—but it was rarer than the bay, for it was necessarily associated with a less common form of building, namely that having a roof running parallel with the street (pl. 31). The gabled structure containing the dormer was much smaller and less roomy than those of similar date still surviving in other provincial cities like Norwich and Oxford. Nevertheless, it persisted in Exeter throughout the seventeenth century and beyond.

Some of the windows, with their simple, square-headed lights, had a stone framework,[4] but the vast majority were framed with wood, and a variety of mouldings were used on the mullions. For example, those at Nos. 225–226 High Street have an ogee moulding both inside and out. At St. Nicholas Priory, however, in the guests' chamber converted to secular domestic use around the same date (in the 1560's), an inserted window has a filleted double-roll moulding on the outer faces and a filleted roll-and-hollow on the inner. At the end of the century No. 67 South Street displays an external ogee and an internal roll (fig. xviii). But the simple ovolo-moulded mullion, rolled on both sides, had already made its appearance by then (Nos. 4–5 Cathedral Yard), and persisted at least to the mid-seventeenth century (No. 227 High Street, No. 40 Alphington Street). By about 1700, however, a square mullion, slenderer than its predecessors and with narrow, rolled angle-mouldings, had been introduced (No. 182 Cowick Street).

The transom, a feature of many large windows, was kept throughout the whole of the period. A window on the second floor of No. 42 High Street (1564) still has one or two lights transomed at a point halfway up the mullion (pl. 13), but later examples were placed nearer the top (pl. 28), with the moulding carried across the underside but with the upper face plainly chamfered. This arrangement is continued in the first floor rear window at No. 227 High Street and in much of the façade, but the central, curving members there

[1]Reed, 'Demolition of Ancient Buildings of Exeter', measured drawing facing 280.
[2]Hooker, *Description of the Citie of Excester*, III, 948.
[3]*Ibid.*, 936.
[4]At No. 196 High Street 'the stone windows of an Elizabethan room' remained in the side wall overlooking Parliament Street until 1914 (Reed, 'Demolition of Ancient Buildings of Exeter', 277).

(*front.*), reminiscent of the Venetian window so popular in the eighteenth century, are unique in the city, and there is no evidence available to indicate whether or not this feature was once incorporated in other buildings erected around the middle of the century. Whatever the case it is hardly likely that there were many, if any, subsequent houses with such enormous areas of glass. Buildings in the latter part of the century had much smaller windows, two or three on each floor, with the leaded lights often divided by a single central mullion crossed by a high transom.

STAIRS   No doubt most of the poorer people, certainly before 1600, had to make do with a stairladder to reach an upper floor or room, especially if this had been contrived in what was originally a ground floor dwelling open to the roof. In the larger houses there might be a newel staircase, a type which persisted from the earlier period and continued to 1700 and beyond, though it was now a less robust structure, always made of wood. A third type, also long-lived and introduced into the best houses in the second half of the sixteenth century, was the framed wooden staircase of the dog-leg or open well variety, which took up more space. Those at No. 67 South Street (pl. 29) and No. 227 High Street are examples of these, and still retain the typical turned balusters of the time.

SANITATION   Of course, the city authorities continued to provide common latrines, and in fact this service was considerably extended early in the period, for on the 4th November 1568 the council agreed that ' there shall be three Common Jakes or Widraughtes made within this city, viz., one in Friernhay, and one at the Town Wall in St. Paul's parish, and the third about the Watergate '.[1] However, at least one of these, that in the Friernhay, later fell into disuse, for in 1665 it was ordered that ' howses of Offices ' for the ease of the citizens were to be re-erected at the Snayle Tower.[2] This fluctuation in the supply of public conveniences is surprising, for one would have thought that the demand was fairly constant. Certainly the great majority of Exeter people had to fend for themselves, in their own back gardens or in the nearest open spaces.

The extent to which the more substantial householders attended to their comfort, and the ways in which they did so, are largely reflected in the documents. Obviously a number of dwellings still survived with the stone shafted garderobe that had been installed a century or two earlier, but this feature is not specifically named in the later records.[3] The Bedford family was apparently content with its six privy houses strategically deployed about the residence for gentlefolk and servants alike, but the nearest thing to this recorded in the less

[1]Hoskins, *Two Thousand Years*, 61.
[2]Walter J. Harte, *Gleanings from the Manuscript of Richard Izacke's Antiquities of the City of Exeter* (undated), 19.
[3]However, there is some evidence that garderobes were still being constructed. Mr. A. W. Everett informs me that lying off the east side of Holloway Street is part of a brick-built mansion, dating from the late seventeenth century and known as Marlborough House. There was a shaft in the centre of the building which descended directly to a cess-pit below ground level. The cess-pit, which appeared to be about 4 ft. square, had slit openings, presumably soakaways, in its sides.

exalted homes was the ground closet built into the new vicarage of St. Thomas after the Civil War.[1] The rest of the citizens were dependent upon the chamber pot, usually a tin one, or the close stool, which was simply a seat with a hole in it and is occasionally described as being accompanied by a pan or an earthen pot. The two utensils are listed in about one-sixth of the inventories, with the close stool alone appearing in one-eighth of them. Some people had both, but practice varied. A dyer in 1640 might have only one chamber pot, though a yeoman over forty years earlier had four, and an innholder, understandably enough, boasted ten in 1625.[2] A merchant might have only one close stool, yet a cutler who died in 1576, leaving an estate worth less than £30 after payment of his debts, had two of them, with an additional close chair for good measure.[3]

The rooms usually mentioned in the inventories as containing the chamber pot, namely the kitchen and the buttery, were those where it was stored and not where it was used. The position of the close stool, however, is a more reliable guide to the habits of the Exeter manufacturing and trading classes. They were not squeamish, it seems. Occasionally, it is true, the close stool would be put in the cockloft, at the head of the stairs or in the gallery, but it was commonly to be found in a chamber on one of the middle floors, and the inventory usually records a bed in the same room. Sometimes, in fact, it was kept in the principal chamber, handily placed for the master and mistress, though the servants perhaps were left to their own devices. Nor was any particular trouble taken to conceal the object from view, and the apothecary who in 1596 had a screen to shield the close stool from the bed in his parlour was an exceptional individual.[4] Yet it was people like these who were enjoined by a sixteenth century physician to sleep with the windows of their chambers closed.[5]

GARDENS

Many of the houses in the centre of the city did not have a garden at all, and even those sites which were not taken up almost entirely by the main dwelling and its associated outbuildings could only accommodate a small one. However, well-to-do citizens often remedied this deficiency by renting gardens elsewhere. Friernhay was a popular area within the walls, and there was space, too, in the north-eastern and south-western quarters of the city. But naturally there was far more land available in the extramural suburbs, and this was far from being fully occupied by those living there, though they tended to have larger gardens. For example, seventeenth century leases describe some dwellings in St. Sidwell's with orchards and gardens extending over as much as an acre. There were others in St. David's, and the expanse of Southernhay

[1]DRO, E/GT (Terriers), document dated 17 February 1679/80.
[2]These three inventories are transcribed in the Appendix.
[3]ECM, Inventory 26.
[4]ECM, Inventory 62. The two closets, probably contrived to take close stools, on the third floor of No. 227 High Street (fig. xiv) indicate a more positive move towards privacy, but it is doubtful if they were inserted before 1700.
[5]John Dover Wilson, *Life in Shakespeare's England* (Pelican edn., 1944), 291.

between the South and East Gates was particularly well developed. By the second half of the sixteenth century stretches of it must have looked very much like a modern allotment, and some details of sixteen of the gardens there have come down to us. They varied between 96 ft. and 220 ft. in length and between 65 ft. and 80 ft. in width, and all but two were rented for 6s. 8d. per annum.[1]

Information about the layout of the gardens is not plentiful. They were often bounded by a wall, or perhaps a hedge, and in a number of deeds they are mentioned together with an orchard, which seems to have been a popular feature. One document, dated 1697, is a little more specific than most in referring to one property, with a herbgarden (kitchen garden) besides an orchard, in the middle-class parish of St. Kerrian's.[2] In the 1670's a basket-maker, John Tucker the elder, had an orchard and hopyard in Magdalen Street, near his house and garden.[3] But gardens, as well as providing food, were often a source of recreation. In 1697 a house in the parish of Holy Trinity formerly occupied by a merchant had, in addition to a kitchen garden and a back garden, another that was known as the best garden, which was probably laid out with some formality and served as a place in which to sit and stroll.[4] The city authorities, to their credit, had long recognised the importance of this aspect. In 1612 they laid out a 'pleasant walke' on Northernhay and set benches there. In 1664 they laid out another walk and planted two hundred young elms, and repeated the scheme on Southernhay three years later.

What was grown in the gardens is hardly mentioned at all. The inventories are concerned with movable goods and usually record only a few tools or some odd stores, and perhaps a well, though one made in 1583 lists 'a woode vyne', valued at 33s. 4d., in the back court of a baker's house.[5] Another document, however, is more helpful. Among property left to Flaye's Alms-houses was a garden in St. Paul's parish and this, according to a brief schedule attached to a lease of 1637, contained the following fruit-trees: 'One Apricocke Tree, One Rennatt Tree, One paire maine Tree, One peppin Tree, One greene henning Tree, One querrindon Tree, One Stubbard Tree, Two Cherrie Trees'.[6]

ROOFS

The roof-trusses remaining in the city that are both original (i.e. dating from 1550–1700) and accessible are relatively few in number, and it would be unwise to generalize too much on the strength of the available evidence. A single example may signify not a type but an expedient, dictated by the requirements of a particular case and also by the materials at hand. However, certain facts are clear. Top floor rooms were either partly contained within the roof-space, or they had a flat ceiling with the roof above this, and cocklofts might be wholly accommodated there. In the first case the arrangement resulted in an open truss which was often similar to earlier examples dating from

[1]Hooker, *Description of the Citie of Excester*, III, 758-761.
[2]ECM, 53/6 Box 93, No. 8.   [3]ECM, D1/40/12.   [4]ECM, Box 49.   [5]ECM, Inventory 33.
[6]ECM, D425. The rennet, pearmain, pippin, ?greening, quarenden and stubbard are varieties of apple.

before 1550. This was natural enough, for the problem, that of providing adequate head room, was still the same. The truss put up in the late sixteenth century and contained in the rear block behind the main building at No. 36 North Street (fig. xv) is very like that shown in pl. 9. It consists of an upright member curving at the top and jointed (though not flush in this case) into the principal rafter, which has a wall-plate of small section let into its upper face. The rafters are halved at the apex and stabilized by a high collar-beam. As in the earlier example the design is given added character by the manner in which the ridge–tree and the purlins (there is only one pair at No. 36) are carried through the rafters. Other trusses, apparently like this and erected at much the same date, still survive at Nos. 3–5 Cathedral Yard. There the curving member fits more neatly into the principal, but the ceilings hide many of the collar-beams and all of the ridge-trees and purlins, so it is impossible to see if the styles are exactly similar.

Another type of open truss, again dating from the end of the sixteenth century, is to be found at No. 18 North Street. A ceiling conceals much of the detail—though there is almost certainly a collar-beam above it—but the most interesting feature, the junction of the upright with the principal rafter, is clearly visible (fig. xv). The method employed is an unusual one, and the form of construction is inherently weak. The principal, instead of resting on top of the upright, is fitted into its inner face—or rather into half of it, for it is set off-centre—and the effect of this is to thrust the upright outwards. The position of the wall-plate is also different, for in this case it is let into the upright. Almost a century after No. 18 North Street was built an open trussed roof was put up at No. 40 High Street, and the arrangement here is again a weak one (fig. xv). The joint is carried too far down for the principals to be considered safely lodged.

In those houses where the top floor was not partly contained within the roof-space, or where the cockloft was wholly accommodated within it, a closed truss was commonly used. In other words a tiebeam was incorporated in the arrangement, and this would usually render a collar-beam unnecessary. Neither No. 46 High Street (fig. xiii) nor No. 67 South Street (fig. xviii) has a cockloft, and the trusses used in these two buildings are probably typical of many put up in Exeter from before 1550 to well beyond 1700. In both cases the principal rafters rest on top of the tie-beams and are halved at the apex (those at No. 67 are also notched). At No. 46 the two pairs of purlins and the ridge-tree are carried through the principals, as in the contemporary open truss, but at No. 67, though the single set of purlins is carried through, the ridge-tree is let into the apex.

From c. 1650 onwards roof construction in the city was dominated by a particular type of truss, which persisted well after 1700. A feature of roofs after 1550 was a tendency for the scantling to become progressively lighter. The example of No. 46 High Street shows how heavy it could be early in the period. By the second half of the seventeenth century it was distinctly thinner. Principal rafters that had once been a foot across in places were now a mere six inches, and the extent to which these tapered towards the apex, a marked characteristic a hundred years earlier, was now negligible. Moreover, this development was accompanied by an inferior arrangement of the roof members. No longer were the purlins and the ridge-tree passed through the principals, for these were too narrow to take them. Instead the principals were halved and crossed at the apex, with the ridge-tree lodged in the ' V ' so formed, and the purlins either rested upon the upper faces of the main rafters or were partly let into them. Despite the lightness of the construction it seems that a collar-beam was not used. However, the new truss was versatile. It could either be used closed in those dwellings, like No. 227 High Street and No. 178a Cowick Street, which had the cockloft contained in the triangle of the roof-space, or it could be used open in cases where the arrangement was more complex, as at No. 4 Cowick Street (fig. xx).

The development of a lighter roof structure was not related to the covering that it had to bear, for, so far as is known, this did not change markedly during the period. Although a high proportion of houses in the extramural suburbs had thatched roofs, particularly in the working-class area of St. Sidwell's, this material was forbidden within the city walls owing to the grave risk of fire.[1] In 1641 when John Hayne, a merchant living in St. Mary Arches parish, was having some repairs done to his roof he paid a boatman 16s. for delivering 3,000 ' shindles ' (shingles) to him.[2] It is possible that these were wooden tiles, but it is more likely that they were the relatively small, stone roofing slates then in use. Stone slates, probably from quarries in the Kingsbridge area, were the standard covering, and these are occasionally mentioned in the inventories. William Spicer, for example, had 500 ' hellinge ' (roofing) stones stored in his garden outside the South Gate (App., p. 109), and in 1616 James Tirrie of St. John's parish had ' healdinge stones with certaine heare ', valued at 20s., in or near his kitchen.[3] The hair—animal hair, that is—was perhaps used for bedding the slates and for keeping out the wind and rain. Unfortunately, Devon roofing slates were inclined to go soft with weathering,[4] so it is doubtful if any still survive in the city from before 1700.

The best houses were fitted with cast lead eaves guttering, which caught the rain and conveyed it to a cistern, usually also made of lead, in the courtyard below. The cisterns were often highly decorated, but so was the guttering, and a late sixteenth century example, having a crenellated outer edge with a running floral motif, is preserved in the local museum. However, the most striking feature on a number of seventeenth century roofs, when viewed from the ground, was the ridge-tile, bearing the figure of a horse and rider, at the apex of the front gable. Apparently this was once a fairly common sight in towns in the South-West, though no examples could be dated before 1600. It is said that they were made at the brickworks at Bridgetown, Totnes, and they seem to have been quite sizeable. One tile that was measured was 22 ins. long, the horse standing on it was 13 ins. long, and the tile, horse and rider together were $13\frac{1}{2}$ ins. high.[5] Until the last war No. 79 Fore Street, erected in the early

[1]Hoskins, *Two Thousand Years*, 60.
[2]Brushfield, ' Financial Diary of a Citizen of Exeter ', 251.
[3]ECM, Inventory 123.   [4]Hoskins, *Devon*, 264.
[5]*DCNQ*, XI, Pt. 1 (1920-21), 264 and illustration facing.

seventeenth century, had one of these on its roof (pl. 30), and was known as The Chevalier because of it, but the building was destroyed in 1942 and the ridge-tile, then unique in the city, went as well. We have seen (p. 21) that a comparable practice was followed in medieval Exeter but in all likelihood the equestrian figure was peculiar to the seventeenth century. It is doubtful if the custom persisted much beyond 1700. An ordinary gable was required to show the figure off, but at the end of our period the hipped roof was being generally introduced into the city, in conjunction with a completely new style of building. It quickly became common, and in fact there was a tendency to convert already existing gabled roofs to the new fashion, as at No. 40 High Street (pl. 39).

BUILDING MATERIALS

COB   This continued to be used throughout the whole of the period— indeed it persisted in the city down to the nineteenth century—but there is no way of estimating at all accurately the amount of work that was done in it. A number of seventeenth century deeds refer to garden walls and property boundaries being built of cob, or ' clobb ' as it was sometimes called, and on one occasion the traditional method of construction is noted down. A lease of 1659 describes a garden on the east of St. Nicholas Lane as having a clobb wall seven feet high besides the coping, and footed with stone.[1]   So far as houses are concerned cob, as a cheap building material easily obtainable, was probably used quite widely in the construction of dwellings for the labouring poor, particularly in St. Sidwell's, though paradoxically the only cob house now remaining in Exeter from before 1700 belonged to one of the most powerful citizens of his time—Sir George Smyth. Old Matford House was erected c. 1600 as his country residence, and there is significance in the fact that it stands well outside the city walls. Building in cob was a lengthy business and adequate working space was necessary, for the walls had to be pared down to the required thickness. That space would not often be available in old Exeter, at least not in the central area. Furthermore, cob walls were frequently of massive proportions, and might be as much as three feet thick. These would take up far too much of the restricted sites within the city, and the amount of living space would be severely reduced. The implication of all this is that what building there was in cob must have taken place largely in the extramural areas, where the pressures of space and time were of less importance.

STONE   This material is occasionally recorded in the inventories. A baker in 1606 had ' free stons ' worth 20s. in his linney,[2] while Alexander Jermyn, a merchant who died two years later, had in his garden ' 96 Foote purbrick stone & iiij stone pillers ' valued at £3 6s. 8d., together with ' 40 seames of Silferton stones ' valued at £1 6s. 8d.[3]   Purbrick, or rather Purbeck, stone is a hard limestone from Dorset used in building and paving, and Silverton stone, quarried at a village a few miles to the north of Exeter, is of the volcanic trap variety. But the physical evidence shows that it was the coarse, red breccia,

[1]ECM, 53/6 Box 100.   [2]ECM, Inventory 75.   [3]ECM, Inventory 99.

more readily available at Heavitree in particular,[1] which was by far the most common building stone used throughout the whole of this period, as it had been in the earlier one.

Bampfylde House (1590's) and Cowick Barton (c. 1600) were built entirely in stone of the Heavitree type, but they were exceptional. The all-stone house in Exeter really belonged to the era before 1550. Nevertheless, the material continued to be widely used. We have seen that the cob walls in the city were footed with it, as a defence against damp and disintegration. Until the late seventeenth century cellars were also invariably lined with Heavitree stone, and chimney-stacks were constructed of it. Down to 1600, if not later, the earlier practice persisted in some of the more imposing houses of having side walls of stone, which could accommodate fire-places and also serve as fire-breaks. On the upper floors these continued to project on shapely corbels, similar to those at No. 41 High Street (fig. xv). There is evidence, too, that in some buildings a stone wall on the ground floor was combined with timber-framing on the upper storeys. An old engraving of a late sixteenth century dwelling, formerly in Catherine Street, illustrates this combination in the two-storeyed facade.[2] At No. 72 High Street (c. 1600), a building rising to three floors, the arrangement was once to be found at the rear.[3]

We know that stone slates were the most common form of roof covering, but they were also used on the facades of many houses. As in the earlier period shop stalls on the ground floor were protected from the rain by stone-slated pentices which flung the water clear (pl. 7).[4] These usually extended across the entire width of the building, and they were also often attached at upper floor levels (pls. 31 and 33). A more comprehensive form of protection for the complete face of a wall was slate-hanging, which at that time was common in other towns in South Devon (e.g. Ashburton, Totnes), and which persisted in Exeter until the nineteenth century. Nearly all of the later work in the city is confined to rear and side walls, and the slates used are simple, rectangular ones, but the early seventeenth century example of the Tudor House (pl. 32) shows that the slate-cutter made a distinct contribution to the architectural ostentation of Jacobean Exeter. In other respects the building is unexciting and Exe Island was far from being the richest quarter in those days, so there are grounds for assuming that such intricate work was displayed on other facades within the city walls. But it is impossible to say how extensive it was, for the Tudor House is the sole survivor.[5]

TIMBER-FRAMING   This method of construction was by far the most common

---

[1]The former immense size of the Heavitree quarries indicates the amount of stone used over the centuries. In 1882 they were reputedly a quarter of a mile long and up to 100 ft. deep (F. T. Howard, ' The Building Stones of Ancient Exeter ', *TDA*, LXV (1933), 334).

[2]Copy in Exeter City Library.

[3]Reed, ' Demolition of Ancient Buildings of Exeter ', illustration facing 280.

[4]Thatch was often used for this purpose in the extramural suburbs.

[5]There is similar slate-hanging on the first floor facade of No. 1 Catherine Street. It was probably inspired by the Tudor House but was applied only thirty or forty years ago.

throughout the whole of the period, and down to *c.* 1650 it was characterized by an extreme sturdiness. This was particularly so in the third quarter of the sixteenth century, when beams and bressummers might be as much as 1 ft. across and upright members 7 ins. by 5 ins. in section. They were necessary to carry the heavy scantling of the roof, where the massive trusses were often no more than five or six feet apart (e.g. No. 46 High Street, Nos. 225–226 High Street). However, from the end of the sixteenth century onwards there was a marked tendency towards a lighter form of construction.

The upright studs which formed the framework of the walls were sometimes set only about 9 ins. apart, and the greatest distance between them was not much more than 1 ft., an arrangement dictated by the methods of infilling. One of these is clearly demonstrated by an exhibit in the Royal Albert Memorial Museum, Exeter; it is of sixteenth century date and was formerly on the site of No. 57 Preston Street (fig. xv). Holes were drilled in the sides of the studs and oak slats were fitted horizontally into these, then mud plaster was laid on this base until it was flush with the faces of the studs. Nos. 46–47 High Street (pl. 12) were among other houses built in this manner. But it had its drawbacks, for it meant that the slats had to be laboriously inserted as the main timbers were being erected. A more convenient procedure, and perhaps a more popular one, is illustrated in the two-storeyed structure behind No. 36 North Street. The central part of this is of late sixteenth century date, put up almost a hundred years after the main dwelling at the front, and at one point the timbering is completely exposed. In this case, instead of holes the studs have a long, continuous groove down their inner sides, and the slats were originally lodged in these (though they are no longer *in situ*).[1] The advantage here was that they could be slid in after the framework of the building had been fitted together.

But the chief significance of the timber-framed technique of building at this time was that it enabled those who could afford it, namely the merchants, to embellish the exteriors of their houses with almost as much extravagance as they brought to the decorative scheme within. It was the facade, naturally, to which the greatest care was devoted, and in the second half of the sixteenth century increased opportunity for display was made possible through the practice of building many houses in pairs, so that the designer had a larger surface area to work on. Nos. 41–42 High Street (pl. 13), Nos. 46–47 High Street (pl. 11), Nos. 225–226 High Street (*front.*), the former Nos. 19–20 North Street (pl. 23) and Nos. 78–79 Fore Street (pl. 30) are all examples of houses built in pairs, and together they illustrate perfectly the external exuberance of the Elizabethan and Jacobean merchant house in Exeter. The vertical studs and the bressummers were often elaborately moulded and carved with running motifs, and the plasterwork between them might be decorated with strapwork designs (pl. 15).

Probably the most striking feature about these buildings was the manner in

---

[1] The same method is used in the Elizabethan extension of a surviving fifteenth century merchant's house at Barnstaple in North Devon (see Bruce W. Oliver, ' The Three Tuns, Barnstaple ', *TDA*, LXXX (1948), 152).

which they sailed out over the street, frequently by several feet.[1] In some cases each of the upper floors—and there might be as many as four—projected over the one below, and as they did so they carried bay windows and gable-ends which thrust the structure further forward. The opportunities for decorative supports at these points were legion, and on the best houses they were fully taken. Elaborately carved window and storey brackets proliferated. They might take the form of human or animal heads, but complete animal figures two to three feet in length also appeared there. Mythological beasts seem to have been among the favourites; for example, Nos. 225–226 High Street have a griffin and Nos. 19–20 North Street used to have a unicorn. Grotesques, often in the shape of men with women's breasts, were also popular (*front.*). Nos. 19–20 North Street even had, on some floors, columns with panelled pedestals and Ionic capitals extending to full storey height. On the ground floor of some of the houses the door-head itself was brought into the scheme, bearing perhaps that symbol of the proud owner or craftsman—the date of the building's erection (pl. 14).

Though architectural display was concentrated in the facade it did not end there. Carved panels in the side wall of No. 46 High Street once overlooked Lamb Alley when it ran from the Close to the main thoroughfare. Oriel windows with carved consoles—modest ones, admittedly—still remain at the rear of No. 18 North Street (pl. 24). It seems that the gallery in particular was sometimes the subject of special treatment. For example, that formerly on the first floor at No. 229 High Street was supported by circular, moulded posts, made of oak and 10 ft. high (fig. xv). The gallery itself, which was about 6 ft. wide, was completely enclosed and the outer wall, containing two windows, was broken up by moulded ribs into an intricate series of rectangular and L-shaped panels. These were originally filled with decorated plasterwork laid on a base of oak pegs or twigs, which were kept in place by grooved boards lying behind the ribs.[2]

No. 227 High Street (*c.* 1650) was still in the great tradition of the earlier merchant houses (*front.*). The grotesques and the carved heads had gone out of fashion by then, but the huge brackets supporting the upper storeys and the gable-ends were nevertheless bold and ornate, and the open, balustraded gallery on the fourth floor was a feature which its forerunners had probably not possessed.

But this was a last fling. A new style of timber -framing was already being introduced into the city. The timbers were now much slighter, and the upright studs were braced by occasional diagonal struts. The major difference, however, was that there was no longer any infilling between the members, and the framework was simply covered with a thin layer of lath-and-plaster (pl. 35). The whole conception was more severe, and certainly more meagre. Nearly all external decoration had gone, and though the bay window remained a fairly common feature, the brackets supporting it were only plainly shaped. More-

---

[1] A by-law of August 1563 required that any person wishing his property to oversail the street should first obtain permission from the city authorities (Hooker, *Description of the Citie of Excester*, III, 936).

[2] A post and part of the panelling from No. 229 is preserved in the Royal Albert Memorial Museum, Exeter. For an exterior view of the gallery when *in situ* see Crocker, *Old Exeter*, Pl. LI.

over, oversailing of the upper storeys was either reduced to a few inches or, in the vast majority of cases, discontinued altogether (pl. 34).

How poorly these new buildings compared with the earlier ones is implied in the documentary evidence. A survey of certain Exeter properties made at the close of the seventeenth century describes, among others, two tenements in the parish of St. Lawrence. They were newly built in 1676 ' and are but thinn, weak buildings, and thereby very subject to repairations '.[1] It may well have been a house of this sort which in 1674 was involved in an incident described by Izacke: ' On Tuesday the nine and twentyeth day of December, the house of one Richard Jewell, within the Parish of St. Sydwell's in the Suburbs of this City casually fell down, about seven of the Clock in the morning of that day, grievously bruised the said Jewell, and destroyed his Wife and a Grandchild therein '.[2] Whether this was so or not, thinness and weakness were indeed two of the salient features of the new style, as is shown by the fact that none of these later structures has survived as well as a number of others put up long before 1650.

This lighter form of construction really came into its own during the decades following the Civil War. In October 1645 about eighty houses outside the South Gate were deliberately burned down by the royalist defenders, who feared an attack from that quarter,[3] and dwellings in St. Sidwell's were also destroyed during the siege of the city. When the war was over the business of rebuilding these began, and part of this process is described in a number of leases, now in the City Library, which refer to the ' late troubles ' and to earlier homes ' consumed by fire '.[4] Some of the houses erected then still (1962) survive in part in Holloway Street, Magdalen Street, and in the lower part of South Street (pl. 34). At the same time others were being raised elsewhere in the city, in St. Sidwell's and across the river in Cowick Street and Alphington Street. They were soon appearing in High Street itself. Despite its inferiority to the old style the new one quickly became established and, so far as dwellings of up to medium size (i.e. three storeys) were concerned, it persisted far beyond 1700.

BRICK There are scattered documentary references to brick from the late sixteenth century onwards. As early as 1578 we find a curious entry in the inventory of the prosperous merchant, Henry James, relating to 'lyme and stones of bricke with the cask '.[5] These were listed among other things in the great court, and were valued at 2s. The same document also mentions brick, kept together with charcoal and an old range, in a chamber which James had at premises belonging to a Mr. Williams. The quantities involved here seem to have been quite small but another merchant, Alexander Jermyn, had 2,000 bricks valued at £3 3s. in his back court when he died in 1608.[6] In what way were the bricks used? We are told that the cellar at Bampfylde House

---

[1] D & C, 4573 1/8. Other houses built in the latter part of the seventeenth century are described in App. p. 123.

[2] Richard Izacke, *Remarkable Antiquities of the City of Exeter*, 177.

[3] Hoskins, *Two Thousand Years*, 72.

[4] See, for example, ECM, 53/6 Box 87, deed dated 29 March 1677; Z1/19/2/4a dated 30 June 1652; D1/40/6 dated 20 September 1656; D1/40/8 dated 2 October 1665; D1/40/10a dated 1 March 1666.

[5] ECM, Inventory 29.   [6] ECM, Inventory 99.

(*c.* 1600) contained original brick groining springing from a square brick pier,[1] and though there is no other direct evidence of its use in house building, brick must have been increasingly employed in some forms of construction during the first half of the seventeenth century.

Certainly this is strongly implied by the choice of brick for the wall which divided the Cathedral into East and West Peter's during the Commonwealth period.[2] It was erected in 1657 at a cost of £150, and the size of the project argues a local familiarity with the material, and also a local source of supply. One or two points support both of these suppositions. A lease dated the 2nd February 1675–6 relates to a close of land of one-third of an acre in Holy Trinity parish which was assigned to Nicholas Potter of Exeter, bricklayer.[3] If Potter's was a recognised local occupation in the mid-1670's, then it is safe to assume that a fair amount of building in brick was already taking place in the city for some time before that date.[4] So far as the source of supply is concerned, it is possible that Dutch bricks used as ballast in returning ships came to Exeter by way of Topsham in the latter part of the seventeenth century. But we know that by 1690 there were already two brickfields opened up in St. Sidwell's parish,[5] and in view of the amount of work that was being done before that date, it seems reasonable to assume that at least a high proportion of the bricks used were being manufactured locally.

Some time between 1679 and 1682 Nicholas Potter erected houses and other buildings on his third of an acre, and in all likelihood these were partly or wholly made of brick.[6] At almost exactly the same time (1679–81) the Custom House, the earliest surviving brick building in the city, was being constructed at the quay. If no houses made entirely of brick preceded it a good number must have followed soon afterwards, under the influence of this fine building.

Yet even in 1700 brick had not triumphed completely. No. 4 Cowick Street (fig. xx) had its chimney-stack, rear and side walls built of brick, but the front was still timber-framed. The imposing facade of No. 40 High Street (pl. 39), the earliest remaining piece of domestic brickwork in the city (*c.* 1700), was only a facade, for the structure behind it is a timber-framed dwelling put up a few decades before. Indeed the timber-framed method of construction continued, as we have seen, well into the eighteenth century. But brick had made its mark. The opening up by 1706 of yet another brickfield near Larkbeare in Holy Trinity parish suggests a minor building boom in the city at the end of the seventeenth and in the early part of the eighteenth century.[7] Of greater significance, however, is the fact that a completely new style and a new sophistication partly derived from Dutch models (e.g. No. 40 High Street) had been introduced into Exeter. A fresh era in its architectural history had begun, one destined to reach its climax a century or so later in the Georgian designs of Bedford Circus, Barnfield Crescent and Southernhay.

---

[1]Dymond, ' Bampfylde House ', 98.

[2]Oliver, *History of the City of Exeter*, 120.

[3]ECM, Z1/19/2/5.

[4]Two leases of 1671 refer to brick walls (ECM, D1/6/5 and D7/5/5).

[5]Hoskins, *Exeter in the Seventeenth Century: Tax and Rate Assessments*, xiii.

[6]ECM, leases Z1/19/2/6a and Z1/19/2/7.

[7]Hoskins, *ibid.* This may have supplied bricks for Bellair. a large house erected *c.* 1700 beside the Topsham road.

PART III

DESCRIPTIONS OF SELECTED HOUSES

(The following properties are listed in alphabetical, not chronological, order)

1   40 ALPHINGTON STREET

This is a dwelling of three storeys, presenting its gable to the street and constructed of timber-framing clad with lath-and-plaster. The rear wall on the ground floor is of brick or stone and may be later. The roof is modern. The structure dates from *c.* 1650 and contains some original features. Among these are the staircase and the oriel windows in the facade, one on each of the first and second floors (which both oversail the street by about 10 ins.). The oriels have moulded sills (roll-fillet-hollow) supported by brackets. (No. 38 has a similar sill on the first floor, but this building, erected at the same time as No. 40, has been almost completely refashioned.) In the first floor oriel the original mullions survive, having an ovolo moulding internally but with no external mouldings. They divide the window (8 ft. wide overall) into three front lights (20 ins. each) and two splayed side lights (7½ ins.). The lintel and jambs are chamfered internally with raised, hollow stops. The original plan survives and is typical of the period. It consists of a front and back room on each floor, with the chimney-stack and staircase lying between them. A ground floor through-entry lies on the east side and opens on to both rooms and directly on to the staircase, which can be approached in no other way.

2   BOWHILL HOUSE, DUNSFORD HILL (figs. iv and v)

Bowhill, situated across the river in the parish of St. Thomas, was erected *c.* 1450 or somewhat earlier by the Holland family which, at various times during the fifteenth century, supplied members of Parliament for Devon, Exeter and Totnes. The building, which is constructed of Heavitree stone and volcanic trap rock, lies a little way back on the north side of the road; it encloses a courtyard on the east, south and west sides, but it may be that the plan was originally quadrangular.[1]

The eastern wing is largely taken up by the great hall, now partly divided into two floors with the screens passage at the south end; this retains its original moulded doorways with pointed arches, but no panelling survives. The hall was lit by four large square-headed windows, each of two lights divided by a transom, and these are almost complete. The lights have cinquefoil heads and signs that shutters were used below the transom; external square labels terminate in human heads. The fireplace, now blocked, lies between the two

---

[1]This description is based on A. W. Everett's account of the building in ' A Note on Bowhill, Exeter ', *Arch. Journ.*, CXV (1958), 203-206.

east windows. The hall roof is still most impressive though dilapidated. Great moulded arch-braces, originally with decorative features at their lower extremities, rise to the collars from a point 3 ft. 6 ins. below the wall-plate. There are two ranges of purlins, and the upper set, 18 ins. by 6 ins. in section and laid flat, support semi-circular coving, a feature found in other roofs erected locally at that time. Each bay is divided vertically by a central moulded rib, with large cusps which once bore a decorative feature; diagonal wind-braces, curved inwards at the bottom, lie between the wall-plate and the lower purlin, and formerly had large bosses at the upper point of intersection. At the north end of the hall there is evidence of a former stud-and-panel partition on the ground floor with timber-framing above, beyond which there was possibly a store-room beneath a first floor private chamber. Much of this part of the building is now missing but it seems that the chamber also had an arch-braced roof, and was reached by a projecting stair rising from a small round-arched doorway with chamfered jambs in the north-west corner of the hall.

To the south of the hall in the range fronting the street was the parlour, formerly gained by a door in the screens passage. The ceiling here is divided by moulded beams into rectangular compartments, though these are subdivided further by moulded ribs of later insertion. In the east wall there is a pair of mutilated two-light windows with cinquefoil heads and stone mullions beneath a single square label. To the north of these is a small pointed arched doorway which formerly opened on to another projecting stair rising to the floor above. The fireplace, now concealed, lies in the south wall.

The room above the parlour was probably the solar. It is now divided by a nineteenth century partition but the open roof of four bays still survives. It is almost identical with that in the hall but less elaborate and of lighter construction. The east wall has been replaced but there may have been a garderobe in the south-east corner. At the west end of this south range on the same floor there is a large room with an open roof of three bays ceiled at collar-beam level. It is of plain arch-braced construction having curved wind-braces below the lower of the two ranges of purlins, and the bays were formerly divided by a central vertical rib.

The original kitchen lies on the ground floor of the west range, having a large open fireplace, with oven, in its north wall; the ceiling has chamfered beams and joists. The room over it has an arch-braced roof of one and a half bays, with wind-braces. The large ground floor room at the west end of the south range was possibly a service room associated with the kitchen, though the kitchen wing originally extended further to the north.

3   3–5 CATHEDRAL YARD (fig. xv)

Here there are three adjoining four-storeyed buildings, each about 15 ft. wide, having cellars lined with Heavitree stone and presenting their gables to the Yard. They are of timber-framed construction and date from the sixteenth century, but they have been generally extended by 1 ft. 7 ins. or more at the rear, and the side and rear walls have been almost completely rebuilt in modern brick. Some timber-framing, however, is visible on the top floor of No. 5, in the east side wall. It consists of comparatively slight vertical studs set 15–18 ins. apart; they are tied with straight, raking struts, but these seem later. The original plan of the dwellings consisted simply of one room to each floor, and there was no oversailing of the upper storeys. But internally few original features have survived. The cellar of No. 5 still retains its flight of stone steps, in the front east corner, leading up to the street, and all three cellars have chamfered beams with ogee stops. On the top floor each building has an oriel window of five lights supported by brackets, and those in Nos. 4 and 5 have their original ovolo-moulded mullions with chamfered, ogee-stopped jambs, and some original fittings. The most important survivals, however, are the trusses, partly revealed in all three structures. The roofs, of two bays (8 ft. 6 ins. to 9 ft. 6 ins. wide), are mostly ceiled at collar-beam level, but a curving collar-beam is disclosed in the centre truss of No. 3. The other components of the trusses are two principal rafters jointed into vertical wall-posts, which curve at the head to follow the line of the principals (fig. xv).

4 1–2 Catherine Street (pls. 1, 19 and 20, fig. vii)

These are a pair of three-storeyed buildings, with cellars, standing on the corner of Catherine Street and St. Martin's Lane, and among the most interesting survivals in the city. They are constructed of substantial timber-framing against a rear wall of Heavitree stone and, judging by the fifteenth century accounts of the Vicars Choral, they were erected c. 1450 as part of a range called Little Calendarhay. They were possibly planned as a group of one-roomed lodgings or 'flats' for resident priests, who ate perhaps in the late fourteenth century hall of the Vicars Choral in South Street. The ground floors of both premises have since been converted into a modern shop, and the facades have also been almost completely rebuilt.[1] The decorated slate-hanging on the first floor of No. 1 was put up only thirty or forty years ago, probably inspired by the Tudor House. Nevertheless, a surprising number of original features remain.

Internally on the ground floor two stud-and-panel screens have survived for the most part, and each dwelling has a garderobe in the rear wall, though that in No. 1 has had its shaft blocked up and that in No. 2 has been cleared out and converted into a cupboard. No. 2 also has a fireplace with a segmental relieving arch, and it may well be that there was once a similar arrangement in the other house, but as the rear wall has been remade in connection with the westward extension it is impossible to confirm this. No. 1 was originally entered from Catherine Street, like No. 2, for the old St. Martin's Gate, taken down in 1819, formerly abutted the west side of the building.

On the first floor there is a further garderobe and fireplace in No. 2, and the mortises for the original studs together with the internal chamfering for the original window (3 ft. 9 ins. wide, which suggests an early date) are revealed on the underside of the bressummer in the facade. Again it is quite possible that there was a corresponding fireplace and garderobe on the first floor of No. 1, but this room is now chiefly remarkable for evidence of early decorative

---

[1] These notes describe the buildings as they were before the further alterations carried out in April/May 1961.

work, of late sixteenth century date, on the spine-beam and on the joists between the beam and the facade (pl. 20). (The original joists on the other side of the beam have been replaced.) There are chevron designs painted on the joists and running tendril patterns on the beam, both in black on a ground of yellow ochre.

The top floor of two bays contains nothing of interest in No. 1, but in its partner the trusses are partly revealed and during the alterations of April/May, 1961 (which saw the removal of the inserted fireplace shown in fig. vii) they were completely exposed. They consist of two heavy principal rafters which are connected to the wall-post by a form of arch-brace, and which are halved and crossed, but not notched, at the apex. There is a single set of purlins and a ridge-tree, which do not rest upon the principals but are passed through them.

The cellars of the two dwellings are not at all alike. That in No. 1 is large and spacious, ideal for storage, with a modern fireplace occupying the point in the rear wall from which the garderobe was originally cleared. That in No. 2, with some cob among the stone lining, is very small and cramped and was built chiefly for the purpose of clearing the garderobes above. Both cellars have inserted stairs, but there is good evidence (chamfering on the beam in No. 1, a cut-back in the stonework in No. 2) pointing to the original entrances to both. Staircases have also been inserted on the other floors and effectively block the entrances to all the garderobes, but there is nothing to indicate the positions of the original staircases or ladders.

If Nos. 1 and 2 were occupied as priests' lodgings, then the practice ceased at the Reformation. They continued to remain in the hands of the Vicars Choral, but deeds deposited in the Cathedral Library show that No. 2 (and probably No. 1, as well) was leased as a business proposition.[1] During the second half of the sixteenth century the lessees were various Devonshire gentry—Hugh Pomeroy and John Prouz (1566) and Nicholas Wyott (1591) —who then sub-let the property. In the course of the seventeenth century, however, it passed directly into the hands of tradesmen, with John Veale, a yeoman of Exeter (1631–2) being succeeded by Stephen Toller, a haberdasher (1664) and Robert Chafe, a shoemaker (1695). The rent remained throughout at 13s. 4d. per annum. The transfer to secular use resulted in a rearrangement of room functions, and the new plan probably consisted of a ground floor shop with a kitchen behind, and a first floor hall with a chamber above.

5   1 THE CLOSE (pl. 19, fig. xvi)

This is a building of four storeys with cellar, presenting its gable to the street and erected on a site which narrows considerably owing to the position of the adjoining St. Martin's Church. The structure, now a shop with living accommodation above, is of late sixteenth century date and takes its name, Mol's Coffee House, from the Thomas Moll recorded in a subsidy of 1595 for St. Martin's parish[2]. It is reputed to have been built in 1596 and a carving

[1] D & C, VC/3122, 3128, 21802, 21717, 21720/1, 21723/4/5.
[2] DCNQ, XXI (1940-41), 25.

of the royal coat of arms of Elizabeth, incorporating that date, was situated until 1806 between the two bays on the second floor before being replaced by the present painted board *c.* 1885.[1]

The side walls, corbelled forward on each floor, are of Heavitree stone. The rear wall may be of stone on the ground floor, but there is timber-framing above. The stack is in the north wall, though the fireplaces have been removed on the lower floors. The facade is remarkable for the great double-bayed window on the first floor, but the two separate bay windows on the second floor have been modernized. The balustraded balcony and Dutch gable above date only from the second half of the last century; they can be no later than 1879, for they are recorded in Crocker's sketch of that date.

Internally the ground floor retains no original features, and neither do the top two floors, which were once two rooms wide and contained two or more chambers on each floor. But the staircase, in the north corner against the rear wall, has a carved newel post, covered with an oak-leaf pattern, on the ground and first floors. The latter is the most interesting in the building, being taken up almost entirely with what was once the principal living room (the kitchen was presumably on the ground floor, where the later wash house is shown in the plan). This is 9 ft. high and contains late sixteenth century panelling incorporating carved, fluted pilasters set at intervals, and bearing a series of forty-six small, painted coats of arms.[2] The double-bayed, mullioned and transomed window extends for seventeen lights across the whole of the facade; the mullions have an external ogee moulding and a hollow-fillet-ogee internally.

6   2–4 THE CLOSE (pl. 19, fig. xvi)

These are three timber-framed buildings of late sixteenth century date, but very much altered. Few original features survive. All three once presented a gabled elevation to the Close, and they consisted simply of a front and rear room on each floor, with a ground floor side passage, as shown in Tothill's plan; a small courtyard and garden lay behind each of them. No. 2 has a massive, central chimney-stack of Heavitree stone lying between the two rooms, with signs of a wooden lintelled fireplace in the rear room on the ground floor. In the same room there is a lateral beam with a triple-roll moulding on the north side. In Nos. 3 and 4 the stacks, also centrally placed, are far narrower and are no doubt later. No. 2 is of three storeys, with the top floor oversailing. No. 3 is of four storeys with cellar, but the top floor is later and must have been added when the facade was remodelled, probably some time in the nineteenth century. No. 4 is of four storeys with a cellar, which is lined with Heavitree stone and contains a well. There is late sixteenth century wall panelling in the first floor front room, though some at least has been inserted subsequently.

---

[1] Crocker, *Old Exeter*, in the account accompanying Pl. XXVI.
[2] Most of the bearers of these are listed in Crocker.

7 7 THE CLOSE (fig. ix)

A former prebendal house erected in Heavitree stone *c.* 1450, this building
was partly remodelled in the late sixteenth century, and drastically altered
in the early nineteenth century.[1] Tothill's plan of 1764 shows the structure
very much as it must have been originally. It occupied a long, wide site with
a large garden and stables at the rear, and the living quarters, which were
probably for the most part of two storeys, were grouped around two court-
yards. Between these was the nucleus of the entire complex, the great hall,
lying parallel with the street; it measured 30 ft. by 24 ft. and probably had
an open roof of three bays. The solar lay to the east of the hall above cellars
or an undercroft, but the newel stair by which it was originally approached
had been replaced before 1764 by an open staircase situated outside the north
wall of the hall. It may well be that the private apartments once extended,
at least on the first floor, into the front block containing the main gateway,
for there was a direct link by way of the narrow strip of building on the east
side of the forecourt. At the west end of the hall an imposing projecting porch
opened directly on to the screens passage, which led in turn to the various
domestic offices. The buttery and pantry perhaps lay to the west of it, in the
positions occupied by the steward's parlour and the closet in 1764, but the
kitchen (with brewhouse adjoining) was accommodated in the rear block and
was connected to the hall by a covered extension of the screens passage.

By the end of the sixteenth century the property was being leased to professional men and gentry, and one or more of these was no doubt responsible
for the alterations which were made at that time, possibly including the
addition of the open staircase to the north of the hall. In 1662 the lease was
acquired by Sir William Courtenay of Powderham, and for two hundred and
fifty years from that date the building served as the town house of the Courtenays. In 1813 the remainder of the lease of Courtenay House, as it was
called, was sold for £1,000 to the recently founded Devon and Exeter Institution
for the Promotion of Science, Literature and Art (the Institution bought the
premises outright in 1908 and is still there), and during the following seven
years the building was largely reconstructed to meet the needs of its new
occupants. The space taken up in Tothill's plan by the small garden, the
hall and the rear courtyard was covered by a double library consisting of two
rooms, each 40 ft long by 30 ft. wide and lit by a domed lantern in the roof
above. The new structure was far narrower than the old one, and behind the
front block the western half of the complex was entirely swept away.

Today no original features remain in the front portion but part of the original
rear block, still *in situ* behind the library, contains considerable evidence of
the late sixteenth century refurbishing. The room shown in the plan as the
larger of the two parlours has a plaster ceiling dating from *c.* 1580. The geometrical designs are defined by single ribs and end in floral sprays; part of the
plaster frieze also survives. There is some wall panelling of much the same
period, together with a carved oak overmantel bearing fluted pilasters and two

---

[1]This building is discussed in a wider context in W. A. Pantin, ' Medieval English Town-House
Plans ', *Medieval Archaeology*, VI-VII (1962-63), 202-239.

round arches. Beneath the arches are two Courtenay coats of arms painted in the eighteenth century.[1] A bay window of six lights, also Elizabethan presumably, now has moulded wooden mullions, which have apparently replaced the stone mullions recorded as being there about fifty years ago. There is a similar window, retaining no original features, on the floor above, which formerly consisted of one room—a principal chamber, perhaps—open to the roof. An attic floor, containing a further two rooms, has since been inserted, but over this another fine decorated plaster ceiling (also *c.* 1580) still survives. It is semi-circular, having been laid on the fifteenth century wagon roof, and, like the one below, is of the single-rib type. The design, based on squares and quatrefoils terminating in floral angle-sprays, is centred on a great, moulded pendant.

8 8, 9 AND 9A THE CLOSE (pl. 2, figs. vi and viii)

In all probability these three properties originally formed a single residence, which was erected *c.* 1450 around a central courtyard. The material used was mostly Heavitree stone, and the east wing, or No. 9a, was built completely of this. It is of two storeys with later cocklofts in the north end. There has been considerable modernization but the original roof remains. It consists of collar-braced principal rafters having unchamfered purlins and crossed at the apex to support the ridge-tree.

The south wing, or No. 9, running along the edge of the Close, is also of two storeys. The ground floor, which is 9 ft high, has thick walls of Heavitree stone and retains a number of original features. In the facade are a single-light and a double-light window, both having wide internal splays, plainly chamfered surrounds and iron bars. To the left of the easternmost window part of a stone door jamb remains in the wall, indicating an entrance which once possibly led directly to the central courtyard. Almost opposite this in the rear wall is a late sixteenth century window of five lights with chamfered mullions. But the most imposing feature on the ground floor is the wide stone gateway at the west end. It has a square head of Beer stone above a four-centred arch having a hollow moulding enriched with formal floral designs. The arms of the Chancellor of the Diocese are placed in the spandrels, though there is no evidence that this was his official residence. The double doors, with raised panels and bolection mouldings, date from the early eighteenth century. To the right within the gateway is a blocked low-arched doorway of Beer stone which once led directly into the south wing. The first floor of this part is unusual in being timber-framed, oversailing only on the south side, where the hollow-chamfered bressummer is supported by curving wooden brackets, also hollow-chamfered, resting on moulded stone corbels. In the rear wall over the gateway there is an oriel window of late sixteenth century date, wooden mullioned with five forward facing lights, now blocked. Bow windows have been added to the facade, and internally cocklofts have been inserted in addition to a number of other alterations. But the original roof remains above the later ceiling, which is itself over 11 ft. from the floor. The

[1]Details of these are given in Lega-Weekes, *Topography of the Cathedral Close*, 176.

principals, halved at the apex, have a cambered collar supported by chamfered arch-braces extending almost halfway down the walls. There are two sets of chamfered purlins but there is no ridge-tree, and the common rafters, also halved at the apex, lie at a distance of about 1 ft. 3 ins. from each other.

The west wing contains a later staircase and also an original two-light stone window in the west wall, both part of No. 9, but the most striking feature in the whole complex is the great hall, now the Law Library and a separate unit. In the south-west corner of this is a doorway (now blocked) of Beer stone, square-headed above a four-centred arch with floral enrichment similar to that at the main gateway. It once opened on to the screens passage, so the domestic offices—kitchen, buttery, pantry and so on—were in the block fronting the Close. The hall has a fireplace, now partly blocked, in the east wall with a window on either side of this and a third in the wall opposite. They have four-centred arched heads and the stone framing is missing, but they were no doubt each originally of two lights divided by a transom.

The principal feature, however, is the single hammer-beam roof divided by four trusses into three bays, each 10 ft. wide with a span of 22 ft. 9 ins. There is a noticeable affinity of style with the great roof at Westminster Hall (1399), but this is by no means an exact copy. Great two-centred arches rise from five-sided decorated stone corbels, and curved braces supporting the associated hammer-beams spring from the same points. The main purlins at collar-beam level have longitudinal arch-braces and the secondary purlins are supported by diagonal struts springing from the wall-plates, with carved bosses at the points of intersection. The intermediate main rafters have attenuated lions sejant at their bases, whilst each hammer-beam terminates in a full-length angel. Those on the two inner trusses hold shields, those on the outer hold books, and the latter figures are quarter turned inwards to face the room, a fact which indicates that the hall was always its present length. The heraldry, however, appears to be later.[1] All timbers are heavily moulded, and many of the interstices are filled with tracery characterized by cusped, ogee heads. There is a coved ceiling above collar-beam level, a distinctive feature found in other, local examples of fifteenth century roofs. In this case it is divided into rectangles by moulded ribs, with carved bosses at the intersections. The area to the north of the hall is now taken up by a brick house, of three storeys and cocklofts beneath a hipped roof, dating from the beginning of the eighteenth century. This must have replaced the original solar wing where the best private apartments were situated, with additional ones probably located in the east wing.

9   10 THE CLOSE (pls. 3 and 27, fig. viii)

This is a building constructed of Heavitree stone, apparently dating from c. 1450, with later features. It is disposed around three sides of a courtyard and is of two storeys except for the north corner of the west wing, which contains an attic. It appears, however, that it was originally of quadrangular plan, having an east wing which is now incorporated in No. 11. The gateway leading from

---

[1] *Ibid.*, 169-170.

the Close is round-arched, surmounted by a hood-mould with square terminals bearing lozenge shaped tablets. It belongs to the same period as the gate, extravagantly studded (pl. 27), which can be ascribed to between 1597 and 1621 on the evidence of Bishop Cotton's arms above. Judging from wall thicknesses and the deviation in the line of the present frontage, the south wing was only about half its present length and was extended when the new gateway was added. Across the courtyard in the north wing the arms of Bishop Oldham (1504–19), with a diagonal cusped light to the left, are placed over the doorway with a moulded two-centred arch opening on to a screens passage. To the west of this is the hall, with two long, square-headed stone windows and the remains of a third in the south wall. One of these has one light, the other two, with external hollow moulding and iron bars. The single-light window obviously replaced an earlier feature, possibly a doorway, for part of a simple stone arch is visible in the wall beside it. Internally over part of the hall there is a flat timber ceiling with moulded ribs and bosses, bearing among others the painted shield of Bishop Lacy (consecrated 1417, died 1455). The kitchen was once in the usual place, across the screens passage from the hall, but this is now part of No. 11. Though much of that building was damaged by bombing in 1942 the original fireplace still survives. It is of massive construction, having a double row of voussoirs, and incorporating a special flue leading from the oven to the main chimney. The purpose of this was to carry off the smoke when the oven was being fired for baking.

The west wing has a small, timber-framed addition containing a four-light window, wooden mullioned with internal ovolo and external ogee mouldings. In the corner beside this is the projecting entrance porch, lit on the ground floor by a two-light, square-headed window similar to that in the hall. Opposite this, sealed and blocked by a modern staircase, is the original wooden doorway leading from the porch; it is wide and low-arched. The west wing contains many modern insertions and alterations, as does the south wing which, however, does contain some chamfered beams, mostly with raised hollow stops.

Above the hall the first floor, part of which contained the solar, was originally divided into two rooms separated by a timber-framed wall incorporating a curved brace. The roof above, though concealed, is apparently of the braced collar type, and in the west room a chamfered arch-brace, descending almost to floor level, is lodged against the south wall. Beside this is a single-light wooden window having a very low triangular head with carved spandrels, and there is a blocked window similar to this in the south wall of the adjoining east room. In the wall opposite is an original stone fireplace with a relieving arch above. The jambs and the massive lintel, which has a rose carved on it, bear a chamfer-fillet-roll moulding. To the right of the fireplace is a single-light stone window, iron-barred and with a cinquefoil head. There is a stud-and-panel screen at the west end of the room.

The chapel over the entrance hall once opened directly off the solar; it is now about 12 ft. by 9 ft. but was originally larger, and has a Decorated east window; it is of three lights with a two-centred arch and traceried head. In the south wall is a square-headed single-light window with cinquefoil head. Above the chapel is a tunnel-vaulted, decorated plaster ceiling almost certainly covering an earlier roof. It is of the single-rib type with floral angle-sprays, bosses at the intersections and a central pendant. It is probably contemporary with the main gate (i.e. between 1597 and 1621). In fact it seems that the house was considerably refurbished in the early seventeenth century, for a fine door frame of that period still remains in the south wing. It has a double roll-fillet-roll moulding with large 'urn' stops, and it stands in what was originally the north outer wall. It is associated with the contemporary timber-framed extension to the west wing, clearly added to improve internal communications in what was then a corridorless house.

10   COWICK BARTON, COWICK LANE (fig. xvii)

The building stands on the present outskirts of the city, and was formerly in open country. It is two storeys high with cocklofts, and is of a modified E-plan, having projecting wings and a central porch surmounted by a cable-moulded gable and a finial. There are modern extensions to the south and west. It is constructed of Heavitree stone, largely covered by modern cement rendering. The roof is of modern slate but almost all of the stone ovolo-mullioned windows are preserved. Most of the original doorways, roll-moulded or chamfered with 'urn' or ogee stops, also survive.

The internal arrangements are conventional. The porch opens on to a central through-passage, with domestic offices to the south and the living quarters (hall and parlour) to the north. The hall has heavily moulded beams (fillet-roll-fillet-hollow-fillet) with simple angle stops, but its outstanding feature is the very large fireplace. This has Heavitree stone jambs with 'urn' stops and moulding similar to that on the beams, and a moulded wooden lintel; then, framing all this, an embattled cornice resting on engaged columns. Surmounting the whole is the date 1657 and the coat of arms of the Baron family, who occupied the dwelling in the seventeenth century.[1] In the north wing leading from the hall is the parlour, which has a plastered beam, a moulded plaster cornice and a plaster tableau of symbolic figures over a simple fireplace with roll-moulded stone jambs and wooden lintel.

On the other side of the screens passage the kitchen is indicated by the simple chamfered beams, and by an enormous fireplace with roll-moulded stone jambs and wooden lintel. This also has a blocked oven. The subsidiary service room in the south wing contains a modern fireplace and oven. A framed staircase is placed in each wing, in the corner nearest the main block.

The chambers on the first floor retain their original fireplaces, of simple design with roll-moulded stone jambs and wooden lintels, though the latter are only chamfered in the room in the south wing. The chamber over the kitchen has a stone-lintelled fireplace surmounted by a plaster tablet portraying a sailing ship. The staircases continue to the cocklofts in the roof.

The property on which Cowick Barton stands was held at various times by the Courtenays and the Russells, Earls of Devon and Bedford respectively, and it was still in the hands of the latter family when the present building was erected c. 1600. They must have been responsible for the insertion in the hall

---

[1]Beatrix F. Cresswell, 'Cowick Barton', *DCNQ*, XVIII (1934-35), 244.

window of armorial stained glass dating from the 1540's. This, showing the Royal Arms with the label argent of the Prince of Wales (later King Edward VI), the initials E P and the Prince of Wales' feathers, was removed some little time before 1920.[1] The building is now (1961) empty but in fair condition.

11 4 COWICK STREET (pl. 38, fig. xx)

This was demolished early in 1962. A three-storeyed house with a cockloft in the roof-space, it presented its main gable to the street and the cross-gable on the west side may have been later. The building had brick walls, largely original, on three sides and a facade of slight timber-framing clad with lath-and-plaster. The structure dated from *c.* 1700 and, despite the conversion of the ground floor into a modern shop, it still contained a number of important original features. The plan was basically the same on each floor, consisting of a front and a back room with a common brick chimney-stack against the west wall. The staircase, rising to the loft, also lay between the two rooms on the first and second floors, but was independent of the stack. On the ground floor the first flight of stairs was placed against the east wall, so this dwelling clearly never had a side entry running from front to rear. No original windows survived and only one original fireplace was revealed; it was of typically simple design, having a wooden, chamfered lintel with a raised hollow stop. The original bressummer supporting the first floor facade was still in position, bearing a filleted roll moulding. The roof-truss was of late type, with the principal rafters notched and crossed at the apex to carry the ridge-tree, and there were two pairs of purlins.

Originally successive storeys oversailed the street by about 6 ins.

12 178A COWICK STREET

This was demolished in June 1959. A building of three storeys and an attic, it presented its gable to the street. It was constructed of comparatively slight timber-framing clad with lath-and-plaster. In appearance it was deceptively medieval, due to the overhanging first floor and to its restricted size (21 ft. long by 12 ft. 3 ins. wide internally), but in fact it was of late seventeenth century or very early eighteenth century date. It had been drastically altered in recent times, particularly on the ground floor, which had been gutted to form a modern shop with the adjoining building; and the solitary fireplace on the first floor was not an integral part of the structure. The original plan was probably similar to the arrangement on the top storey, i.e. two rooms to each floor with the staircase, which rose to the cockloft, in the rear north-west corner. The roof of two bays had a central truss of late type, with the principal rafters halved and crossed at the apex to support the ridge-tree. A single pair of purlins was let into the upper face of the principals and there was no collar-beam.

13 181A–182 COWICK STREET (fig. xix)

These were demolished in June 1959 as part of a road widening scheme. They

[1]*DCNQ*, XI, Pt. iv (1920-21), 127.

consisted of a pair of three-storeyed houses presenting their gables to the street
and constructed of comparatively slight timber-framing clad with lath-and-
plaster, but with a rear wall of stone up to first floor level. They dated from
c. 1700, and both had suffered subsequent alterations. The front rooms on
the ground floor had been converted into modern shops, and some drastic
additions had been made to the structure of No. 181a. The front gable of No.
182 had been cut back to form a half-hip, but otherwise this member of the
pair was in a better state of preservation. The plan on each floor was basically
the same, and consisted of a front and a back room with a chimney-stack of
Heavitree stone lying between them. On one side of the stack there was a small
intercommunicating room, and on the other was the staircase. On the ground
floor the staircase was directly accessible only from the entry, which extended
from the street to the garden behind the dwelling and also opened on to the
ground floor rooms. The entry had a door at both ends and was an integral
part of the structure. Nineteenth century fireplaces had been inserted, but
when one of these was removed a simple stone fireplace was disclosed, having
a wooden chamfered lintel with ogee stops. The splayed window of four lights
in the ground floor stone wall retained its original mullions, which were square
in section with beaded angles; the corresponding window in No. 181a also
survived but had no splay. The original plan consisted perhaps of a shop with
kitchen behind on the ground floor and chambers above, though the first
floor front room may have been a parlour. Possibly the kitchen was detached
at the rear of each dwelling, preceding a nineteenth century kitchen with a
room above which stood in this position at No. 182.

14   THE DEANERY, THE CLOSE

This is a two-storeyed stone house containing work of several periods.
Much of the walling appears to be of thirteenth or fourteenth century date;
further remodelling was done in the fifteenth century, and in the eighteenth
and nineteenth centuries considerable alterations were made. The building
as it now stands consists of one long range of uneven width, with a projecting
wing on the north side; this contains a fifteenth century chapel having a
three-light east window and a ceiled wagon roof. The main block was
entered on the south side, at a point marked by an entrance tower which was
probably erected in the thirteenth century; however, early remains of this are
scanty owing to eighteenth or early nineteenth century alterations. The entrance
no doubt led to a screens passage, but this no longer survives, though a pointed
arched doorway at the north end is still *in situ*. To the east of the passage and
to the south of the chapel were the domestic offices (later alterations make
it impossible to work out the original plan here), and the living quarters lay
to the west. On the ground floor there is a room with a flat fifteenth century
ceiling, a fifteenth century fireplace in the north wall, and two-light square-
headed windows to the south.

However the most important rooms lay on the first floor. The hall was
situated above the ground floor room just described, and had fourteenth
century trefoil-headed windows in the north wall (one of these is still exposed).

On the same side of the room a mutilated early Decorated chimney-piece is concealed by a fine fifteenth century example formerly in the Precentor's house. The latter fireplace has splayed, panelled jambs, and a lintel covered with cusped tracery and bearing heraldic shields. Engaged columns terminate in small, crocketed pinnacles embracing an embattled parapet of stiff flowers in the Perpendicular style. In the south wall tall window openings were altered in the eighteenth century, and these now have semi-circular heads above stained glass by Peckitt, dated 1762. There is also at the east end a minstrels' gallery with twisted balusters. However, the most striking feature is the roof. Moulded arch-braces rise from decorated stone corbels and there were originally pendants at the point where they meet. There are two sets of purlins and decorated intermediate ribs set vertically between the principal trusses; the ceiling is coved above collar-beam level. To the west of the hall was the solar, also with an arch-braced roof. A fourteenth century fireplace still remains in the north wall here, its stone lintel decorated with four quatrefoil panels.

15   16 EDMUND STREET (pl. 4, fig. x)

In December 1961 the structure was encased in baulks of timber, raised on hydraulic jacks and bodily transported to a new corner site, about fifty yards away opposite St. Mary Steps Church. It has since been completely restored. The following notes describe the building as it was before the operation.

A very dilapidated dwelling dating from c. 1500, timber-framed on three sides with a west wall of Heavitree stone. It is of three storeys and orginally had a cockloft in the roof-space. A corner house, its upper floors oversail Edmund Street and Frog Street, and the oblique dragon-beams involved in this type of construction are supported on the ground and first floors by massive, triple-headed corner posts. This style of framing is characterized by large curving braces on the upper floors; there is usually one pair to a bay except on the first floor north elevation.

On the north elevation there were four main posts on the ground floor, though one of these is now missing. This and two of the others divided most of the space into two equal openings, forming plain shop arcading; the smaller, westernmost bay which has a chamfer over it, probably contained a window or a door, though the proximity of the fireplace makes the latter less likely. The frontage is taken up by a dwarf stone wall with wooden mullioned windows above, all modern. The first floor, which oversails by 1ft. 11½ ins., has an original traceried window of two lights, each having cinquefoil heads pierced by two small quatrefoil lights above. The stone party wall, remade in recent years, oversails on the first floor but not the second, which projects by about 1ft. 8 ins. Here there are two original traceried windows, one having one light and the other two. Both have cinquefoil heads, and the tracery above consists of small cusped lights.

On the ground floor of the east elevation, behind a small modern extension, a post, now missing, once defined another arcaded bay 5 ft. to 6 ft. wide, and to the south of this a chamfer on the wall-plate indicates that there was once a door there. On the first floor there is an inserted seventeenth century oriel window with ovolo-moulded mullions and shaped brackets; it has three lights to the front and a splayed light on either side. On the second floor the studs are modern replacements and an oriel window has been removed, though it is preserved inside the building. It is similar to the one below but rougher, with chamfered mullions. The roof is recent but an early photograph shows that the original one also presented its gable to Edmund Street.[1] The old truss included three sets of purlins with protruding ends, and a small window of uncertain date lit the cockloft. The latter feature, however, took up only the eastern half of the roof-space; the western half consisted of a full storey with a cross-gable. This was also of uncertain date, but it is probable that it was a later addition.

Internally on the ground floor there is a single room with a brick fireplace let into the stone wall, and a small rough staircase rises in the south-west corner. Both are modern but the originals occupied the same positions. Though space is restricted it is likely that a small shop and kitchen were once accommodated here. The first floor also consisted of only one room (the hall) containing a fireplace, but on the second floor there were two chambers. Here the soffit of the cross-beam running north-south has seven mortises for studs, with a long mortise (about 1 ft. 4 ins.) for a doorhead at either end.

All three storeys are of equal height, about 7 ft. 6 ins. Beams are simply chamfered but joists are left plain. The scantling is very heavy. For example, the ground floor cross-beam measures 13 ins. x 13 ins. in section, the post supporting it is 12 ins. x 8 ins., the ground floor corner-post is 13 ins. x 11 ins., the ground floor east wall-plate is $10\frac{1}{2}$ ins. x $7\frac{3}{4}$ ins., the joists above the ground floor are $7\frac{1}{2}$ ins. x $6\frac{1}{2}$ ins., an arch-brace in the south wall on the first floor is $8\frac{1}{2}$ ins. x $4\frac{1}{2}$ ins., and the studs in the south wall of the second floor are $7\frac{1}{2}$ ins. x $5\frac{1}{2}$ ins. The infilling consists mainly of modern pressed sheeting, but the original method is indicated on the second floor—studs there have holes bored in their sides at 7 ins.—9 ins. centres. Cross-rods were fitted into these, a latticework of twigs or wooden slips was woven, and mud plaster was laid on this base.

16 166 FORE STREET (fig. xi)

This was demolished for redevelopment in March/April, 1958. The greater part of fig. xi is based on the measured drawings made by Mr. A. W. Everett, F.S.A., during demolition, and these notes owe much to his recollections of the property over the last fifty years. The plan, which is partly conjectural, has been reconstructed with close reference to the O.S. 1/500 map of Exeter, 2nd edn., 1891. No. 166 dated from c. 1500 and, as it survived in 1958, was a two-storeyed dwelling with spacious cocklofts, and was built of Thorverton stone with internal timber-framed partitions. There were two rooms on the ground floor, one a large hall, the other probably a parlour, and both were lit by windows overlooking a side-passage to the south. Each contained a large fireplace with relieving arch, the first having a massive stone lintel, the second a wooden one of almost equal proportions. A wooden newel staircase rose from the hall to another extensive room on the first floor (probably the

[1]National Buildings Record.

principal chamber) containing a sizeable window with splayed sides and sill and a wooden lintel. In all likelihood this was originally divided into four lights by moulded stone mullions. A further chamber, over the parlour, had a fireplace with a stone lintel. The stairs continued to a long range of roomy cocklofts under a roof divided by six trusses into five irregular bays. The trusses consisted of two principal rafters joined by a cambered collar-beam (that in the north end wall had a straight collar, probably to take the studs more easily), and supported near their lower extremities by short posts curved at the head and resting on the tie-beam. The principals were halved and notched at the apex, and had a ridge-tree and three sets of purlins let into their upper faces.

At the further end of the complex and opening off the hall was a smaller structure, demolished well before the war but clearly recalled by Mr. Everett. It had a round-headed door and two windows in the east wall and was almost certainly the kitchen. A well stood nearby in the passage. The fireplace, cockloft and the door leading to the passage, all shown in fig. xi, are conjectural, but they seem very fair assumptions in the context. That part of the structure which survived until 1958 stood just over 30 ft. away from Fore Street, but there was evidence (the remains of the west party wall of Thorverton stone, corbelled out over the street) that the building originally stretched as far as the main road. A stone-lined cellar extended across the width of the site and above it there would be space for another two ground floor rooms, with a through-entry beside them and with further chambers and cocklofts over. In view of the ample living accommodation already provided, it is unlikely that the domestic quarters took up the whole of the missing portion. On the assumption, then, that the house was built for a very prosperous merchant, a shop with warehouse over has been postulated for the front section, though it probably included additional sleeping accommodation as well.

17 15 FROG STREET (pl. 18, fig. x)

This was demolished in the summer of 1961. It was a two-storeyed dwelling situated outside the city walls where frontage space was more freely available, which accounts for the comparatively wide site and for the roof running parallel with the street. The building was of timber-framed construction, with a stone party wall on the east side and a rebuilt wall of modern brick to the west. It had suffered very considerable alteration in the past, and was extended at the rear in the eighteenth or nineteenth century, but the original plan was easily discernible. A side entry, with a door at the Frog Street end, still ran through to the backyard (never big enough to accommodate a garden even before the extension), and the single ground floor room (the hall) opened off this. It contained a fireplace in the east wall and the stairs or ladder must have risen originally in a back corner, probably in the south-west. On the first floor, oversailing the street, were two chambers, the eastern one being the larger; the dividing, studded partition, running from north to south was almost completely preserved and visible. It incorporated a truss consisting of two principal rafters with tie-beam and collar-beam, two sets of purlins and a ridge-tree. The inter-communicating door was at the south end. The house probably dated from the second half of the sixteenth century, and was an example of a type reflected in Elizabethan probate inventories of local middling tradesmen.

18 40 HIGH STREET (pl. 39, fig. xv)

This is a timber-framed building, dating from the second half of the seventeenth century, to which a brick facade was added *c.* 1700. It is of three storeys with cockloft. The cellar or cellars below extend to the rear of a later building across the courtyard behind the main block. They have walls of Heavitree rubble, with the remains of stone steps in the front east corner. The ground floor is occupied by a modern shop, but the original plan is retained on the top two floors. It comprises a front and rear room, with a newel staircase rising against the west wall, beside the rear room. There are no signs of original chimney-breasts. The courtyard is now glassed over, and an enclosed first floor gallery leads to the building at the rear. Stairs to the gallery have balusters of seventeenth century type, but these may be inserted or copies, and there is no clear evidence that the rear structure is of any great age. The only original features visible internally are in the cockloft of the main block, where, in the roof of three bays, the lower parts of the trusses are revealed. These are unusual in that the wall-post, curved at the head to align with the principal rafter, is halved with it to make a vertical, weak joint instead of a strong, horizontal one (fig. xv).

The roof-line is at right-angles to the street, but though the original rear gable is still *in situ*, that at the front was hipped *c.* 1700 to conform with the new facade. The latter survives on the first and second floors in an excellent state of preservation. Betraying Dutch influence, it consists of three narrow bays, the central one projecting slightly, with the whole ensemble framed by quoins and surmounted by a very full, moulded cornice. Each bay on both floors contains a window with voussoirs and a moulded plaster cornice above, except the centre window on the second floor which has a more imposing, plaster segmental pediment. The undersides of the voussoirs in the central bay are shaped to form a flat ogee arch. The first floor cornices are surmounted by sunken rectangular brick panels, and those on the second floor by ellipsoidal panels.[1]

19 41–42 HIGH STREET (pls. 13 and 14, figs. xiv and xv)

These are a pair of timber-framed dwellings presenting their gables to the street and erected in 1564, according to a carved doorhead which still survives (pl. 14). They are of three storeys with cocklofts, and have cellars lined with Heavitree stone. There is an east side wall of the same material, corbelled forward on each floor (fig. xv), and the west wall was no doubt once of similar construction. The two properties have now been converted into a single premises, and the ground floor has been completely gutted to form a

---

[1]Other brick houses or facades contemporary with No. 40 High Street, but no longer surviving, are illustrated in Crocker, *Old Exeter*, Pl. XI (No. 102 Fore Street) and in A. E. Richardson and C. L. Gill, *Regional Architecture of the West of England* (1924), 85.

modern shop. However the original plan is clearly discernible on the upper floors, and consists typically in each case of a front and rear room with a newel staircase lying between them. The arrangement on the ground floor was probably similar. (The fireplaces are situated in the stone east wall, and those inserted later, including apparently all those in No. 42, have been omitted from fig. xiv.) Behind this main block is the courtyard, now glassed over, with a more recent building beyond it.

A number of original internal features have survived. In the cellar of No. 41 some of the stone steps leading to the street remain in the front east corner. In the same building, in the first floor front room (8 ft. high), which could have been either the principal chamber or the parlour or the hall, there is a heavily moulded beam and window lintel (the window itself is just over 10 ft. wide). In the east wall there is a concealed fireplace (possibly of fifteenth century date and therefore earlier than the timber-framing), with stone jambs, apparently granite, and an oak lintel.[1] On the second floor, in the front rooms of both buildings, the beams are simply chamfered, with raised hollow stops, but the wide oriel windows still retain their ovolo-moulded corner mullions, and that in No. 42 also has transoms and diagonally set iron bars in the side lights. It seems likely, therefore, that both of these windows, originally having five forward facing lights, were once transomed. Both sets of stairs continue to the cocklofts, where some of the trusses are almost completely exposed, revealing collar-braced principal rafters halved at the apex, with two sets of purlins and a ridge-tree let into their upper faces. The structure oversails at both front (third floor by about 1 ft., second by about 1 ft. 8 ins.) and rear (third floor by about 1 ft., second by about 10 ins.). The jettying is emphasised by the square oriel windows in the facade, which project over curving brackets. The brackets on the first floor of No. 41 are of a more sophisticated type, but the window differs from the others and seems later. The windows and wall surfaces of the top two floors are protected by pentices.

20 45 HIGH STREET (pl. 11, fig. xiii)

This is a three-storeyed building with cellar presenting its gable to the street, and erected on a very narrow site (about 9 ft. 6 ins. wide); it extends to an eighteenth century house at the rear, about 54 ft. from the main road. No. 45 is of timber-framed construction, and oversails at first floor level, though the facade has been considerably altered. The front half of the roof has been raised slightly in recent times (the original height is shown in fig. xiii). The cellar is lined with large squared blocks of Heavitree stone, and there are signs of the stone steps that originally led to the High Street; but the present internal entrance is at the rear on the ground floor. The ground floor itself has been completely gutted and extended at the rear to form a modern shop. There are beams on the first floor bearing ogee mouldings and the original plan is clear; it is repeated on the top floor and must once have been echoed on the ground floor too. It consists, or consisted, simply of a front and a back

---

[1]A drawing of this, with notes, by Miss E. Lega-Weekes is in the proprietors' hands, and there is another copy in the Exeter City Library.

room, served by a staircase centrally placed against the west wall. There are no signs of any original fireplaces in the building (the present ones are obvious insertions) and the early occupants possibly had to manage with braziers. In view of the narrowness of the site it seems most unlikely that there was once a ground floor entry running from front to rear.

It is clear that before the erection of No. 45, probably *c.* 1600, this particular site was an open space (see dn. 21), and Lamb Alley, now a cul-de-sac leading from the Close, once continued right through to the High Street. In all probability the site now occupied by the eighteenth century house at the rear was formerly a courtyard accessible from High Street and the Close.

21 46–47 HIGH STREET (pls. 11, 12 and 25, fig. xiii)

A pair of houses originally three-storeyed (No. 47 now has an additional floor) presenting their gables to High Street, and erected on narrow sites extending to Lamb Alley at the rear. Both are constructed of substantial timber-framing over cellars lined for the most part with large, squared blocks of Heavitree stone, and they date from *c.* 1550. No. 46 is the better preserved, though the oversailing facade has been considerably refurbished and the roof hipped at the front. But on the coved second floor vertical bands of spiralling, beaded moulding still survive, and a carved wooden figure flanks these at the east corner. The woodwork below it is defaced, as is the whole of the corresponding section of the west corner, but it appears that both points were originally occupied by a standing wooden figure surmounting a half-length angel bearing a heater-shaped shield.[1] The cellar of No. 46, which now has an internal entrance at the rear on the ground floor, still retains in the front west corner four of the stone steps that formerly led up to the High Street. The ground floor itself, originally two rooms deep and probably with a side through-entry, has been completely gutted to form a modern shop, but the east wall was recently exposed for a time, revealing near the street front a slightly curved arch with spiral moulding similar to that on the second floor facade. The cellar wall was also carried above ground level to support the timber-framing above.

The original plan is retained on the first floor, and consists of a front and a rear room with the staircase lying between them. Far more features have survived at this level. The wide window at the rear has been modernized but the original lintel remains bearing two separate, external roll mouldings. In the front room much of the timber-framing is visible, with studs 8 ins. or more wide and only 10 ins. to 1 ft. apart. But the most distinctive feature is the window in the east side wall near the facade; it is of three lights, moulded and iron-barred, with flat-arched heads. In all probability a further eight lights formerly extended across the whole of the facade, as shown in fig. xiii. This same room, once the hall or principal living-room, also has hollow-chamfered beams and wall-plates, and a simple triple-roll plaster cornice. Whether this was once part of a more ambitious plaster ceiling it is now impossible to say.

[1]William Cotton, *An Elizabethan Guild of the City of Exeter* (1873), illustration facing 44.

The framed staircase which, judging from the balusters, was renewed in the latter part of the seventeenth century, must once have descended directly to the ground floor (now gained by a modern stair in a rear extension). It still continues to the top storey, where the basic plan is repeated; the front room here was no doubt the principal chamber. This floor, coved out at front and rear, is now unceiled, revealing an original roof of seven bays with the trusses comprising chamfered tie-beams supporting massive principals. The latter are halved at the apex, with the ridge-tree and two pairs of purlins passing through them. The front gable has been hipped at a later date. The rear window has been replaced but two chamfered door frames with flattened arches remain *in situ*, and a blocked window, this time of four lights, stands in the east wall over the corresponding one below. In the facade, though not visible from outside, there are substantial remains of the window of eight lights with flattened arches, which once ran across the width of the building. At one point in the rear room the infilling between the studs is revealed and is shown to consist of riven oak battens slid between the studs, down grooves in their inner faces, and then plastered over (pl. 12).

There are no signs of original fireplaces in No. 46, but the house was clearly built for a very prosperous merchant. Some hints of the former splendours of the facade are still apparent, and the building was further ornamented on the east side for No. 45, which now stands there, is a later structure (*c*. 1600) and occupies what was formerly part of Lamb Alley.[1] In fact at two points in No. 45, on the first and second floors near the facade, the outer east wall of No. 46 is shown covered with a series of juxtaposed wooden panels, about 2 ft. 7 ins. long by 8½ ins. wide and looking like small bench-ends. They are carved, with a trefoil design at the head, a blank heater-shaped shield below this, and a quatrefoil in a square frame at the lower end. Whether these are confined to that part of the wall near the facade or whether they extend over a larger area, it is not possible to say.

From the High Street No. 47 bears no resemblance to its partner. The facade has been completely rebuilt in a different style, and the roof has been hipped and raised to provide a further floor, though it seems likely that some of the original trusses, similar to those in No. 46, have been re-used.

The building has two cellars, a front one over 50 ft. in length, and one at the rear in line with this and going back another 20 ft. or so. The latter, now almost completely filled with rubble, is about 4 ft. lower. The former has traces in the front east corner of stone steps leading up to the main street. There was once a well, now filled in, towards the rear of this cellar and near the east wall.

The ground floor, with the cellar entrance at the rear, has been completely gutted to form a modern shop, though it was probably two rooms deep originally, with a side through-entry. There are few original features visible on the upper floors, but these do retain the original plan, comprising a front and back room with the staircase lying between them, though the proportions and certain other details are not identical with those in No. 46.

[1] Note by A. W. Everett, *DCNQ*, XXIII (1947-49), 135.

In the wide rear window on the first floor part of an original jamb remains, with a hollow-fillet-ogee moulding similar to that on the blocked windows in No. 46.   In the corresponding window above on the coved second floor the outer moulding, of two separate rolls, survives on the original jamb and lintel.   But the most important feature in the whole building is the first floor open gallery, a wooden structure about 7 ft. long by 2 ft. 9 ins. wide.   It leads, over what was once the court, to a later, featureless block a further two or three rooms deep at the rear, and this takes up the remainder of the site. The gallery retains its original balusters, which appear to be of late seventeenth century type, so indicating the date when the rear block was erected.

22   225–226 HIGH STREET (*front.* and pl. 15)

These are a pair of timber-framed houses of five storeys presenting their gables to the street.   They were originally occupied by leading merchants and were reputedly erected in 1567, according to an inscription (placed just inside the main doorway) commemorating their restoration in 1907.   There appears to be no documentary evidence now available to support this, but the remaining physical features are typical of that period.   Both dwellings once had similar rectangular plans, consisting on each floor of a front and rear room with the stairs lying between them.   There may well have been a further building across the courtyard behind the main block.   Unfortunately in each case the original rear portion of the latter has been almost completely demolished, and all that remains of it (as much as is visible) is the cellar or cellars—about 40 ft. long and lined with Heavitree stone—lying behind No. 225.   The front portions of the two dwellings have long been combined to form a single property, and until recently this served as part of the premises of the local newspaper. A large single staircase has been erected where the two separate staircases formerly stood.   Internally most of the rooms were almost completely refashioned in 1907, and there are no signs of any fireplaces, original or otherwise.   On the first and second floors there are ranges of windows running across the entire width of the facade, and both of these incorporate two fine bays of seven lights each, which retain their original wooden mullions, with internal and external ogee mouldings.   No doubt there was a hall or parlour, with principal chamber above, situated here.   Standing near the windows are moulded posts supporting a beam running just inside, and parallel with, the facade, but these are probably later, inserted features.   The top floor is ceiled at the level of the cambered collar-beams, but the lower parts of the trusses and one set of purlins, all clad in lath-and-plaster, are easily distinguishable.   The trusses are about 6 ft. apart and the scantling used is no more than $3\frac{1}{2}$ ins. thick, which possibly indicates that the slate-covered roofs are a fairly modern rebuilding.

In the facade the ground floor (1907) and the third and fourth floors (some years earlier) have been remodelled, but the very fine woodwork on the first and second floors, though cleaned and repaired in 1907, is substantially original.   This includes three large carved animal brackets supporting the oversailing top two storeys, a series of carved consoles (human and animal figures, the former often with women's breasts) and moulded studs beneath the ranges of windows, carved friezes (rose and running tendril motifs), and plaster panels bearing black and white strapwork designs below the windows on the second floor (those on the first floor are modern copies). Individual floor heights are as follows: ground floor = 8 ft., first floor = 8 ft. 4 ins., 2nd floor = 7 ft. 7 ins., 3rd floor = 7 ft. 5 ins., 4th floor = 7 ft. On the first floor each of the original dwellings is 13 ft. 6 ins. wide and the front room goes back about 18 ft. The top two storeys oversail by about 3 ft. 6 ins.

23   227 HIGH STREET (*front.*, fig. xiv)

This is a timber-framed building, once a merchant's house, containing over twelve rooms and dating from *c.* 1650. It has a cellar well over 40 ft. long and lined with Heavitree stone, but the structure above is not completely regular. The front portion consists of four storeys with a cockloft in the roof-space and this part, together with the large staircase behind it, is housed beneath a single wide gable presented to the street. However, the portion to the rear of the staircase has no cockloft and is surmounted by a pair of gables running in line with the other. It seems that the gables echoed the internal plan which probably consisted, on the upper floors at least, of one large room at the front (e.g. forehall on the first floor, principal chamber on the second) with two smaller rooms side by side at the rear.

Much of the property is now occupied by a modern shop and a great part of the interior has been substantially altered, but certain important features survive. Originally a ground floor through-entry ran along the west side of the building, and remaining flagstones there are possibly original. In the rear wall on the first floor there is an original transomed and ovolo-mullioned window, six lights wide, and it may once have extended across the whole width of the dwelling. On the second and third floors the seventeenth century staircase with turned balusters still remains, and rises to the cockloft where the original trusses are revealed. The principal rafters, typically slight for the period, are halved and crossed at the apex to bear the ridge-tree, and there are three sets of purlins. Considering the span of the roof it is surprising that there were originally no collar-beams. The trusses in the two rear gables are not visible.

The facade, with oversailing upper storeys, supported by boldly carved brackets, was tastefully restored in 1878 and is largely original. It is notable for continuous ranges of mullioned and transomed windows on the first and second floors, each having a large, arched centre light; the lower range also incorporates a pedimented oriel. On the third floor there is an arcaded gallery with its original balustrade, and behind it another continuous range of mullioned and transomed windows with the two outer lights having arched heads. In all likelihood the gallery once extended across the whole width of the building (the asymmetrical pattern of the arched windows suggests this), and was at some later date curtailed to allow the insertion of two small closets. These have side windows looking on to the gallery, but they are so small and set so high that it seems they were meant to afford ventilation rather than light, and it is possible that a close stool was accommodated in one or both of the closets.

At the far end of the site on which No. 227 is situated is another, separate structure incorporating an earlier, smaller dwelling. As it now stands it is three storeys high and apparently of late seventeenth or eighteenth century timber-framed construction, but there is a cellar lined with Heavitree stone and the rear stone wall is almost certainly of the same material. On what was once the first floor there remains a blocked fireplace with chamfered jambs of Heavitree stone and a lintel of volcanic trap rock with relieving arch above. It dates probably from the early sixteenth century when the original building must have been erected.

24   12 MARY ARCHES STREET (fig. x)

Demolished in the summer of 1963, this was a three-storeyed house presenting its gable to the street. It was constructed of comparatively slight timber-framing clad with lath-and-plaster, and had two chimney-stacks of Heavitree stone. The structure was erected in the second half of the seventeenth century, and was basically of rectangular plan, though this had been distorted to fit a curious, elbowed site. It had suffered very considerable alterations in the past, including the rebuilding of much of the east end of the rear wing, and the ground floor front room was in recent years a business premises. However, it appeared that it had consisted originally of a main living-room or hall fronting the street, containing a large fireplace and with stairs against the rear wall. The narrower portion accommodated a further two rooms and one of these, having a fireplace with a chamfered wooden lintel, was probably the kitchen. The chambers, with fireplaces in corresponding positions, were similarly disposed on the first and second floors. The roof-truss, which could be inspected in the wing, was of late type, consisting of two principal rafters halved and crossed at the apex to carry the ridge-tree, and bearing a single pair of purlins on their upper faces.

25   8 MILK STREET (fig. x)

This was erected in the early fourteenth century and destroyed in the air raid of May, 1942. Fig. x and the following notes are based on the recollections of Mr. A. W. Everett, F.S.A., who inspected the remains soon after the raid, and on the O.S. 1/500 map of Exeter, 2nd edn., 1891. The plan shown here is a reconstruction, not based on measurements, so it does not claim to be accurate in detail. The dwelling, which had been much altered in its lifetime, consisted of a cellar with two storeys above, and stood fronting Milk Street, with an alley immediately to the rear. It had thick walls of Northernhay volcanic trap rock and the facade was originally timber-framed. The house was of a common medieval type, with the cellar rising three feet or so above ground level; this had not had a vaulted stone roof originally. The original ground floor, supported by wooden beams and joists and accessible by steps leading up from the street, consisted of two rooms, the front one (hall) having a fireplace and garderobe in the north wall. The garderobe had a small slit window overlooking Milk Street, and was apparently cleared from the street. The room at the back contained a two-light, shouldered-arched window of early fourteenth century date, and in the east corner there was evidence of a former stone newel stair leading to the upper floor, which had a further fireplace in the rear wall.

26 'THE NORMAN HOUSE', CORNER OF PRESTON STREET AND KING STREET (fig. x)

This building was damaged in the raid of May, 1942 and was subsequently demolished. It first really came to light when part of the West quarter was being cleared at the beginning of the First World War, and the city council decided to restore it. A plan of the structure was made at the time, and this is substantially reproduced in fig. x. There was considerable controversy over the interpretation of the structure, which was predominantly a mixture of Norman and fifteenth century features.[1] Miss Prideaux claimed that portions of the original twelfth century masonry remained undisturbed and were sufficient to indicate the early rectangular shape of the building (marked by heavy black lines on the plan). This walling was mainly of Heavitree stone with occasional blocks of volcanic trap rock, but some carved work in Salcombe stone also survived. This comprised the head of a Norman doorway-arch in the north wall, bearing chevron, lozenge and pellet designs, part of a small semi-circular arch, possibly the remains of a window, over the later fireplace in the south wall, and sections of an internal cornice marked with an interlaced lozenge design. There were also scattered fragments of Norman moulding incorporated in later walling.

The fifteenth century and later developments (these are represented by hatching in fig. x) resulted in the replacement of the rectangular plan by one resembling a parallelogram, and the conversion of the structure into two separate dwellings. Each consisted of two storeys with a cockloft in the open roof, and they were divided by an oak partition. On the ground floor this and the other partitions there were of stud-and-panel construction, but on the upper floors they consisted of vertical studs with an infilling of oak battens, which were then plastered over (cf. No. 46 High Street). The roof added in the fifteenth century was collar-braced, with the collar supported by moulded arch-braces. The east gable wall above wall-plate level was timber-framed, with cambered tie-beam, collar-beam and vertical studs.

A fourteenth century door with a pointed or two-centred arch already stood at the south end of the through-passage in the western dwelling, and in the fifteenth century a doorway with a flattened arch was placed at the north end. Another, probably similar, was placed beside it in the eastern dwelling (which did not have a through-passage), but was later blocked. It seems that in the fifteenth century the eastern dwelling had two ground floor rooms, one containing a fireplace with a massive lintel of Heavitree stone, and in the western dwelling there were three ground floor rooms, which were provided in the late sixteenth century with a single-ribbed plaster ceiling bearing Tudor rose and

[1]See E. K. Prideaux, 'Remains of an Ancient Building in Exeter', *DCNQ*, VIII, Pt. 1 (1914-15), 161-170; also 237-240 in the same volume; and *DCNQ*, IX, Pt. 1 (1916-17), 4-5, chart facing 16, and 49-51.

fleur-de-lys motifs. A somewhat similar ceiling was also installed on the first floor of the eastern house.

With such a confusion of evidence, which can no longer be checked, the Norman House invites idle speculation. However, the fact that Heavitree stone is not recorded before the end of the fourteenth century, together with the presence of scattered pieces of Norman moulding built into the walls, suggests that it was, after all, largely a fifteenth century building incorporating fragments of twelfth century work. The dividing partition was by no means complete when the structure was recorded, and it may be that there were originally not two dwellings but only one, consisting of a central through-passage with living quarters on the east side and the domestic offices on the west. This, however, would result in a house of about nine rooms, a large number at such an early date.

27 18 NORTH STREET (pl. 24, fig. xv)

A timber-framed building, this has a north party wall of Heavitree stone and presents its gable to the street. It is of four storeys with cellar, lined also with Heavitree stone and once approached by stone steps from the courtyard at the rear. The front part of the cellar has been deepened, and the ground floor above lowered as a result of this. The alterations were no doubt made *c.* 1900, when North Street was widened on the west side; at the same time about 8 ft. was removed from the front of the building and a new facade erected. The house was also damaged by enemy action in 1942.

Nevertheless a surprising amount of evidence survives, enough to give a clear picture of a typical merchant's house of *c.* 1600, the date when the building was put up. The plan is a common one. A through-entry runs along the south side and retains much of its original oak partition with ovolo-moulded studs and chamfered rails; the original doorway to this, with ogee moulding and 'urn' stops, remains *in situ* at the rear. The entry opens on to a central dog-legged staircase lying against the north wall between a front and a rear room, each having a fireplace in the north wall. This plan is repeated on the upper floors. The staircase is not original (though its position is unchanged), but dates, on the evidence of the turned balusters, from the latter part of the seventeenth century and is similar to others found elsewhere in the city (e.g. No. 40 Alphington Street). It seems that certain improvements were effected at that time, for other features date from the same period, e.g. the bolection moulded fireplace in the rear room on the second floor, and the moulded over-doors on the first and second floors. The original trusses survive on the top floor, but they are only partly visible beneath the ceiling placed just above a pair of purlins. However, enough is revealed to show that the principal rafters are partly halved into the head of the wall-post, and there are no curving members (fig. xv). On each of the first and second floors at the rear (the first floor oversails here) an oriel window has survived which consisted originally of three forward and two splayed lights. The lower one is still supported by three carved brackets with rosettes beneath the sill, strapwork on the face and scrolls on the sides. Similar brackets supporting the higher window almost certainly survive beneath modern plasterwork.

Behind this front block across the courtyard are the remains of what must have been the kitchen. It is now almost completely demolished, but certain features are clear. The rear block extended across the whole width of the site, about 16 ft., and went back a distance of 28 ft. 6 ins., enough space for at least two rooms. It had walls of Heavitree stone on the north, west and south sides, but the side facing the front block across the court was timber-framed. Against the north wall is the lower part of a great projecting fireplace, 6 ft. 6 ins. wide at the back with splayed sides. It is situated about 8 ft. from the timber-framed front.

This rear block once rose to a height of three storeys, a fact proved by the survival of what is the most important feature of all on the site, in that it is the only remaining example left in the city. This is the timber-framed double gallery on the north side, consisting of a second floor gallery directly over a first floor one, and constructed to connect the two blocks of building. Both galleries are 3 ft. 9 ins. wide and 16 ft. long and were originally supported by posts on the ground floor. They are enclosed (as they probably were originally) and disguised by later work, but the lower one still has internally the familiar ogee-moulded, ' urn '-stopped doorway opening on to the front block, and the corresponding doorway above was not removed until 1942.

28 36 NORTH STREET (pl. 10, figs. xii and xv)

These premises lie at right-angles to the street, and extend altogether for about 140 ft. along the site, containing work of several periods.[1] The front block is the most interesting; it is timber-framed between side walls of Heavitree stone, that to the south being an integral part of No. 37. This part of the structure was erected as a merchant's house c. 1500, and had an unusual plan which is repeated, with minor differences, in only one other surviving house in the city, No. 38 North Street. This plan originally consisted of a central hall open to the roof, lying between front and rear sections that were each of two storeys; the front section probably contained a shop with the solar or principal living-room above, and the rear one a parlour beneath a first floor principal chamber. A through-entry, which still remains, ran along the south wall and (judging from the interrupted chamfering on a beam) was possibly 1 ft. or so wider at the parlour end; and directly above the entry, connecting the solar and principal chamber at first floor level, was a gallery. Finally, below the whole block there was a cellar, lined with Heavitree stone. It is still there and stretches the whole length of the building, but it is only as wide as the hall and does not extend beneath the entry.

No. 36 has since been drastically altered. The ground floor has been lowered by about 2 ft., the internal timber-framed partitions removed, and the open hall divided by an inserted floor. This may have been done in the late eighteenth or early nineteenth century, when the front section was raised by a further storey and the gabled elevation replaced by a rectangular facade

[1] This building is discussed in a wider context in W. A. Pantin, ' Medieval English Town-House Plans ', *Medieval Archaeology*, VI-VII (1962-63), 202-239. See also W. A. Pantin, ' Some Medieval English Town Houses: a Study in Adaptation' in *Culture and Environment: Essays in Honour of Sir Cyril Fox*, ed. I. Ll. Foster and L. Alcock (1963), 466-470.

which was brought forward by 2 ft. (Inside the building traces of the over-sailing first floor can still be seen in the north wall.) The structure is now empty and in a very dilapidated condition. Despite this a surprising number of original features survive. Three chimney-stacks are accommodated in the north wall. The shop at the front never had a fireplace, but that in the hall is still *in situ*. It is 6 ft. wide with a corbelled stone hood; the jambs and corbels bear a recessed ogee moulding, and the lintel has a plain hollow one. A similar smaller fireplace, now half blocked, remains in the parlour. On the first floor, a stone relieving arch and part of a moulded jamb is all that remains of the solar fireplace, but the one in the principal chamber is well preserved. It has no hood, but bears the recessed ogee moulding with semi-pyramidal stops. It is made of Thorverton stone and presumably those on the ground floor ,now covered with many coats of whitewash, are of the same material.

The hall is lit by a great splayed window in the north wall, overlooking open ground behind No. 35 (pl. 10). It rises to an external wooden lintel, chamfered with raised hollow stops, placed about 1 ft. 3 ins. below eaves level. It is now modernized and partly blocked but it must originally have consisted of four transomed lights. The hall was probably gained directly from the side entry by a door at its east end, for owing to the proximity of the hall window and the parlour fireplace there would not have been much room for a screens passage there. It seems that the upper floor was originally reached by a wooden newel stair in the north-west corner of the hall. This is indicated by two windows which appear to have lit the stair, and which survive one above the other. That on the ground floor has iron bars set in a wooden frame, chamfered externally, and that on the first floor an iron grille embedded in the surrounding stonework.

On the first floor part of the original partition between the principal chamber and the hall is still *in situ*. It incorporates a tie-beam and collar-beam, and the former has in its soffit the mortises for the studs, placed 2 ft. 6 ins. to 3 ft. apart, with groups of two or three holes between them. Twigs or narrow slips of wood were fitted into these, so providing a base for the infilling of mud plaster. At the south end of this partition there remains a post with a shouldered-arched head, part of the doorway leading to the former gallery. But the most imposing feature in the whole building is the arch-braced roof, and much of that over the hall (three bays) and rear section (two bays) is still intact. The truss consists of principal rafters which rest *on* the north wall but *against* the south wall (part of No. 37), being supported on timber posts. These principals are halved at the apex, with three pairs of purlins and a ridge-tree passing through them. The purlins have two pairs of wind-braces between them, the upper set being inverted. The two pairs of arch-braces beneath the collar make a continuous curve from wall to wall.

Behind the main block, across a courtyard which is now covered over, lies an L-shaped rear block 58 ft. long. This is of two storeys (though there is an additional attic at the east end), mostly timber-framed against a thick north wall of stone and brick. The range contains work of different periods. The section nearest the main block extends across the width of the site and was clearly the original detached kitchen (there are signs of a large fireplace in the north wall) with a through-entry to the south. Evidence of a doorway in the main block suggests that the principal chamber there and the chamber over the kitchen were once connected by a gallery running along the south wall. The remainder of the range was lit by an open side passage, also to the south. It appears that *c.* 1600 the kitchen block was extended eastwards by two rooms, and a new kitchen was introduced. A ground floor room in this section contains a large stack, and there are other original features above on the first floor. The studs in the partition here are now exposed, and have grooved sides into which oak battens were slid as a base for the infilling. The original roof-trusses are revealed and consist of collar-braced principal rafters halved at the apex, with a ridge-tree and a single pair of purlins passing through them. One rafter rests on the north wall, the other is jointed into the vertical wall-post, which is curved at the head to accommodate it (fig. xv). The final east-ward extension was made in the mid-eighteenth century when, it appears, the accommodation in the front block was deemed inadequate and the main living-quarters were transferred to the rear block. At the far end of the site a large, first floor drawing-room or principal chamber was added (panelling and a carved wooden chimney-piece still remain) and other parts of the range were refurbished at the same time.

29 38 NORTH STREET (pl. 22, fig. xii)

A wide, timber-framed building, this has side walls of Heavitree stone, that on the north still being corbelled forward on the upper floors.[1] The chimney-stacks are accommodated in this wall, but no original fireplaces survive. No. 38 was erected *c.* 1500 as a merchant's house, and originally consisted of a hall open to the roof and centrally placed between front and rear sections, which were both of three storeys. The structure presented a single gable to the street, and was similar in most respects to No. 36 nearby. Around 1900, however, the front part was raised by a further storey and was given a double gable. At the same time the building line, including the south wall, was brought back by 3 ft., the ground floor was opened up completely for business purposes, and the first floor was also considerably affected. Nevertheless, a considerable amount of evidence remains. On the ground floor, though there is no sign of the original shop which must have occupied the frontage, the hall of three bays is still open to the roof, and the side through-entry still lies against the south wall. Formerly, perhaps, the entry contained a door opening on to the east end of the hall, but if there was a screens passage here it must have been located within the rear room (which may have been a buttery). Other-wise, it would have cut across the great splayed hall window which survives, partly blocked, in the north wall, and overlooks open ground on the site of No. 37.

The front room on the first floor was the original solar, or principal living-room, and a later insertion, part of a magnificent Jacobean plaster ceiling, is still *in situ* there (pl. 22). It is of the single rib type, crowded with floral

[1] The structure is also described in Pantin, ' Medieval English Town-House Plans ', 231.

and animal motifs. Due to the rebuilding of the front only half of the ceiling
remains, the other half reputedly having been removed by the Rev. Sabine
Baring-Gould to his house at Lew Trenchard. As in No. 36 the solar at No.
38 was connected with the rear room on the first floor by a gallery running
along the south wall over the through-entry, and in fact a modern one occupies
this position today. Over the greater part of the main block is a very fine
arch-braced roof. Principal rafters (halved at the apex, with three pairs of
purlins and a ridge-tree passing through them) are secured by a cambered
collar-beam, beneath which the two sets of chamfered arch-braces make a
continuous curve from wall to wall. The roof, now ceiled just below the level
of the middle purlins, probably once had the curving wind-braces that still
survive in No. 36.

Across the courtyard immediately behind the main block is the old kitchen,
timber-framed with a north stone wall containing a massive stack. The fireplace is now concealed but it seems that a flue from the oven led to the main
chimney, carrying off the smoke when the oven was being fired for baking
(cf. No. 11 The Close). There is a first floor chamber above and this is connected
to the front block by an enclosed gallery of comparatively roomy proportions.
It is timber-framed but has no distinctive features to suggest the date of its
erection. Beneath it in the courtyard is a well, now covered over.

30   OLD MATFORD HOUSE, WONFORD ROAD (fig. xvii).

There has been a building on this site since c. 1250 at least, but the present
house was erected c. 1600 as a country residence for Sir George Smyth (knighted
1604), a very wealthy merchant and three times mayor of Exeter. It was not
built before 1592, for the Lay Subsidy Roll of that year for Wonford Hundred
does not record any payment by Sir George.[1] The date of erection was most
probably some time between 1596 and 1604, judging by two deeds deposited in
the city archives. The first of these, dated 26 March 1596, refers to the lease
of a pasture to George Smyth of Exeter, Esquire. However, by the 20 September 1604 when another pasture was leased, the lessee had become Sir
George Smythe of Madford, Knight.[2]

The ground plan of Old Matford House is in most respects typical of the
Elizabethan country house, in that it consists of a hall and screens passage
in the main block, with two cross-wings and a projecting porch. The east
wing probably once contained the domestic offices, with extra living accommodation, including a parlour, in the west. The building is of two storeys,
having an additional cockloft at the front of the east wing, and it is constructed of cob, with three chimney-stacks of Heavitree stone and timber-framed
internal partitions. The porch has a low-arched entrance of moulded stone
with the Royal Arms of Elizabeth I above. In the screens passage there is a
simple stud-and-panel partition on the east side, but that on the west or hall
side is more impressive, being divided by heavily moulded vertical and
horizontal members. Several original moulded doorways (roll or double-roll

[1]Public Record Office, Exch. K. R. Subsidy Rolls, E 179 101/408.   [2]ECM, D387 and D1695.

with ' urn ' stops) still survive. The roof is of modern slate, but must have been thatched originally.

A few years ago the structure was empty and decaying, and its restoration has resulted in certain additions and insertions, including an extension at the rear and a new doorway in the facade. Most of the windows are also new but two original examples remain in the north front, one of four lights on the ground floor and one of three lights in the cockloft. Both sets of mullions in these have external ovolo mouldings, but internally those on the ground floor have an ogee moulding and those in the cockloft a straight chamfer. In the first floor chambers certain plaster details survive. These include sections of moulded cornice, and in particular fleur-de-lys designs and coats of arms (of Sir George Smyth) in the principal chamber over the hall. In the southernmost room of each wing the bases of certain roof-trusses protruding from the ceiling are covered with fluted plasterwork or plaster figures.

31 67 SOUTH STREET (pls. 28 and 29, fig. xviii)

This is a three-storeyed dwelling, dating from *c.* 1600, with double gables fronting the street. It is of timber-framed construction with two chimney-stacks of Heavitree stone, but the rear wall has been rebuilt or refaced in modern brick. The ground floor has been gutted to form a modern shop, but there must once have been three or four rooms there, two at the rear, a kitchen and another service room, and perhaps a shop and associated room at the front. It is clear from the position of the stacks that there was never a side entry running from front to back.

Fortunately the original dog-legged staircase with turned balusters has survived, and the centrally placed spacious landings admirably serve all the rooms on the first and second floors. Easily the most impressive room in the house is the first floor hall, with a magnificent mullioned and transomed window, sixteen lights in width, extending across the whole facade. The central eight lights project over supporting brackets, and the original window fittings, including the diagonally set iron bars to which the windows were attached, still remain. This spacious room also has an elaborately moulded, plastered beam and cornice, and large, stylized plaster flower motifs set in the corners of the two panels into which the ceiling is divided. Among the flowers and plants represented are the rose, the tulip, the thistle and the vine. A bolection moulded fireplace, probably of late seventeenth century date, has replaced the original one. There are a further two rooms at the rear, the western one containing a defaced original mullioned window of three lights.

The top floor consists of four chambers, and the pair at the front of the dwelling still retain their original oriel windows of six lights, with supporting brackets and moulded mullions and lintels. The original roof of five bays still survives for the most part in the southern gable; the other half is inaccessible. The roof-truss comprises two principal rafters, halved and notched at the apex, with the ridge-tree let in at the top but with the single pair of purlins passed through the principals. The door-frames on the first and second floors are chamfered, but the fireplaces are blocked by modern grates. However, one on the top floor was partly exposed for a time, revealing a chamfered wooden lintel with raised, hollow stops.   Most of the others must have been of similarly simple design.

32 THE TUDOR HOUSE, TUDOR STREET (pls. 31 and 32)

A house of four storeys and cellar, having its roof parallel with the street, it is about 26 ft. 6 ins. wide by about 20 ft. deep. Individual floor heights are as follows: ground floor, 6 ft. 9 ins.; first floor, 7 ft. 6 ins.; second floor, 8 ft. 1 in.; third floor, 8 ft. 9 ins. to collar-beam level. The plan is a simple one, two rooms on each floor with a newel staircase, not original, rising centrally against the rear wall. There are fireplaces in each room, one stack being in the north side wall, the other in the east rear wall. No original internal features remain; even the beams are encased and the top floor, half in the roof with two dormer windows overlooking the street, is ceiled at collar-beam level, so the roof-truss is not visisble. Externally the side and rear walls have been rebuilt or refaced with modern brick, and the only original features are to be found in the timber-framed facade. There is an ovolo-mullioned window of five lights in the south room on the ground floor, and on the first floor there are two ovolo-mullioned, five-light oriel windows, each supported by three brackets. These upper windows are protected from the weather by a pentice, and this device is repeated on the second floor which, it is clear, also originally had two similar oriel windows.

However, the most interesting feature of all is the slate-hanging which is now restricted to the first floor, though it once extended over the whole facade— or over the second and third floors at least—until it was removed some time during the first half of the nineteenth century.[1] The remaining portion, and this is not complete, consists of small, intricately carved pieces of slate individually pegged on to the main structure, and incorporates three shields, each enclosed in a laurel wreath. These are now somewhat damaged but were once charged as follows: (i) on the right, as one faces the building, a Tudor rose crowned; (ii) in the centre, two coats impaled, first a holy lamb passant, second ermine three crowns in chief; (iii) on the left, a lion rampant crowned. These last two shields seem to relate to the family of Sir Simon Leach (d. 1637) of Crediton, and this would indicate that for part of the seventeenth century at least the dwelling was the Exeter town house of the Leaches.[2] If this is accepted then the slate-hanging probably dates back to soon after 1625, when Sir Simon was knighted. This would accord with the physical evidence, for the windows suggest that the house was erected in the early seventeenth century. Sir Simon did not own the house (it is not mentioned in his will) and it may be that it was leased from the Tedder or Tudder family. The latter are recorded as having owned property on Exe Island from the sixteenth to the eighteenth century, and they may well have given their name to the Tudor house (this would explain the shield bearing the Tudor rose) and to Tudor Street.[3] The building is in very poor condition (1961).

[1]Crocker, *Old Exeter*, in the account accompanying Pl. XVII.
[2]Beatrix F. Cresswell, ' Tudor House, Exe Island ', *DCNQ*, XIV (1926-27), 1-5.
[3]*DCNQ*, XV (1928-29), 185-186, 207.

33 11–12 West Street (pl. 5)

Two houses erected *c.* 1500, No. 11 standing on the corner of West Street and Stepcote Hill. Both structures are timber-framed with distinctive curved braces (cf. No. 16 Edmund Street), and present their gables to West Street. They have a stone party wall between them and there is a rear wall, corbelled on the north or Stepcote Hill side, still surviving behind No. 11; it is patched but is mainly of Heavitree stone. This wall once extended to take in No. 12. The facades have been restored and the two structures, No. 12 in particular, have been largely rebuilt so that they now incorporate a further two properties —Nos. 15–16 Stepcote Hill.

Both dwellings have modern shops on the ground floor, but No. 11 is the better preserved of the two. It is of three storeys and the first floor oversails on the west side by 2 ft., though this does not occur on the north side, where the timber-framing rests on a ground floor wall of mixed Heavitree stone and volcanic trap rock. The second floor, however, oversails on both sides by about 1 ft. 6 ins. This building originally had two rooms on the ground floor, probably a shop with a kitchen behind; there was a large first floor hall, with two chambers over this. The stairs rose in a rear corner and there was a fireplace, also at the rear, on each floor. In fact the original fireplaces remain on the first and second floors, that on the latter having ogee-moulded stone jambs and lintel with a relieving arch above. Other remaining features include a window of two lights with cinquefoil wooden heads in the front chamber on the second floor, and below this a blocked wooden doorway, tall and narrow with a four-centred head. This once opened directly off the hall on to a short external stone stair affording access to Stepcote Hill.

No. 12 is of four storeys but narrower, about 10 ft. 4 ins. wide internally. The first floor oversails by 2 ft. 6 ins., and the second and third, which are in line, by about 1 ft. 10 ins. The scantling is heavy. Two beams on the ground floor, chamfered with simple hollow stops, are $11\frac{1}{4}$ ins. x $11\frac{1}{4}$ ins. in section, and joists on the first floor measure $5\frac{3}{4}$ ins. x $7\frac{3}{4}$ ins. Again this building originally had one or two rooms on each floor, probably with a domestic arrangement similar to that in No. 11.

APPENDIX

Transcripts of Original Documents

Nine of the following thirteen documents are probate inventories, drawn principally from the Orphans' Court Collection in the Exeter City Library, though some examples which have found their way into the Devon Record Office have also been used. They have been selected with a view to presenting a series of detailed pictures of Exeter domestic interiors roughly between 1550 and 1700, covering as wide a social range as possible. The remaining documents consist of property surveys and deeds from the same period, together with an account of house repairs which dates from 1387–1388. All but one of the documents have been recently transcribed by the author and, with the exception of the headings of the deed and the inventories, they are reproduced here with only minor alterations, namely, the omission where necessary of the repetitive word ' item ' and the occasional substitution of Arabic for Roman numerals. All editorial insertions are enclosed by round brackets.[1]

I   D & C, 5154

(*Translated from the Latin*)

An account of the cost of repairs to certain houses between Michaelmas 1387 and Michaelmas 1388.

Firstly concerning the house of Walter Helyere, viz., in timber for 1 door and a latrine and for repairs to windows in the rooms	6s	
in boards purchased for 1 gutter, for the doors, windows, rooms and doorways (*ostiis*)	4s	2½d
in hatchnails[2] and boardnails, ' Spekys Twystys ',[3] hooks and staples for the windows		18d
in ——lagers[4] for the doors and for the thresholds (Threschstolys)	2s	2d
in payment to a carpenter for 5 days at 5d per day	2s	1d
in payment to a carpenter for 3 days at 5d per day		15d

[1] In the inventories many obscure words have been left unexplained when they are not directly relevant and do not affect the documents' significance. Most of them are defined in *Farm and Cottage Inventories of Mid-Essex, 1635-1749*, ed. Francis W. Steer, Essex Record Office Publications, No. 8 (1950). This is an excellent introduction to the world of the probate inventories, and it is pertinent even to the domestic conditions found in a city like Exeter during the sixteenth and seventeenth centuries.

[2] Doornails.

[3] Spikes and twists. Spikes were large nails and a twist was that part of the hinge that was fixed to the door and twisted into an eye for hanging on to the jamb.

[4] The first part of the word is missing. It may be ' door-ledges ', the wooden cross-bars fixed on the back of a door to brace it.

to Walter Gyst working on the same buildings for 5 days at 3s 4d per week	2s	10d
to Thomas Tyelere, carpenter, working at the same place for 1 week at 5d per day	2s	6d
for the purchase and carriage of 5,500 stone slates	20s	4¾d
for the purchase of 2,250 stone slates at 2s 9d per 1,000	6s	2¼d
for their carriage		13½d
for the purchase of 900 laths at 4½d per 100	3s	4½d
for 3,350 lathnails for roofing and plastering	4s	7d
for 6 quarters and 4 bushels of lime at 10d per quarter	5s	5d
for 2 quarters of lime purchased at 12d per quarter	2s	
for 29 loads of sand		21d
for the purchase of 7,000 pins at 2d per 1,000		14d
in payment to one tiler for 1 week at 5d per day	2s	6d
in payment to the said tiler for another week at 5d per day	2s	6d
in payment to two assistants for the same for a week, both at 4d per day	4s	
in payment to one assistant for the same for 2 days at 4d per day		8d
to the aforesaid tiler for a week at 5d per day	2s	6d
to his assistant for the same period at 4d per day	2s	
for 10 tons of stone purchased for ' onysys bord '		7d
to a tiler for 1 week at 5d per day	2s	6d
to his assistant for the same period at 4d per day	2s	
for 4 bushels of lime		5d
for 10 loads of clay and 11 loads of earth for plastering		10½d
for straw and dung		5d
for 7 bags of water for the same work		3d
for making an angle wall		6d
2 bags of water		1d
for 150 laths for plastering		7½d
for 4 bushels of lime purchased for the same work		5d

Sum £4 11s 5½d

in repairing the houses of Stephen Coppe, John Cristowe and David Glasyer, viz., for 500 stone slates purchased for the aforesaid houses		20d
for 2 quarters of lime purchased for the same at 10d per quarter		20d
for 10 loads of sand		7½d
for 150 laths		2½d
for 250 lathnails		5d
for 1,500 pins		3d
in payment to a tiler for 2½ days at 5d per day		12½d
in payment to his assistant for 3 days at 4d per day		12d
for 2 tilers for 2½ days	2s	1d
for 14 lbs of lead purchased for the gutter over the shop of William Ok		15d
1 lock purchased together with 1 staple for the house of John Gurdeler		7d

Sum 10s 9½d

in repairing the house of David Glasyere. Firstly for 350 stone slates priced at 4d per 100		14d

for the purchase of 150 laths	2½d	
for 150 lathnails	3d	
for 4 bushels of lime	5d	
for 2 loads of sand	1½d	
for 500 pins	1d	
to Walter Helyere, tiler, for work on the aforesaid house for 2 days	10d	
to his assistant for the same period	8d	

Sum 3s 9d

on the house of Thomas Cryditon, saddler (no details)

Sum of all expenses 105s

II ECM ORPHANS' COURT, INVENTORY 3

Robarte Mathewe, baker, of Trinity parish.   Inventory made 30 August 1564.

In the Halle

Inprimis A table borde a Carpet a framed forme & a benche	10s	
vpon the Cobbarde one chardger 5 platters a basen 4 podengers 5 sawcers 7 podegedyshes one tynen quarte a salte & 2 erbe pottes	21s	
a Cobbarde with a cobbarde clothe	10s	
4 candelstyckes a morter & a pestle & a broken chafyngdyshe	6s	8d
a shyppe cheste	4s	
a peare of harnys & 2 bylls	8s	
2 quyshens (cushions) & the stayned clothes	5s	
2 brushes & a Rubber		6d
a ywen bowe with 18 shotyinge arrowes	6s	
an olde Chayre		4d
Summa £3 11s		6d
a Taffyta doblete & a canvas doblete	5s	
one cote of clothe & 2 Jaketts of clothe	16s	
one cloke	6s	
2 gownes	27s	
2 peare of hosen	4s	8d
a cappe & a hatte	2s	
Summa £3		8d

Lynnen

4 bordclothes	8s	
4 towels	4s	
14 napkyns	5s	
7 peare of shetes & one odde shete	26s	8d
4 pyllowes tyes	5s	
an olde cobarde clothe		4d
5 shyrtes	13s	
Summa £3	2s	

Yn his chamber

3 fether beddes 3 bolsters & 3 pyllowes	53s	4d
3 couerletts one of taptyer (tapestry) & 2 playne	16s	4d
a ioyned bedstede & a tester	5s	
2 blankets	2s	6d

the paynted clothes	3s	4d
an olde flocke bedde	2s	
20 pownde of woole	16s	
2 cofers & a borde	2s	
a remlet (remnant) of Cersye contayninge 2 yards & halffe	5s	
Summa £5	5s	6d

plate

one desen of Syluer spones	£3	
a stondinge cuppe with a couer parciall gylte	£3	
a stone cuppe with a couer gylte	26s	8d
Summa £7	6s	8d

Im the kychen

3 brasse potts & a posnet	13s	4d
2 panes a stelle panne & 2 lytell cawdrons	13s	4d
a fryinge panne & 2 gose pannes		20d
4 olde candelstyckes		16d
5 platters 3 Sawsers 3 podengers & a tynen quarte potte	9s	
a broche & 2 pothanginges		16d
2 dogges a fyer peke a fyer panne an awndyron	2s	
a table & 2 formes	2s	
a cobbarde		12d
a borde clothe		8d
4 stoninge cuppes		8d
a botell		2d
3 dosen of trenchures		3d
an old peare of bots & spores (spurs)	2s	
a syltinge (salting) tubbe		6d
in woode	6s	
a cowpe kayg (coop cage) & a tubbe		12d
a mouldynge trowe (trough) & a boshell		18d
Summa	57s	9d

In the bakhouse

7 sackes	6s	
a sacke of whete	20s	
in other stuffe remayninge in the bake house to the value of	13s	4d
Summa	39s	4d

In the shoppe

an old fether bedde & a bolster a peare of shetes & a tester	8s	
an olde mantell		6d
2 spinninge tornes		20d
a peare of Cardes		8d
an olde bedstede & a coffer		12d
a horse & a saddell	26s	8d
Summa	38s	6d
Summa totalis £39		23d
In Redy mony	12s	
In desperat detts	20s	

fer the lease fer terme of yers   £6 13s   4d
(on dorse) he awyd (owed) to Roger Matheu for a Gildyng   26s   8d

Appraisers: John German, Sylfester Weste, Thomas Babcoonbe,
          Henrye Waller.

III ECM ORPHANS' COURT, INVENTORY 31

John Dynham, weaver, of St. Paul's parish.   Inventory made 13 May 1583.

(m.1)   In the hall
Inprimis the table borde forme & benche   6s   8d
one newe Cubberde with a presse to the same & a Cubberd cloth
    vppon it   26s   8d
one olde Cubberd   5s
one Chest and an olde Coffer   13s   4d
two Chaires & a stoole (glossed ' one chair ')   20d
a bedsteed and a paynted tester to the same   4s
fyve Cushens & a matt vppon the benche   12d
the paynted Cloathes about the hall (glossed ' one paynted clothe ')   3s
a fether bed a dust bed a fether bolster a flock bolster a fether pyllowe
    and a peare of blancketts   20s
two bowes a sheafe of Arrowes & a black byll   4s

          In the Chamber
three bedsteedes and three paynted testers to them, and the paynted
    cloathes about the Chamber (glossed ' one paynted cloth ')   11s
a fether bedd a flock bed a fether bolster & a flock bolster a fether
    pyllowe a blanckett a sheete and a Couerlett of Tapistry Worke   20s
a flock bed two dust beds a fether bolster two little fether Pyllowes
    a peare of blancketts a Couerlett a flock bed 1 bolster & two olde
    Couerletts   19s   4d
foure Coffers and a shippe Coffer   8s
a litle olde borde and two hampers   14d
a peece of Clowte leather   16d

          In the Chamber ouer the shoppe
A table borde, a benche two olde formes & a Carpett   5s
a bedsteed and an olde Coverlett   2s   6d
A paynted Cloth   2s

          In the two shoppes
three loomes and two queele tournes   53s   4d
two sleas and harneys & three setts of staves   6s   8d
a litle table borde foure tubbes and a standerd two stooles two
    bucketts a Cradle olde paynted Clothes and other olde trashe   4s

          In the garden
a heape of stones   8d

          In the out Chamber
two bedsteedes a flock bed A Dust bed and two olde Couerletts & a
    bolster   5s

In the out Shoppe

A Warpinge tree a Gaggle a Plancke a tvrne a hanner a hand Sawe
    a peare of Pynsers and other olde trashe   3s   4d

In the Stable & ouer the stable

the Woode ouer the stable and A Grynding Stone in the Stable   6s

In the Kytchen

a table borde a benche a forme & a ioyned stoole   2s   6d
an olde Cubberd a bearer to sett barrells on two shelfes and a lether
    bottell   20d
a Cage for poultrye and two shelfes ouer it   12d
a Spytt a goose pan a frying pan two gredirons a peare of tonges
    three pott hanginges three pott Crookes and other olde Iron
    (glossed ' one gredyron ')   6s
12 Pewter platters and a pewter bason 12 Pewter poddingers 8
    sawsers & 5 tynne spoones   20s
six brasse potts and three Posnetts   33s   4d
foure brasse pannes & a litle Cawdren   13s   4d
two pottell potts of tynne three quarte potts of tynne three pynte
    potts of tynne & fyve flower potts of tynne (glossed ' dyneham ')   4s
seven Candlesticks a bason of brasse two Chafing dishes & a litle
    salte of tynne (illegible gloss)   4s   8d
three score and two poundes of yarne   £5   8s   4d
two peare of slyders and a peare of stockens   6s   8d
one Jerkyne   3s
one dublett   8s
two Cloakes   38s
two Gownes (glossed ' one gowne ')   33s   4d
a peare of Dowles sheets (glossed ' a pawne ') & one Canvas sheets   10s
two peare of Canvas sheets   4s
two Canvas borde Cloathes   3s   4d
three sherts & 6 bands   6s   8d
one yarde of fyne Canvas   2s   6d
4or yards of Irrishe Canvas   14d
one Dyaper borde napkyn and sixe Canvas napkyns   2s
2 Pyllowebecres (glossed ' mr dynham ')   12d
three drinckyng glasses and 2 Cupps   8d
three peare of gloves   6d
in monye   £4   1s

Pawnes

one Cassock 2 kyrtles of sylke & a Couerlett lyeth for 40s   40s
two platters and a sawser of Pewter lyeth for 12d   12d
one brasse pott lyeth for sixe shillinges   6s
two peare of sheets lyeth for 10s   10s
a peece of olde Damaske lyeth for 2s   2s
halfe a dosen of syluer spoones lyeth for 33s 4d   33s   4d
one syluer spoone lyeth for 3s   3s
one Goblett and a Couer to it of syluer double gilted lyeth for £7   £7
half a dosen of syluer spoones lyeth for 10s   10s

Debts

Nycholas Grenoe oweth	26s	8d
mr Symon Knyght oweth	£3	
Wylliam Knolles oweth	26s	8d
Sumes Gyll Wydowe oweth	20s	
Thomas Edbury of Tvton in the parishe of Credyton oweth	£4 10s	
mr Nicholas marten oweth	£35	

A revewe made the 18 of maye folowyng

an Iron shvuell & an olde garden rake	8d
a bundell of lastes	4d
Chirckcole	6d
lyme	4d
an olde rack & an olde plancke for a mavnger	2d
4{or} olde Costs & an olde Cowle	8d
a Conye hutche	4d
2 bushels of Rye & half a bushell of meale	5s
a hatt & a Cappe	20d
a playing tables & an olde breade grater	8d
a Carpett	20d
a litle brasse morter & a pestell of Iron	12d
an olde mantell	4d
a Rathe	4d
Summa £90	13s 8d

Appraisers: John Tvcker, Thomas Jordane, Edmond Coke.

(mm. 2-4 are executors' accounts)

IV   ECM ORPHANS' COURT, INVENTORY 60

Richard Hedgland, joiner, of Exeter. Inventory made 10 March 1596.

Inprimus one Cubborde	5s	
2 stooles & one olde Chayre	2s	
one peece of Seeling[1] and the Benches	3s	
the stened Clothers	3s	4d
one standing bedstede	11s	
a Fether bed one fether bolster & on flocke bolster	20s	
on pare of shittes and a Coverlet	16s	
one old bedsted	2s	6d
one plater and towe poddyngers of tyn		20d
one Latten[2] Candell sticke		8d
one Tynnen Cuppe A Tonne of Tynne and a salte of Tynne		12(d)
a peper Corne		2d
one Brasse Croke	3s	
one Brandize one pare of pothangings and a fleshe hooke		8d
on drypen pan and three spones of Tyn		3d
on Cuppe of stonne		2d

[1]Wainscot.
[2]A brass-like alloy.

on worken bynche		16d
Certen Tymber and other old Trashe aboute the house	8s	
Sum' Totalis ys	£3 19s	5d

Appraisers: Thomas Stonynge, William Joyce.

V ECM Orphans' Court, Inventory 70

John Fawell, yeoman, of the parish of St. Mary Major. Inventory made 28 November 1597.

Imprimis all his wearinge apparell	£4	
one belsalte double gylte, one lyttle goblett double gylte one Cuppe of Stone couered and footed withe syluer parcell gylte and one syluer goblett prysed att	£6 13s	4d
Nyneteene siluer spoones pryced at	£5	
Monye in his purse	20s	
his Corne in the barne	£3 10s	
Debts due to hym good and badd	£7 10s	
one Cowe priced att	40s	
one pigge priced att	6s	8d
a lease of the howse wherein he dwelt	£7	
a lease of two Closes of ground in St Sydwells made from one Willyam Mylford alias Challys priced att	40s	
a lease of a garden made from one Hannyball Ratclyffe priced att	40s	
In the hall		
three tablebordes one sydebourde and Fower Formes pryced att	33s	4d
one Settell and two Cupbordes	30s	
the Cylinges (seeling) & benches about ye hall	26s	8d
the paynted clothes about the hall	3s	4d
one Muskytt with his furnyture	20s	
one paire of Iron Dogges one paire of Andyrons one Iron barre and one paire of tonges pryced att	6s	
halfe a dozen of olde Cushions pric'	2s	
In the broad Chamber		
two standinge bedsteads and two truckle bedsteads priced att	40s	
fower featherbeds fower feather boulsters fyve pillowes & fower Ruggs	£8	
one framed tableborde one sydebourde one fourme one benche & one ioyned stoole	13s	4d
two olde Carpetts & two olde Couerletts	26s	8d
In a lyttle Chamber within the broadchamber		
one bedstead one featherbed one boulster one quilte and one lyttle Carpett	26s	8d
In the Parlour		
one standinge bedstead and one olde truckle bedstead pryced att	£5 3s	4d
two Featherbeds two Featherboulsters and fower feather pillowes pryced att	£3 10s	
two Ruggs one Carpett one blanckett and fyve Curtaynes pryced att	40s	

one tablebourd one fourme benches and Cylings with a Portall[1]
    priced att   20s
two olde Chests pryced att   4s
one Chaire of Strawe & two Iron Doggs   4s   6d

In the lyttle Parlour

one featherbed one featherboulster two pillowes one rugge one old
    bedsteade one lyttle fourme one lyttle rounde table & two lyttle
    Iron Dogges in the Chymney   40s

In the backe Chamber

two featherbeds two featherbolsters and two olde Couerletts pryced att   40s
two olde standinge bedsteads pric'   12s

In the Chamber ouer the parlor

two featherbeds two featherboulsters one olde flockbedd and 2 olde
    Couerletts   £3 10s
two standinge bedsteads one truckle bedstead one lyttle Sydeborde
    one ioyned Stoole, & one olde Cheste priced att   33s   4d

In mr Glanvyles Chamber

two Featherbeds one featherboulster one flocke boulster two Feather
    pyllowes & two white rugs with ye Curtaine   £3 2s   6d
one standinge bedsteade one trucklebedstead one lyttle tableboard &
    one olde Coffer pric'   20s
ye paynted cloathes in ye same chamber   20d

In the Gallyrie

one featherbed one flockbedd one dustbed one featherboulster one
    flockbolster two feather pyllowes three Ruggs and one olde quilte
    pryced att   46s   8d
two olde bedsteads & one Coffer pric'   8s

In the Schollers Chamber

three olde flockbedds one boulster two olde bedsteads & one olde
    square table   18s

In the Chamber over the gate

one featherbedd one featherboulster one featherpillowe one olde
    flockbed two old flocke boulsters one Rugge & one olde quilt   46s   8d
one standinge bedsteade one trucklebedstede one square bourde one
    olde fourme one stoole one olde benche and one Carpett pryced att   16s

In another Chamber ouer the gate

three featherbeds three feather boulsters three feather pillowes and
    three Couerletts pryced att   £6 6s   8d
two standinge bedsteades one truckle bedstead one table boarde two
    fourmes two ioyned stooles one Cheste & one olde carpett   52s

In the Buttery

pewter vessell one hundred and six pounds pryced att   40s
one pottle pott three quarts three pints fower tynninge Chamberpotts
    six brasen Candlestycks six tynnen candlesticks one pestell &
    morter fyue lyttle salts fower lyttle olde tynninge Cups and
    a goblett   16s   8d

[1]A small entrance lobby made of wainscot.

seaven stoninge Cups & one Jugge pric'   18d
two old Cupbords two plancks a frame to sett Drinke vppon and
   other trifles   5s

In the Cellar
one boatvate two syltinge tubs one sardge and a lyttle barrell pryced   6s   8d

The Naprie
thirtie paire of Sheets good and badde priced att   £8
one & twentie pillowtyes pric'   25s
three dozen & halfe of Common napkyns & two dozen of Diaper
   napkyns pric'   30s
thirteene bordcloathes good & badde   40s

In the Kytchin
three brasen potts & one posnett   20s
two pannes of brasse fower Caulderons two olde Skilletts & two olde
   Chaffindishes   22s
two brandyses sixe Crooks of Iron, one yron barre in the Chymney
   one fryengpan three pothooks fower spitts & one fyrepanne   20s
two Drippinge pannes   6s
fyve olde tubbs two Cowles two old plancks one spinninge turne
   with other olde trashe priced att   10s

In the stables
the haye priced att   £6 13s   4d
the Racks & Maungers priced att   20s

In the lynney[1] in the backcourte
two olde tubbs one hogesheade three olde barrells & one olde
   bourde pryced   3s   4d
two paire of Sheets two pillowtyes one Crocke one Carpett thirteene
   pounds & halfe of pewter, beinge a pawne left with the testator for
   certen mony the value not knowne to the Executrix   40s
                 Summa totalis   £132   4s   2d

Appraisers: Thomas Poyntington, Roger Powle, John Vugle.
(Sheet 2 is an executor's account)

VI ECM ORPHANS' COURT, INVENTORY 85

Willyam Spicer, (merchant, city of Exeter).   Inventory made 25 June 1604.

In the Shoope

	£	s	d
(Goods, mainly kersies =	554	12	1)

In the Seller vnder the Shoope

	£	s	d
29 pe(ces) of Wayneskots att 3s 4d pe(ce) is	4	16	8
31 quarters att 3d pe(ce) and is		7	9
4 boards 4 Tressells & 1 hoghead		3	4
in Woade and 1 pe(ce) of old Tymber is	1	0	0
Some is	6	7	9

[1]An outbuilding generally having a lean-to roof and an open front.

In the Halle

1 squeare tabell Board att 10s		10	0
1 Tabell board and 2 formes att		13	4
1 side board with a Coubord att		6	8
4 frame stoolles & 1 footte stoolle att		3	6
2 Cheares 2 lowe stooles & 1 payre of tabells is		6	8
2 Carpets of Dournex & 1 lyttell saye Carpet		6	8
6 old grene Cushines att		1	6
2 mapes in frames & 1 storrie at	1	10	0
45 yeards of seellinge at 20d per yeard	3	15	0
14 paines of glasse in the hall & gallery (contains) 50 Footte att 4d per foote and is		16	8
Some is	8	10	0

In the Parler

1 Drawinge Tabell board of Walnovt tree	2	13	4
1 Court Coubord att		13	4
1 Lyttell side tabell board att		6	0
6 frame stooles att 10d & 1 fourme 2s 6d		7	6
2 Cheares with stiche Cloth backs and 2 Imbrodred stooles is		13	4
1 Lyttell Roane (i.e. from Rouen) Cheare & 1 foot stolle		3	4
12 pictoures and 1 storrie		15	0
1 Ironne backe 1 payre of billowes and 1 payre of Snoffers		4	6
1 Windid Instrument or organes	8	0	0
6 grenne Chussines att 1s pe(ce)		6	0
1 Lookinge glasse is		4	0
2 old Carpets att		4	0
1 Courtt Cubberd Cloth frenged att		3	0
16 paines of glasse with 3 Casments (contains) 48 fout		18	0
68 yeards of seelinge att 2s is	6	16	0
4 yeards of Broad Cloth browne blue at 13s 4d per yeard and is	3	3	4
1 blacke Mournynge gowne att	3	10	0
1 Skarlett gowne att	16	0	0
1 gowne of Browne blue faced with bouge gardid att	5	0	0
1 gowne faced with foynes gardid with vellet	7	0	0
1 gowne faced with Satten att	7	0	0
1 gowne faced with Boudge welbid (?wellid) with vellet	2	6	8
1 gowne faced with boudge gardid with velvet	3	0	0
1 nieght gowne att		16	8
1 french Russett Clooke with Loopes att	2	10	0
1 Clooke with Rousett Loopes att	1	10	0
2 old Clocks with a payre of Basses		13	4
1 blacke sattayne doublett Cutt	1	13	4
4 doublets att	1	10	0
1 Jerkin of Raysed Velvet att	1	0	0
1 Cloth Jerkin with Roussett Lace & 1 payre of Cuffes att	1	6	8
1 bl(ue) Cloth Jerkin with Velvett Lace		15	0
1 k(ersey) and 1 grogoran Jerkin att		6	8

1 payre of bl(ue) Velvett breches with 2 payre of Clothe breches att	2	0	0
2 hats and bands		10	0
6 payre of Wostid hoose		10	0
3 nieght Cappes att		6	8
2 Rownde Cappes att		4	0
1 silke napills (?Naples) gerdiel with 3 payre of gloues		11	0
6 shirts att	1	0	0
5 whitt and wrought nieght Capes att		3	4
12 hand Circhers (handkerchiefs) att		8	0
3 payre of boot hosses 1 payre of topes and 4 payre of sockes		4	0
12 Rouffe bands & 8 payre of handefalles	1	10	0
3 yeards ¾ of bl(ue) satten att 6s 8d	1	5	0
3 yeards of tabye grogoran att 6s		18	0
1 gilt rapier and dager with girdill and hangers	1	10	0
2 silver Clapses for a clook		5	0
1 head peece gylt 1 feather 1 leading stafe Lead with gould and sylver	1	6	8
1 girdell and dager att		3	4
1 Ancient of blacke and Red sarcnet	1	10	0
2 payre of boots 2 payre of shoos and 1 payre of slipires att		8	0
1 mottley Clooke bagge att		2	0

Some is	95	4	0

In the fore hall

1 drawinge tabell bord att	2	5	0
6 frame stoolles att		5	0
7 yeards of greene sarge att 5s 4d	1	17	4
2 Remnants of bayes (contains) 19 yeards att 14d yd	1	2	2
1 Chere with grene Cloth frenged with silke		13	4
1 payre of Verginalles att		15	0
1 great Iland Cheast att	2	6	8
113 Reames of w(hite) pott paper att 4s ye Reame	22	12	0
1 greene sarge Carpett (contains) 7 yeards ½	1	13	4
1 Tourkey Carpett att 6s 8d		6	8
1 greene silke quylt att		6	8
1 Carpett stript (contains) 5 yerds ½ att		10	0
1 greene Carpett for a side board		4	0
1 Tapestrie Coverlett	2	13	4
1 Cremsine Rougge	2	0	0
1 Carpett of Tapestrie		13	0
6 nedell worke Cushianes and nedell worke Bourder att	1	6	8
6 greene Cushianes att		6	0
6 Arrowes (?Arras) Cushianes with the pyllowes	2	0	0
1 L: windowe Cushiane with nedell worke		10	0
2 squeare nedell worke Cushianes		6	8
2 Coverings of nedell worke for stooles		4	0
1 bourder of Nedell Worke for a Court Cobard		5	0

28 paines of glasse with 6 Cassements (contains) 84 footte att 4d
per Footte is

	1	8	0

Some is   46   9   10

In the Chamber owuer the foore Hall

1 Drawinge Tabell boord	1	10	0
6 frame stooles		5	0
1 stript Carpett		5	4
1 Lyttell Compting Chest with a frame		6	8
1 Cheare with greene frenge		5	0
1 payre of brasse Andirons with 1 fire pann Lungs (bellows) 1 Latten panne	2	10	0
1 payre of Verginalles with a ferme (?form/frame)		6	0
1 fether bead 1 woll(en) Mattrese with 1 feether bolster and 2 pyllowes att	3	0	0
greene Rouge and 1 payre of Blanckets	1	10	0
1 payre of sheets 1 payre of pyllotyves		8	0
12 yeards of seellinge att		12	0
48 footte of glasse with 7 Cassments	1	8	0
1 old Chest		2	0
the hangings of greenne k(ersey)	1	10	0

Some is   13   18   0

In the Inner Chamber

1 standinge Beadsteed and tronkell bedsteed		13	4
1 flocke beed 1 w(hite) rugge 1 grenne coverlett		15	0
1 side bord 10s 1 Chere 8d is		10	8
1 short stript Carpett		3	4
1 payre of Andirons & 1 payre of dogs topt with Lattine		12	0
1 payre of Tongs 1 fire panne 1 payre of byllowes		1	6
6 paines of glasse (contains) 9 Foote with 1 Casement		3	4

Some is   2   19   2

At the Stayer Head

1 Brushinge bord		1	0
1 Close stoolle		3	4
1 Lantrone and 1 glasse Lantrone		4	0
6 paines of glasse (contains) 9 footte with A Casement		3	4

Some is   11   8

In the foore Cocke Lafte

1 frame for a Chayre		2	6
A tabell of glasse		3	0
1 old strawen Chayre 1 old dore of seellinge with 1 flaskett ande is		4	0

old tymber old Roopes & old Irone	6	8
2 buffe skines	4	0
16 paines of glasse with 4 Casements (contains) 28 foote att 4d foote & is	9	4

	Some is	1	9	6

In the Chamber over the parler

1 standinge beadsteed	3	0	0
1 Tronckell bedsteed with a foot stepe		5	0
1 fether beed 2 bolsteres 2 pyllotives and 1 mattrese	3	0	0
1 greene Rouge & 1 payre of blankets		13	4
5 greene k(ersey) Curtaynes with the Curtayne Rods		10	0
1 flocke beed & 1 fether bolster		8	0
1 blue Ruge & 3 blankets		10	0
1 payre of sheets 1 payre of pyllotives		6	8
1 Iland Cheest	2	0	0
1 sea Cheest with 5 boxes		6	8
the staynd Cloth with the seellinge		13	4
1 Troncke 1 Cheest bandid with Irone	1	0	0
1 Lyttell Tabell boord & 1 box for bands		8	0
2 windowe Courtaynes with the Curtayne Rods and 1 Lyttell payre of Dodgs		2	6
1 Lookinge glasse 1 broush 1 Roubber		2	0
11 paines of glasse with 1 Cassement (contains) 28 foote att 4d foote and is		9	4
1 payre of Crim(son) and greene Mocado Courtaynes frenged and is	1	13	4

	Some is	15	8	2

In the Mayds Chamber

1 presse 15s 1 greate Chest 8s is	1	3	0
1 brusshinge bord 4s & 4 Lyttell flaskets and 4 hampers		8	0
1 standinge bedsteed & 1 tronckell bedsteede		8	0
1 flocke bed and one fether boulstere 1 payre of sheets & 1 Rouge with other od tryfells		10	0
the glase Windowe with 1 Casement & 1 Courtayne		3	4

	Some is	2	12	4

The Linninge in the barde Cheste

5 payre of dowles sheets	2	0	0
5 payre of pyllotives 3s per payre		15	0
1 damaske Tabell Clothe 1 Towell with 18 tabell napkings att	3	10	0
2 diaper tabell Clothes 2 towells with 3 doz napkings	3	10	0
1 damaske Towell		10	0
2 Courtt Coubbard Clothes of Cutt Worke		3	4
9 bord Clothes of Canvas and dowles	2	0	0

	£	s	d
3 side bord Clothes		6	8
3 dozen oₗ Tabell napkings	1	0	0
3 Longe Towells & 3 shortt towells		6	8
Some is	14	1	8

The Linninge In the Cheste in the maides Chamber

	£	s	d
6 payre of Canvas sheets	1	16	0
3 dozen of Tabell napkings	1	0	0
2 dozen of old tabell napkings		6	0
2 side bord Clothes		2	6
1 payre of pyllotives		2	0
12 Course shourtt tabell Clothes		6	0
10 Canvas towells and 7 dowles towells		6	0
2 Longe Towells		2	0
In old Lyninge		6	0
Some is	4	6	6

The plate

	£	s	d
1 greate sylver saltte doble gilt (contains) 22 ozs ½ att 6s per oz is	6	15	0
1 secke (?sack) Cupe doubell gilt (contains) 23 ozs ½ att 6s per oz is	7	1	0
2 silver bolles & 1 goblett doubell gilt (contains) 50 ozs ½ att 6s per oz is	15	3	0
1 sylver Tankerd doubell gilt (contains) 19 ozs at 6s	5	14	0
1 Challis doubell gilt (contains) 12 ozs ¾ 5s 6d oz	3	10	1
1 Trencher salt doubell gilt (contains) 2 ozs ½ at 6s		15	0
3 whitt sylver booles (contains) 19 ozs ¾ att 4s 8d	4	12	2
12 sylver spones (contains) 17 ozs ¾ att 4s 8d	4	3	10
2 stone Cupes Coverred & fottid with sylver doubell gilt (contains) 17 ozs att 6s per oz is	5	2	0
Some is	52	16	1

In the Chichen

	£	s	d
296 lbs of pewter att 6d per lb is	7	8	0
63 lbs of brassen pannes and other vessell att 7d per lb and is	1	16	9
172 lbs cf brasse potts att 5d per lb is	3	11	8
3 Ironne kettells & 1 Iron pot		11	0
1 settell and 1 Rownd bord		12	0
1 bassen and yewre		2	6
1 gallon 1 pottell 1 quart pot of tynne		13	2
1 Cullender 1 pye plate & 2 Lyttell plats		2	6
2 spout potts 1 quart 1 pynt		2	6
1 quart pott 1 yewre		2	6
4 Flower potts 6 sallts & Coupes		3	0
7 Candellsticks		5	10
4 pynt potts		2	6

	£	s	d
1 Lyttell sestrene (cistern) of Tynne		2	4
7 Candell sticks of Brasse	1	0	0
1 Candell sticke & 1 perfumynge pott		2	6
1 Ironne barre in the Chymley		4	0
4 Irones in the Range of the Chymney & 1 dodg		3	0
200 lbs of Irone spits Racks & Irone stoufe att 2d per lb is	1	13	4
one Jacke and the pe(?ce) being ½ C (50 lbs) of Leade		13	4
1 Coubberd		1	8
1 warmynge panne 1 Ladell 1 skimer 1 dripinge spoune		3	0
1 Mustard Mill 1 Chayre and 1 frame stoole		2	6
1 Coope 2 shelves 1 drypynge panne & 1 fryinge and other Tryfells		6	8
6 paines of glasse with one Casement (contains) 16 foote att 4d per footte and is		5	4
1 plancke bord and the shelves in the Chichinge		8	0
1 Chere and 2 Lowe stooles		1	8
Some is	**21**	**1**	**3**

In the butterye

	£	s	d
1 Amerey 5s 1 Coubberd 12d 1 Candell Coffer 6d is		6	6
12 dozen of trenchers		2	6
1 gibbe 2 baskets 2 Treyes 1 gimlet		1	6
5 glasse bottells and drinking glasses and other Erthen dyshes in all is		6	8
Some is		**17**	**2**

In the Chamber over the Kitchen

	£	s	d
1 tabell boord with a frame		5	0
2 Cheasts 6s 8d 1 payre of doggs in the Chymney 2s 6d is all		9	2
1 gimpresse 6s 8d 1 Cheare 8d		7	4
1 beadsteed and 1 Tronckell beedsted		16	8
1 feather bed 1 boulster 1 pyllowe with one payre of blankets	3	13	4
17 panes ½ of glasse with one Casement (contains) 40 foote and is		13	4
9 willo' of Twiggs			6
Some is	**6**	**5**	**4**

In the Servants Chamber

	£	s	d
1 beadsteed 1 Tronckell bedsteed		6	8
1 feether bed & 2 floucke bolsters		13	4
2 drome Coverings and is		6	8
10 paines of glasse (contains) 25 foote att 4d foote		8	4
1 stille 8s 1 pye panne of lattine 6s 8d		14	8
2 muskets and 5 Callyvers with 2 flasks and tichebox	1	10	0
2 head peces 3s 4d 1 swords 2 dagers 1 welshe hooke 1 bro(wn) bill is all		10	0
1 Costlett	1	0	0

1 frame to mak Lace 1 hachet & 6 wedges & dyvers other trifills of Irone work is all		10	0
Some is	5	19	8

In the backer Chamber

3 old Coffers 3 suger Cheestes 1 Childs Chare(?) 1 Lanren (?lantern) and other Tryfells		6	8
sacke of barley malte		15	0
1 neste of boxes with baskets and whisks		2	0
Some is	1	3	8

In the backe Loft

16 bords 1 suger Cheast & other tryfells		12	4

In the Seller

in Salte by Estimatione	10	10	0
6 Caske & a trendall		10	0
6 bushells of barley		15	0
Some is	11	15	0

In the Entrye at the backe Doore

2 Cowells with Covers 1 tub 2 tressels		2	0

In the Stabell

1 Racke and manger 1 showell 1 picke 1 lader 1 donge evell & is		5	0
1 presse for k(erseys)	3	0	0
3 saddels 13s 4d 1 gildinge £6 13s 4d is	7	6	8
3 sowes of Lead (contains) 3 C att 7s per C (100) is	1	1	0
in bords & ½ inche bords	2	6	8
in old Tymber and woode	1	0	0
1 wheele barrow 1 hand barrow & other tryfells		8	0
Some is	15	7	4

In the Entrey of the gardon

1 Coope with other peces of Tymber		6	8
in stonnes in the stabell and Court		2	0
		8	8

In the gardon

1 well boucket with a rope and Chayne		3	4
1 payre of garden sheeres with a whetstone		1	0
1 shelfe 1 benche & scertayne stonnes		2	0
Some is		6	4

In the Seller vnder the Kitchen

1 plancke boord		6	8
2 gibbes 1 bracke		3	0
1 Irone morter and pessell		3	0
2 boushels of Wheate 2 boushels of Rye 1 bushell ½ of mealle and is	1	2	0
3 powdringe Toubes and salt toubes		2	0
in ½ barrells and Costes		5	0
1 bountinge huche 2 sargs dawe (dough) toubes and other Caske		6	8
2 shelfes 1 great treinge (wooden) platter with earthen poots and pannes		2	0
Some is	2	10	4

In the gardon without Southgate

5 C of hellinge (roofing) stonnes with a pigs trowe & Dunge is in all		4	0

In the Barnne

3 seeffes 1 reepe 2 hooks 1 forke & rake 1 picke 1 wantingestaffe		2	0
1 windsheete (?winnowing) & other old Canvas		2	0
in wood and tymber		2	6
In donnge 5s and 2 pe(ces) of tymber 5s		10	0
in barley in the barnne	3	0	0
1 Close of wheate (contains) 4 akeres att 45s	9	0	0
1 Close (contains) 5 akers of beanes and pease att 30s	7	10	0
Some is	20	6	6

At St Georges Cliste

1 Reeke of Woode (contains) 15 doz: att 6s is		4	10	0

At Lyme

12 tonnes of Lead les 4 C beinge 212 pe(ces) att £7 5s	85	10	0

At the Kaye of Exon

33 pe(ces) of Lead (contains) 36 C att £7 5s is	12	17	0
in Wm Bulles hand of Wells 4 tonnes of Lead att £5 13s 4d	22	13	4
Some is	35	10	4

In aduenturs Abroade

In the hands of John pottle att Roane (Rouen) £87 17s 6d	8	15	9
in the hands of Robertt Tawley in St Mallowes (St. Malo) 4 ballots of Ordynarie Couller k(ersies) (contains) 16 in ech att 30s per pe(ce) & is	96	0	0
12 pe(ces) of Web inalles (?in all) att 23s pe(ce) is	13	16	0

more by ablle(?) of deptt in the said tawleyes hands 276 and is   27 12 0
in the hands of Robt Tawley in St Mallowes 1 ballott (contains)
  16 pe(ces) of Ordynarie Coullers k(ersies) at 30s pe(ce) is   33 0 0
1 ballott of Whitt K(ersies) (contains) 16 pe(ces) att 27s   21 12 0
in the hands of Michall Spicer for the Ilands and is   8 10 0

Some is   209 5 9

In the Counter

26 lb ½ of yellowe wax att 13d lb and is   1 8 8
28 lb of Cuchanelle att 33s 4d lb is   46 13 4
1 bord 1 deske 1 neste of boxes 1 benche with the seellinge and 1
  shelfe is all   1 0 0
2 bibell 1 Cronycle with 2 other books and is   2 10 0
1 voyder for the tabell 1 hamer 1 grassinge knyfe 7 quire of paper
  with other tryfells & is   8 0
2 standishes 1 payre of gould waieghts 1 seale Topt with sylver
  with other tryfells & is   4 0
in (?)k(ersies) in talle £875 6s 6d att 13d per £(?) exchang   903 15 4
in Corrant money and is   301 19 5
the glasse windowe paines (contains) 9 foote att 4d 1 dager 1
  payntid quarrell of glase is   5 0
in kercerie(?) Warres (wares) and is   14 10 0
a lease for 66 yeares to Come of the howse wherin m^rs Spicer now
  dwelleth att £3 15s Real   320 0 0
a lease for 46 years to Come of a garden and stabell in watter beare
  street att 5s Real yeare   20 0 0
a lease for 2 Closes with out southe gate & one Tenement for 40
  yeares yf Robertt Edmontes so Longe shall Live att £8 yeare   6 13 4

Some is   1619 7 1

(Good debts = £300 4s 10d

  Doubtful debts = £662 0s 4d)

The some totall of all this booke is in all   3822 14 8

(Debts due and owing by the said William Spicer = £144 18s 0d)

Appraisers: Mr Waltar Borowe, Mr John Lant, Mr John Shere, Roger Phipes.
(Executors' accounts follow)

VII ECM ORPHANS' COURT, INVENTORY 148

William Knowslye (inn holder), of the city of Exeter. Inventory made 4 January
1625.

£   s   d

In the kitchen Camber

A fether bed 2 bovlsters and a pillowe poz (avoirdupois) 105 lbs ½
  at 7d per lb is   3 1 6
a bedsteed & truckell bed   1 6 8

2 ovld syde bovrds & a forme	5	0
a Clowse stovle & 2 broaken chayers	3	0
a Rvge and a syd table Carpett	10	0
a pear of greene Say Curtens	8	0

In the fawlcon

A Bedsteed vallance & on ovld table bovrd	12	0
the stayned Clovthes of the same Chamber	13	4

In the Roze

A fetherbed performed 117 lbs at 10d per lb	4	17	6
mor on fetherbed performed poz 87½ lbs at 8d per lb	2	18	4
a Bedsteed and truckell bedd	6	0	0
a table bovrd 7 stovles & a chayer	1	8	0
a Livery bovrd		5	0
a Silke quilte and on orise (Arras) Coverlett	3	0	0
5 Cushings & a dornex Carpete		18	0
2 windowe Cushings & a Callaco Carpet		4	0
Curtaynes and vallance to the bede		10	0
a binch within the bovrd		3	4
a Ruge vallued In		16	0

In the Anker Chamber

A fether bed performed poz 109 lbs at 9d per lb is	4	1	9
a Bedsteed & trovckell bed		12	0
a peare of ovld Curtens		2	6
a Ruge and on ovld Carpet		18	0
a lyttell syde bourd a stooll and on ovld Chayer		4	0

In the Catt & Fyddell

A fetherbed performed poz 110 lbs at 8d per lb	3	13	4
a bedsteed and truckell bed	1	10	0
3 ovld Curtens and on ovld vallance		6	8
a lyttell table on ovld Chayer & 2 binches		5	0
one Ruge		10	0
Stayned Clovthes		3	4

In the Staie

A fether bed bovlsters & pillowes 131 lbs at 8d	4	7	4
a Ruge		18	0
a Bedsteed & truckle bed	1	6	8
3 ovld Curtaynes and vallance		8	0
3 ovld Cushings & one ovld Carpett		5	0
on ovlde table bovrd a broaken Chayer on lyttell bench & a broken stoulle		6	0
ovlde stayned Clovthes		4	0

The stagg Chamber

A fether bed bovlster & 2 pillos 116 lbs at 10d per lb	4	16	8
mor a Fether bed & 2 pillos 76 lbs at 8d per lb	2	10	8
on ovld flocke bovlster		2	0
on Ruge	1	0	0
on other Ruge		6	8

a Bedsteed and truckell bede		2	0	0
the Curtens			12	0
2 syde bovrds 4 Joyne stovles on ovld furme and on ovld Chayer			14	0

	60	3	3

2 ovld Carpetts an 4 ovld Cushings	7	0
In the 2 littell shelffs and a bench	1	4

In the Red Lyon

A fether bed 2 pillowes 2 bolsters 104 lbs at 10d per lb	4	6	8
mor one bed bovlster & pillowes 75 lbs at 7d per lb	2	3	9
an ovld Bedsteed and truckelbed		12	0
an ovld Rvge and quilte		18	0
Curtens and vallance		8	0
2 ovld Cushings and one ovld syd Carpete		1	6
2 stovles a Syd bovrd and an ovld Chayer		4	4
a Cheste		8	0

the Chamber within the kitchinge

A fether bed bovlster & 2 pillowes 99 lbs at 10d per lb	4	2	6
on ovld dust bed		2	0
a Bedsteed and truckell bed		7	0
2 ovld Rugs and on ovld Couverlett		12	0
2 Chests and 2 ovld table bovrds		17	0
a Sovrde (sword) pavnd is		8	0

The butt Chamber

A fether bede 2 bovlsters 2 pillowes 98 lbs at 10d per lb	4	1	8
a Bedsteed & truckell bed		15	0
4 ovld Rugs at	1	0	0
one ovld flocke bed and 2 flocke bovlsters		10	0
2 ovld Curtens		2	0
a table bovrd and 2 ovld fourmes		11	0
Impellment in the next howse Cost	4	0	0
a Chest		6	0
3 ovld Cushings		1	0

In the Bell over the Seller

A Fether bed bovlster & 2 pillowes 81 lbs at 9d per lb	3	0	9
a Coverlett		9	0
a Bedsteed & truckellbed	1	0	0
a table bovrd 3 formes and a binch		18	0
a flocke Bovlster		1	6
the Stayned Clovthes		10	0

In the 2 Cuppes or Syd parler

An ovld bedsteed 2 dust beds on ovld Coverlet	10	0
on ovld table bovrd a forme and a binch	5	0
3 ovld Carpetts and 3 ovld Cushings	7	0

In the parler

2 Cubberds	2	0	0
a table bovrd 6 stowlls and a Chayer		16	10

	£	s	d
a Carpet and 5 Cushings		12	0
a gvilt Lether Cushinge & 2 Cubberd Clovthes		5	0
3 ovld windowe Curtaynes		1	0

In the hall

	£	s	d
2 table bovrds and a forme		17	0
a Corslet perfurmed	2	0	0

In the kitchinge

	£	s	d
In Pewter dishes 170 lbs at 9d per lb is	6	7	6
5 payer of tininge Candelstiks		10	0
12 quarte potts at 16d per pece		16	0
12 pynts at 8d the pece		8	0
3 London quarts		5	6
2 pottell potts and on halffe pynte		4	0
2 pie plats		2	0
11 lbs of ovld Broucke pewter Candellstiks		7	4
10 Chamber potts of tynne		10	0
48 lbs of Brasse panes & Cavldrons at 10d per lb	2	0	0
162 lbs of crocke mettell at 6d½ per lb is	4	7	9
116 lbs of Iron worke at 3d per lb is	1	9	0
100 lbs of Iron bars & ovld Iron at 2d per lb		16	8
2 govspans to friing panes and a saving Iron		10	0
	59	12	7

	£	s	d
A Capen Coope a syd bovrd 4 shellfes 2 Joyn stoules	1	2	0
In Bacon		16	0
a dresser 2 shelues & a trendell		6	8
a Copper furnes	1	10	0
3 hogs	2	0	0
1 Reeke of hard wood in the Covrte	2	0	0
5 Brewinge vessells & 6 lyttell tubbes		12	0
a geebe (gib, i.e. iron hook)		1	0
2 brasse Candelstiks a Chaffer a pessell & morter		11	0

the Lyninge

	£	s	d
A diaper Bovrd clovth and 2 dozen napkings	1	0	0
a Canvas Bovrd clovth & 1 dozen napkings		14	0
a Canvas bovrd clovth & 1 dozen napkings		11	0
a Canvas table clovth & 1 dozen napkings		10	0
4 short table clovthes		7	0
2 Canvas table clovthes		8	0
4 Canvas table clovthes		14	0
1 ovld short table clovth & 2 dozen napkings		13	0
6 pear of Covrse sheets ovld & waren (worn)	1	5	6
23 dovles pillotyes 18d pec	1	14	6
15 Covrse hand towells at 8d pec		10	0
1 pear of holland sheets	1	0	0
3 pear dovles sheets at 18s per peare	2	14	0
3 pear dovles sheets at 15s per pear	2	5	0

5 pear dovles sheets at 14s per pear	3	10	0
1 pear of Canvas Sheets		8	0
5 pear of ovld Canvas sheets at 5s	1	5	0
4 pear of covrse sheets for trovkell beds		16	0

his apparrell

A Tawnye sute with Silke and govld Lace	2	10	0
a Sute of mixt stufe	1	4	0
2 Sarge dubletts	1	0	0
2 Clovcks	4	10	0
a hatt and band		5	0
a fustien dublett		5	0
3 peare of worsted hose		10	0
Sherts bands Cuffs and handkerchers	2	0	0
an ovld movrnige cloacke		5	0

The plate

A guilte salte poz 10 oncs $\frac{1}{2}$ at 5s 6d once	2	17	9
A parcell gvilte salte 10 oncs $\frac{1}{2}$ at 5s is	2	12	6
13 bolls 12 spunes 112 oncs $\frac{3}{4}$ at 4s 10d onc is	27	4	11$\frac{1}{2}$
In mony in the howse	9	0	0

In the ovter backe Seller

5 hgheds of Beare at 10s hogs	2	10	0

In the Castell

2 Reecks of ovcken fagotts 30 dozen at 14s dozen	21	0	0

In the drinckinge Roumes

An ovld pecs of seeling 2 drinkinge bovrds & binches		7	0
a dry fate (vat)		3	0
4 ovld Barrells and tubbs		5	0
2 peare of tabells a pear of bellowes & a grater		5	0

In the stables

In haye to the vallewe of	15	0	0
2 Racks & 2 Mavngers		8	0
3 tone and halffe of empty hogsheds 2s 6d pec	1	15	0
9 butts and Pypes at 4s per pece	1	16	0
	126	16	10$\frac{1}{2}$

In the wine seller

4 empty hogsheds 2 empty butts		17	0
a scoringe table			6
2 ovld chests & one ovld bovrd		1	6
a plancke & a deall bovrd		2	0
the bearers with a povdringe tube		6	0
mor 2 empty butts		8	0
2 tons 1 hogshed of ovld gascon win £12 per ton	27	0	0
3 butts of ovld sak at £17 per pece	51	0	0
a Cantell (portion) of Sake	1	10	0
a pype and halffe Canary win at £17 pipe	25	10	0

a Remaynder of tente (a Spanish wine)	1	15	0
a hogs and halffe of newe gascon wine	7	0	0
In good dept owing by divers Severall persons to the som' of	13	17	0
	129	7	0

desperat depts			
humfrye Ball of Chidley the elder oweth	**7**	**0**	**0**
Roberte White of Tiverton	1	3	0
	8	3	0

The totall some besyds the desperate depts of his Inventory amovnteth to in all—£375 19s 08d½

I Say 375—19—08—½

depts owinge by wᵐ Knoweslye at the tyme of his death

diewe to m' Mvncke	18	10	0
diewe to humfrye Cursyn	39	0	0
diewe to wᵐ Terrell	36	0	0
diewe to Beniamyn Rysdon	10	0	0
diewe to Gilberte Sweete	590	0	0
	603	10	0

Appraisers: Richard Sweete, Thomas Awton, Phillipe Horne, William Cowme.

VIII DRO, E/CTI 73

Stephen Avstyn, dyer of the parish of Saint Edmund. Inventory made 17 June 1641.

	£	s	d
In the Kitchen			
Imprimis Nyne pevter dishes		13	6
one Chamber pott of pewter Fower Sawcers one Sallt & one Candell sticke		2	8
one brase Candell stick & A pestell & morter		2	0
Three smalle brasse Crockes	1	0	0
one brasse Crocke		10	0
Tooe Calderens tooe skilletes and one brasse ladle		16	0
Three spitts and one gridiron		2	0
Two pares of pot hangines & 2 flesh hookes		2	6
one paire of Andirones		5	0
one frying pane & one saving Iron and Tooe hanging Crookes		2	0
one driping plate			6
one Tabellbord one settell & one ioyned stoole		10	0
one old Cvbbord		2	0
in other implements belonging to the kitchen		2	0
in another Roome old bord		2	0
in woode and old implements In the shoppe		3	0

In the Halle

15 pewter dishes	1	2	6
4 Tynnen Candel stickes and one salte		15	0
6 Sawcers & 6 pewter dishes		2	0
one qvart & one pinte of Tynne		4	0
one tablebord one Joyned stoole & one Chare		2	0
one presse Cvbord & A Chest	1	15	0
one hie bed steed & A trvckell bed steed	1	0	0
Three Bedds	1	13	0
2 fether bolsters & Three pilloes	1	6	8
too Rvges one Cover leets & A pare of blanckets	1	6	8
one lidell tabell bord one Joyned stoole & too old Coffers		8	8
one oll bedsteed & 2 old Rvgges		15	0
one bibell		5	0
7 pare of sheetes & one olld sheet	3	12	0
5 pilloties	0	6	8
3 tabell Clothes 12 tabell napknges & 2 hand towells	1	4	0
3 shvrtes 2 bandes & 2 Capes		10	0
6 Cvshinges		6	0
one littell wyne bolle	1	0	0
his oune wareing apparrill	2	10	0
for 5 hoges wch ware sold	5	0	0
Three more sold		15	0
Tooe pigges in the hovse	1	5	0
for old implements		6	0
Svm' totale	31	6	8

Appraisers: George James, William Fille.

IX   D & C, DEED 375

(This document, which records two large houses in detail, is dated the 23rd June 1655 and relates to the sale of certain ecclesiastical property as a result of the temporary abolition of bishops, deans and chapters during the Commonwealth period.)

(i) '. . . all that Mesuage or Tenement with the appurtenances Commonly called or knowne by the name of the Archdeacon Cottons house alias the Archdeacon of Totnes house scituate lying and being in the Churchyard or Close of the late Cathedrall Church of St Peter in Exeter haueing the said Close on the South part thereof the Lady Reynolds house on the West part Tills Lane on the North part and the Lady Chambers house and Mr Helliars house on the East part Consisting of an Entrie leading out of the aforesaid Conteyning Nynty Six Foote in length and Nyne foote in breadth into a Large Hall One Hall and two Parlours at the vpper end thereof with Three Cellars one Butterie a Large dineing Roome over them and Three Lodging Chambers over them of One Yeard on the Left hand of the said hall towards Tills Lane haueing a Kitchin with a Larder a Pastrie within it and a Chamber over them. Off two Woodhouses and one Chamber over them on the left hand And on the right hand of the aforesaid yard Of two Stables and Lofts over them with a Lodging for a Groome by the said Stable on the North side of the said yard and of one Gallerie on the East side of the said yard with two Chambers over itt Which said Housing and Yard Conteyne from North to South One Hundred and Twelue foote more or Lesse and from East to West One Hundred and Forty foote more or Lesse And one Garden on the East side of the said House Conteyning Nynety Six foote more or Lesse and Fifty foure Foote more or Lesse in Length And also the ground and Soyle of the said Houseing Yard Garden and other the Last mencioned Premisses and every of them Conteyning in the whole halfe an Acre more or Lesse . . . ' (The annual value of the above property was 50s. The materials of the tenement and buildings were valued at £50 above the cost of pulling them down.)

(ii) ' . . . all that Mesuage or Tenement with the appurtenances Commonly called or knowne by the name of the Chanters House alias Newgate scituate lying and being within the said City of Exeter haueing the way that Leadeth to the Palace gate on the East part thereof the way that leadeth to the gate by the Beare Inne on the North part thereof and the house of Mrs Webb on the Southeast part thereof Conteyning in breadth from East to West One Hundred and Twenty Foote more or Lesse, and from North to South in depth Nynety two Foote more or Lesse In Houseing Consisting of one Gatehouse with one Roome on the Right hand two Roomes on the Left hand and Foure Chambers over them Of one Court within the said Gate Conteyning Forty foote square more or Lesse of one Woodhouse on the Left hand of the said Court and a Stable with a Loft over the same Of one Porcch Leading into a faire hall on the right hand of the same Court Of one Hall two Parlours one Kitchin two Butteries and Three Sollers[1] over all Within the second Storey of one Dineing Roome and Nyne Chambers and in the Third Storey of two Chambers and of one Roofe over them Conteyning Twenty Foote Square more or Lesse And also of one Chamber by them covered with Slate And all that Garden with the appurtenances lying and being behinde the same Mesuage or Tenement Conteyning One Hundred and Tenne foote more or Lesse In breadth And Seaventy two foote more or Lesse in depth And all that Stable with the appurtenances scituate and being behinde the said Garden Conteyning in Length Fifty foote more or Lesse and in breadth foureteene foote more or Lesse And also one Tryangular Yard with the appurtenances lying and being on the South side of the said Stable . . . '

X   D & C, 4573, 1/1

(Undated, second half of seventeenth century.)

A survey of seuerall houses belonging to mistris Agnis Martin without westgate in the seuerall possessions of the persons heareafter mencioned

Viz.   Zacheus Crabb two grownd Roomes parte of a messuage & tenement in Froglane in St Edmonds parish for which he payeth yearely 2–14–0 & is discharged of Reparacions & Taxes worth Cleare of Reparacon—£2 6s

George sandford holdeth one shopp & 2 Chambers ouer Late in the possession of John huett for which he payeth £5 per annum & is to hold it for 6½ yeares from the 1 of 9ber (i.e. September) 69 being parte of the foresaid tenement in froglane & is worth per annum but £4—the planchins[2] are much decayed & is to be Cleared of Reparacons & Taxes—worth besids Reparacion—£4

[1]Solars.   [2]Planks, floorboards.

Isaac wolland (& his vnder tennants) hold one shopp & 2 Chambers & a throung[1] betwene them & 2 lynneys[2] peradioyning to the foresaid house in Froglane late in the possession of Thomas Caseby for which he payeth £9 per annum & hath as I ame informed an Estate of 5 yeares yet to Come in it at the same Rent & to be discharged of Reparacons & Taxes as aboue—this was formerly sett for £6 per annum worth per annum Cleare of Reparacion—£7 10s 0d

John Collings holdeth one growND Roome & a Chamber ouer for which he payeth yearely £3 16s & was late in the possession of Johan Beuill widow& is next adioyning to the foresaid tenement & better in Repaire then any of the foresaid tenements but to be discharged as aforesaid—£3 8s 0d

Mistris Ax now Called mistris Smith widdow holdeth two tenements next adioyning to the former & in the same Courtelage one of them in the possession of phillip Tamlyn for which he payeth yearely £5 & to be discharged as aforesaid the other tenement is in the possession of Thomas huggins for which he payeth yearely £3— in these two tenements mistris ax Claymeth an Estate of 5 yeares as I ame informed Cleare of paying of any Rent which must be Considered in the purchas mr Tamlyns house Consisteth of a backshopp an Entry & a hall and one Chamber ouer & Thomas huggins his house Consisteth of one growND Roome & a Chamber mistris Ax holdethe by the same Lease one garden plot now in the possession of Roger tedder in Bunney lane in St Edmonds & worth per annum £1 10s in all worth aboue Reparacion £8— £8 0s

Mr John Munguell holdeth a Littell tenement in Bunney lane for the terme of two middle aged liues vnder the yearely Rent of 11s & is worth per annum aboue the said Rent £3 10s—this house is very badly built & gon much to decay for want of Reparacions it Consists of 2 vnder Roomes & a Chamber & Cockloft and a garden with a little throung Betwene mr Joseph pinces house & this—see mr Munguells Lease worth aboue Reparacions—(£)2 15s

Mr Mathew Lacy holdeth one tenement for the terme of the lyfe of Thomas Lacy aged 38 yeares vnder the yearely Rent of six pownds this house Consisteth of a kitchin & a large growND Roome now deuided into three littell Roomes, & one other growND Roomes Called a shopp, & a littell Roome one dyhouse a large woodhouse a Lynney a loft ouer a stable & seller all in one large Courtelage & is worth per annum aboue the Rent & Reparacion £8—this tenement is in Bunney lane in St Edmonds parish —£8

mistris Ellenor Dabinett holdeth in mary lane in St mary Stepps one messuage or tenement Consistin of one shopp one kitchin & 2 Chambers for the terme of two middle aged liues vnder the yearely Rent of 1–13–4 & is worth per annum aboue the said Rent & Reparacions 5–0–0

Mr Edward hill holdeth one Tenement in mary lane aforesaid vnder the yearely Rent of £4 10s Consistin of one growND Roome & 2 Chambers very badly Repaired & is worth per annum Cleare of Reparacions £3 10s

Mr Joseph Foxwill holdeth one tenement adioyning to the foresaid tenement Consistin of a growND Roome & 2 Chambers ouer & payeth yearely £3 8s & to be discharged of all things & is worth aboue Reparacion £3 per annum when tis in Good Repaire but now it is very bad & gon much to decay for want of Reparacions —therefore I Count it (£)2 10s Cleare

---

[1]A drang, i.e. a narrow passage.
[2]A linney, or linhay, is an outbuilding generally having a lean-to roof and an open front.

XI DRO, E/CTI 207

John Hingston, city of Exeter.   Inventory made 23 December 1675.

	£	s	d
His wearing Aparrel and bookes	10	0	0
Searges lying in London and Exon	108	0	0
In good debts	270	0	0
one Chattell (lease)	110	0	0
2 Roues of Racks In ye fryers	40	0	0
1 Bill given his son John	54	0	0
money in ye house when he deceased	25	0	0
	617	0	0

In ye dining Chamber

	£	s	d
for Linning	14	8	0
5 silver Boles great and small	10	0	0
4 silver dishes	2	0	0
14 silver spoons	4	4	0
2 sugar Dishes	1	16	0
1 table board	1	10	0
4 Joyne stools		6	0
6 Rushia Chaires	1	12	0
1 great Chair		5	0
1 Livery Cuberd	1	0	0
2 Carpets 6 Cushions and on Cuberd Cloth	3	0	0
6 ordenary Cushions		6	0
1 pair of brass andirons and one pair of Iron andirons with brass heads 1 fire pan and 1 pair of tongs	2	0	0
6 Holland Chaires		6	0
1 stool and 1 litle Chear		5	0
1 remnant of searge	1	10	0
1 Holland round table board		8	0
10 pictures		10	0
	45	6	0

In ye lower study

	£	s	d
1 dozen ½ of Buckerom	4	10	0
1 spruse Chest 1 seller of Bottles 1 ver Box		15	0
1 glass Cage		1	6

In ye chamber adjoyning

	£	s	d
1 press Cuberd and 1 trunck	1	10	0
1 rodden Chair 2 stooles and bellows		10	0
1 featherbed 2 feather bolsters 2 rugs with Curtayns and vallans and 1 bedsteed	8	0	0

J

In ye upper fore Chamber

1 Great Chest and 2 other chests and 2 truncks	1	10	0
1 litle box and 1 litle truncke 1 bed 1 rug 1 bolster 4 pillows 1 Cradlerug and bedsteed	6	10	0
	68	12	6
1 pair of andirons with brass heads 2 pair of tongs brass heads 1 table board 1 fire pan 2 stools 1 Chear		10	0

In ye upper study

2 boxes and 1 bedpan		5	0

In ye Chamber adjoyning

2 Looking Glasses		9	0
1 press Cuberd	1	0	0
1 table board and three joyn stools		6	0
1 Cheare 1 stool and 1 littel truncke		3	0
1 pair of andirons and 1 pair of dogs		4	0
2 rugs 1 featherbed 2 bolsters on bedsteed and 1 trucklebedsteed 4 Curtins and Vallins	8	0	0
1 pear of blankets 1 litle pillow		4	0

In ye Cocklafts

2 bedsteds 2 flock beds 1 feather bed and rug	2	12	6
1 press Cuberd 1 Hanging press	1	0	0
5 pillars 1 bolster 1 blanket	1	10	0
1 distill and 1 Crim bick (limbeck)	1	0	0
	17	3	6

In ye kitchin

202 lbs in puter dishes at 9d per lb	7	11	6
56 lbs in brass kitles at 10d per lb	2	6	8
194 lbs in brass potmetle at 7d per lb	5	13	2
1 pair of pewter Candlesticiks		7	0
1 pair of brass Candlesticks		6	0
4 brass Candlesticks		5	0
3 peuter Candlesticks 1 flagon and 1 salt		10	0
3 brass Chafing dishes 1 skillet 1 pewter pint 1 snuff pan and 1 latine pan		15	0
2 warming pans		10	0
Holland clome and Glassies	1	0	0
1 Jack 4 spits 2 iron dippinge pans 1 pair of Racks 4 gridirons 1 toster and 1 trey	2	13	0
1 table board 3 joyn stooles and 1 rodden Chair		10	0

In ye room and (?under) ye press chamber

1 Iron beeme		2	6
2 qrs of Coal	1	10	0

1 old Cuberd 1 old Coffer 1 old puncion		8	0
12 timber vessels and stiller	2	0	0
	43	11	4

In ye brew house

1 furnace and brewing vessel	3	0	0

In ye press chamber

2 packing presses and papers	9	0	0
2 iron bars and six planks	1	4	0

In ye shop

1 packing press	5	10	0
9 swages		3	0
1 skrane 1 burling board 6 Irons		8	6
3 pair of sheers and Handles and mattin		2	0
	62	18	10

In ye Spence

2 standards 1 dresser board 1 chopping board 1 Coope 3 shelues		10	0
timber in ye court		12	0
for things not seen and unprized		10	0
the total sume	740	3	4

Appraisers: William Dyer, Ambros Page, Christopher Taylor.

XII PRINTED BY H. TAPLEY-SOPER IN *DCNQ*, IX, Pt. 1 (1916-17), 241-242.

Charles Rewallin, virginal maker[1] of the parish of St. Sidwell's. Inventory made 5 July 1697.

	£	s	d
Imprimis his wearing apparell		15	0
one chest in the lower fore chamber	1	5	0
Fyve joynt stools in the same room		3	0
fower chares in the same chamber		6	0
Three boxes and part of a tabell board		6	3
on jack, on spit, on pare and irons and **one pare of dogs**		7	0
two pare of tongs, on firepan and a pot brooke		1	6
one pare of billis (bellows) and a turner of grinding stone		1	0
five stilling irons and on corn bag and on form		2	6
In the higher fore chamber two brass pots and one iron pot		10	0
three brass Kittles on skillet and on pestell and Mortar		8	0
two pewter dishes & on flagon & three candlesticks		2	0
on dissen of tranchers & a salt box		1	0

[1] A virginal made by Rewallin is preserved in the Royal Albert Memorial Museum, Exeter.

in the Easter high chamber on tabell board and on form	3	o
on bed and bedsted	15	o
Three trunks and two boxes	6	o
in the high back chamber on Argon (organ) & on spinet and on littel cabinet	17 5	o
In the loft on half hed bedsted & two boxes	6	o
fower score Argon pipes & Lumber in the house	2 0	o
for old iron	7	o
for goods not seen and unpraysed	5	o
for an organ at the Globe (Inn)	15 0	o

The whole sum is   40 15   3

Appraisers: Martha Rewallin, Richard Venner, Christopher Sandford.

XIII   D & C, Deed 518

St. Sidwells.

A Survey of severall of mr. Longs Tenements lying in St. Sidwells taken by James Bond this 27. June. 1699.

Scituation.	of what it consists.	Rent per Annum to ye Church.	value per Annum aboue the rent.
	The highest Tenement consisting of two ground roomes, a garden being a rodd of land square, with two chambers & a cockloft.	£1 6s 8d	£1 os od
	The lowest Tenement is one low roome with a chamber over, a little drang[1] for a Garden, & a Woodhouse behind it.		
In Longbrooke Streete.	These granted in one Lease.		
	The Mounthouse is next adjoyning, & consists of one ground roome with a chamber over, & then a Cockloft, and behind it a little drang or garden (Garden; together with a Plott o ground, formerly an Orchard; containing from the East part, to the West part, about one hundred foot; and from the North to the South, taking in the Southern Wall, about ninety six foote; And is now 19: March. 1723. in possession of Richard Bedrugges Junior) These are 3 little Tenements	£2 os od	worth nothing aboue ye rent

[1]A small open space.

inhabited by poor people & gone much to decay.

This Tenement consists of a parlour and Kitchin. over them two chambers, & a cockloft
    behind these a Court.

In St. Sidwells Streete a little below the Church as you goe up on ye right hand.

behind that severall Outhouses answering the buildings fronting the Streete.
    then another Little Court & pump. and behind the whole, a garden well stored with fruit trees, being about a quarter of an Acre.
    New built by mr. Long about twenty yeares agoe; this Tenement & the Mounthouse granted in one Lease.

£2 13s 4d   £11   0s 0d

In St. Sidwells Street on the right hand next below the Pound.

Another Tenement being two dwellings. The highest consisting of one low roome and a workhouse, one chamber over, and a Cockloft.
The lowest is one low roome & a workehouse, over them two chambers and a Cockloft
            behind that.
    A Court and brewhouse
A garden runns down in a long strapp behind both, being halfe an Acre and twelve rodds, or thereabouts.
    All the houses built by mr. Long (as he affirmes) since the Restauration.

0   4 0   £5   0s 0d

The Cellar under the high School is about 39 foote in length & 24 foote in breadth
    it lyeth now void in hand.

£0   1s 0d   £3   0s 0d

St. Sidwells.

A Survey of the Widow Maurys Tenement there, taken by James Bond 27. June. 1699.
A ground room with a chamber over. then a little Court.
behind it, another ground room, with a chamber over.
    And behind that a greene plott or Garden.
    Note this 4s. is a new increased rent to ye Church.

£0   4s 0d   £ 3   0s 0d

GLOSSARY

Arabesque — a flowing, interlaced type of ornament.

Barrel Vault — a continuous arched roof or ceiling of semicircular or semi-elliptical section.

Bay — the space between roof-trusses and between wall-posts, not necessarily defined by internal walls. Also the vertical division of a facade by fenestration.

Bead — a small convex moulding of semicircular section.

Bolection Moulding — a projecting moulding framing a panel, doorway, fireplace, etc.

Boss — a projecting decorative feature placed at the intersection of ceiling ribs.

Brace — an inclined subsidiary timber, usually arched, inserted to strengthen a framework. When it connects the rafters to the purlins it is called a *wind-brace*, as it is preventing distortion from wind pressure.

Bracket — a supporting member projecting from the face of a wall.

Bressummer — a load-bearing beam running along the face of a building.

Cable Moulding — a moulding of rope-like appearance.

Camber — the slight rise or upward curve sometimes given to an otherwise horizontal member, such as a collar-beam.

Capital — the top part of a column or pilaster.

Cartouche — a panel with an ornamental frame, usually bearing an inscription or armorial device.

Chamfer — the oblique surface obtained by cutting across the right-angled edge of a beam, jamb, lintel, etc., at an angle of about forty-five degrees.

Collar-beam — a horizontal beam connecting a pair of rafters (principal rafters usually) and placed between the apex and the tie-beam.

Console — a bracket of uniform width with a curved profile.

Coping — the protective capping to a wall or gable.

Corbel — a projecting supporting member built into a wall.

Cornice — a projecting, continuous, decorative feature running along the top of an internal or external wall-face immediately below the ceiling or the roof-line; also along the top of an ornamental fireplace.

Cove, Coving — a concave surface.

Crenellation — battlement.

Crocket — a carved, formalized leaf ornament repeated at regular intervals.

Crucks — pairs of roof supports rising from ground level, or not far above it, and curving over to meet at the apex.

Cusp — in tracery the pointed projection between the leaves of a trefoil, quatrefoil, etc.

Dado Rail — a moulded board running horizontally along the lower part of an interior wall face.

Dragon-beam — a beam running diagonally to the corner of a building, so permitting oversailing of an upper floor on two adjacent sides.

Engaged Column — a column attached to a wall.

Festoon — a carved garland of flowers and fruit hanging between two points on a wall.

Fillet — a narrow flat band or member separating curved mouldings.

Finial — a decorative feature at the apex of a gable.

Fluting — vertical grooves in the shaft of a column or pilaster.

Foil — the almost circular shape formed by cusping. A *trefoil, quatrefoil* and *cinquefoil* consist respectively of three, four and five of these shapes.

Four-centred Arch — a pointed arch each half of which consists of two segments taken from the circumferences of different circles.

Frieze — in an interior that part of the wall immediately below the cornice or ceiling.

Hammer-beam — a short horizontal timber projecting from the top of a wall and helping to support an arch-braced roof-truss.

Heater-shaped — triangular with curved sides.

Hipped Roof — a roof having sloping instead of vertical ends. In a *half-hipped roof* the slope begins well above eaves' level.

Hollow — a concave moulding.

Jetty — the projection or oversailing of an upper floor.

Label — an external moulding projecting above an arch or lintel and designed to throw off rainwater.

Lantern — a turret on a roof, with windows in the sides to light the interior of the building.

Light — one of the main subdivisions of a window between the jambs and the mullions.

Linenfold — carved representation of a piece of linen laid in vertical folds.

Lintel — a horizontal beam or stone bridging an opening.

Lozenge — a diamond-shaped motif.

Mortise — the slot in a timber designed to receive the end, or tenon, of another member that is being jointed to it.

Moulding — a regular ,continuous, contoured surface consisting of a series of adjacent planes and curves.

Mullion — a vertical bar dividing a window opening into lights.

Newel Stair — a spiral stair.

Ogee — a shallow S-shaped curve.

Open Truss — a type of roof-truss that omits the tie-beam.

Oriel Window — a bay window supported above ground level by corbels or brackets.

Ovolo — a convex moulding.

Pediment — a low-pitched triangular gable sometimes used as a decorative feature above doors, windows, etc.

Pendant — a hanging decorative feature.

Pentice — a lean-to roof.

Pilaster — a flat shallow column attached to a wall.

Principals, Principal Rafters — these are the pairs of heavy sloping timbers running from the eaves to the ridge and placed at intervals to form the main roof-trusses; they support the purlins and ridge-tree which in turn support the lighter *common rafters.*

Purlin — the longitudinal roof member lying between and parallel with the wall-plate and the ridge-tree.

Putto (pl. *Putti*) — figure of a small naked boy.

Quoin — a corner-stone.

Rail — horizontal member in a timber frame such as a partition or a door.

Relieving Arch — an arch placed over a lintel to relieve it of much of the weight of the wall above.

Reveal — the vertical side of a door or window opening between the frame and the face of the wall.

Rib — a long narrow member in the decoration of a plaster ceiling.

Ridge-tree — in roof construction this is the longitudinal member at the apex.

Roll — a convex moulding.

Screens Passage — the cross-passage opening on to the service rooms (kitchen, buttery, etc.) and formed by screening off one end of the hall.

Segmental Arch — an arch curved like a segment of the circumference of a circle.

Shouldered Arch — an arch having a step in the curve on either side.

Soffit — underside.

Spandrel — the area between the head of an arch and the rectangular frame enclosing it or between the heads of two adjacent arches.

Splay — the obliquely angled surface created by cutting back the masonry around a door or window opening, for example.

Stop — the termination of a chamfer. This can take many forms, e.g. simply cut off at an angle, hollowed out to make a concave curve, shaped like an urn in profile or like a pyramid cut vertically down the centre.

Strapwork — a form of decoration consisting of flat, interlacing bands.

Stud — vertical timber in the wall of a timber-framed house.

Stud-and-panel — a method of making a partition which consists of fitting flat wooden panels between vertical studs.

Tie-beam — a horizontal timber connecting pairs of rafters at the foot to prevent the roof from spreading outwards.

Transom — a horizontal cross-bar in a window.

Tunnel Vault — a ceiling of semicircular section.

Two-centred Arch — a pointed arch formed by the intersection of two identical segments of the circumference of a circle.

Undercroft — a vaulted room partly or wholly below ground level.

Voussoir — a wedge-shaped stone or brick used in the construction of an arch.

Wagon Roof — a roof of semicircular or semi-elliptical section formed by closely set, arch-braced rafters.

Wall-plate — a longitudinal timber laid on top of a wall.

Wall-post — a vertical wall-timber supporting the end of a main beam.

BIBLIOGRAPHY

Manuscript Sources

CITY OF EXETER MUNIMENT ROOM
    Deeds
    Maps
    Orphans' Court Inventories
EXETER CITY LIBRARY
    ' Clippings ' files on various Exeter streets and buildings
    Old drawings and photographs
EXETER CATHEDRAL LIBRARY
    Bailiffs' Accounts
    Collectors' Accounts
    Deeds
    Property Surveys (MSS. 4573)
DEVON RECORD OFFICE
    Inventories
    Terriers
NATIONAL BUILDINGS RECORD
    Photographs
BRITISH MUSEUM
    Maps
PUBLIC RECORD OFFICE
    Subsidy Rolls

Printed Sources — Books

Bibliography of Exeter, Historical Association Leaflet No. 9 (1908).

Cotton, William, *An Elizabethan Guild of the City of Exeter* (Exeter, 1873).

Cotton, W. and Woollcombe, H., *Gleanings from the Municipal and Cathedral Records relative to the history of the City of Exeter* (Exeter, 1877).

Cresswell, Beatrix F., *Rambles in Old Exeter* (Exeter, 1927).

Cresswell, Beatrix F., *A Short History of the Worshipful Company of Weavers, Fullers and Shearmen of the City and County of Exeter* (Exeter, 1930).

Crocker, James, *Sketches of Old Exeter* (London, 1886).

Dymond, Robert, *The History of the Parish of St. Petrock, Exeter, as shown by its Churchwardens' Accounts and Other Records* (Plymouth, 1882).

Freeman, E. A., *Exeter*, 5th impression (London, 1901).

Harte, Walter J., *Gleanings from the Common Place Book of John Hooker* (Exeter, undated).

Harte, Walter J., *Gleanings from the Manuscript of Richard Izacke's Antiquities of the City of Exeter* (Exeter, undated).

The Description of the Citie of Excester by John Vowell alias Hoker, ed. Walter J. Harte, J. W. Schopp and H. Tapley-Soper, 3 vols., Devon and Cornwall Record Society (1919-47).

Historical Manuscripts Commission, *Report on the Records of the City of Exeter* (London, 1916).

Hoskins, W. G., *Industry, Trade and People in Exeter, 1688-1800*, History of Exeter Research Group, Monograph No. 6 (Manchester, 1935).

Hoskins, W. G., *Old Exeter* (London, 1952).

Hoskins, W. G., *Devon* (London, 1954).

Exeter in the Seventeenth Century: Tax and Rate Assessments 1602-1699, ed. W. G. Hoskins, Devon and Cornwall Record Society, New Series, II(1957).

Hoskins, W. G., *Two Thousand Years in Exeter* (Exeter, 1960).

Izacke, Richard, *Remarkable Antiquities of the City of Exeter* (London, 1681). Also 2nd edition, enlarged and continued down to 1723 by Samuel Izacke (London, 1724).

Jenkins, Alexander, *History of the City of Exeter*, 2nd edition (Exeter, 1841).

Lega-Weekes, Ethel, *Some Studies in the Topography of the Cathedral Close, Exeter* (Exeter, 1915).

MacCaffrey, Wallace T., *Exeter, 1540-1640* (Harvard, 1958).

Letters and Papers of John Shillingford, Mayor of Exeter 1447-50, ed. S. A. Moore, Camden Society (1871).

Oliver, George, *The History of the City of Exeter* (Exeter and London, 1861).

Pickard, Ransom, *The Population and Epidemics of Exeter in Pre-Census Times* (Exeter, 1947).

An Original MS. of John Hooker, Chamberlain of the City of Exeter, 1555, ed. H. E. Reynolds (undated).

Salzman, L. F., *Building in England down to 1540* (Oxford, 1952).

Shapter, Thomas, *The History of the Cholera in Exeter in 1832* (London and Exeter, 1849).

Stephens, W. B., *Seventeenth-century Exeter—a study of industrial and commercial development, 1625-1688*, History of Exeter Research Group, Monograph No. 7 (Manchester, 1958).

White, W., *History, Gazetteer, and Directory of Devonshire* (Sheffield, 1850).

Worth, Charles, *The History of the Suburbs of Exeter* (London, Exeter and Plymouth, 1892).

Guide to St. Nicholas Priory, Exeter, revised Joyce Youings (Exeter, 1960).

Printed Sources—Articles

(Brief articles in *Devon & Cornwall Notes & Queries* are not included)

Adams, Maxwell, ' An Index to the Printed Literature relating to the Antiquities, History and Topography of Exeter ', *TDA*, XXXIII (1901).

Barley, Maurice, ' A Glossary of Names for Rooms in Houses of the Sixteenth and Seventeenth Centuries ' in *Culture and Environment: Essays in Honour of Sir Cyril Fox*, ed. I. Ll. Foster and L. Alcock (London, 1963).

Brushfield, T. N., ' The Financial Diary of a Citizen of Exeter, 1631-43 ', *TDA*, XXXIII (1901).

Clarke, K. M., ' Records of St. Nicholas' Priory, Exeter ', *TDA*, XLIV (1912).

Colby, F. T., ' The Heraldry of Exeter ', *Archaeological Journal*, XXX (1873).

Constable, K. M., ' The Early Printed Maps of Exeter, 1587-1724 ', *TDA*, LXIV (1932).

Cordingley, R., ' British Historical Roof-types and their Members: A Classification ', *Transactions of the Ancient Monuments Society*, New Series, IX (1961).

Cresswell, Beatrix F., ' Tudor House, Exe Island ', *DCNQ*, XIV (1926-27).

Cresswell, Beatrix F., ' Cowick Barton ', *DCNQ*, XVIII (1934-35).

Donaldson, E. A. ' The Inventory of the Goods and Chattels of Mr. Richard Bevys, late Mayor of Exeter, 1603 ', *TDA*, XLI (1909).

Dymond, R., ' Bampfylde House, Exeter ', *Archaeological Journal*, XXXI (1874).

Dymond, R., ' The Old Inns and Taverns of Exeter ', *TDA*, XII (1880).

Emery, Anthony, ' Dartington Hall, Devonshire ', *Archaeological Journal*, CXV (1958).

Erskine, Mrs. A. M. and Portman, D., ' The History of an Exeter Tenement (229 High Street) ', *TDA*, XCII (1960).

Everett, A. W., ' A Note on Bowhill, Exeter ', *Archaeological Journal*, CXV (1958).

Fox, Aileen, ' The Underground Conduits in Exeter, Exposed During Reconstruction in 1950 ', *TDA*, LXXXIII (1951).

French, Kathleen and Cecil, ' Devonshire Plasterwork ', *TDA*, LXXXIX (1957).

Harte, Walter J., ' Illustrations of History from the Act Book of the Chamber of the City of Exeter, 1560-1581—Pt. II ', *TDA*, XLVI (1914).

Harte, Walter J., ' Some data for assessing the population of Exeter at the end of the Seventeenth Century ', *DCNQ*, XX (1938-39).

Hoskins, W. G., ' The Population of Exeter ', *DCNQ*, XX (1938-39).

Hoskins, W. G., ' English Provincial Towns in the Early Sixteenth Century ', *Transactions of the Royal Historical Society*, 5th Series, VI (1956).

Hoskins, W. G., ' The House in the Town ', *The Listener*, 13 June 1957.

Hoskins, W. G., ' The Interior of the House ', *The Listener*, 27 June 1957.

Howard, F. T., ' The Building Stones of Ancient Exeter ', *TDA*, LXV (1933).

Joce, T. J., ' Exeter Roads and Streets ', *TDA*, LXXV (1943).

Jope, E. M. and Dunning, G. C., ' The Use of Blue Slate for Roofing in Medieval England ', *Antiquaries Journal*, XXXIV (1954).

Morris, P., Thorneycroft, W. and Brown, T., 'Report on the Underground Passages in Exeter', *Proceedings of the Devon Archaeological Exploration Society*, I, Pt. 4 (1932). *Notes and Gleanings*

Oliver, Bruce W., 'The Early Seventeenth-Century Plaster Ceilings of Barnstaple', *TDA*, XLIX (1917).

Oliver, Bruce W., 'The Three Tuns, Barnstaple', *TDA*, LXXX (1948).

O'Neil, V. H. St. J. and Russell, P., 'The Old House known as Number Five, Higher Street, Dartmouth', *TDA*, LXXXIII (1951).

Pantin, W. A. and Rouse, E. Clive, 'The Golden Cross, Oxford', *Oxoniensia*, XX (1955).

Pantin, W. A., 'Medieval English Town-House Plans', *Medieval Archaeology*, VI-VII (1962-63).

Pantin, W. A., 'Some Medieval English Town Houses: a Study in Adaptation' in *Culture and Environment: Essays in Honour of Sir Cyril Fox*, ed. I. Ll. Foster and L. Alcock (London, 1963).

Parfitt, E., 'Archaeological Discoveries in Exeter, made during April and May, 1878', *TDA*, X (1878).

Pearson, J. B., 'The Canon in Residence', *TDA*, XLVIII (1916).

Prideaux, E. K., 'Remains of an Ancient Building in Exeter', *DCNQ*, VIII, Pt. 1 (1914-15).

Reed, Harbottle, 'Demolition of Ancient Buildings of Exeter during the last Half Century', *TDA* LXIII (1931).

'Report of the Summer Meeting at Exeter', *Archaeological Journal*, CXIV (1957).

Russell, P. and Everett, A. W., 'The Old House known as Number Thirteen, Higher Street, Dartmouth', *TDA*, XCI (1959).

Smith, J. T., 'Medieval Roofs: A Classification', *Archaeological Journal*, CXV (1958).

Stephens, W. B., 'Roger Mallock, Merchant and Royalist', *TDA*, XCII (1960).

Transactions of the Exeter Diocesan Architectural Society.

INDEX

A NOTE ON THE MEASURED DRAWINGS

Unless otherwise stated solid black represents stone walling or the ends of beams and joists in section; stipple represents brick. Diagonal hatching consisting of closely set, broken lines denotes later infilling. Ordinary broken lines usually designate beams and joists in plan, but occasionally they represent conjectural attempts at reconstruction. Where original window mullions survive they are shown, while a simple straight line indicates that the window is a modern replacement or insertion. An arrow associated with a staircase signifies that it is rising.

Plate 1. Nos. 1-2 Catherine Street before the recent
alterations

Plate 2. No. 9 The Close, once the wing of a large, quadrangular house erected in the
fifteenth century

Plate 3. No. 10 The Close, showing the entrance, with the chapel above, in the
north corner of the courtyard

Plate 4. No. 16 Edmund Street, which has now been removed to a site opposite the church of St. Mary Steps

Plate 5. Nos. 11-12 West Street, at the foot of the medieval Stepcote Hill. The West Gate once stood before these houses and part of the city wall can be seen on the left

Plate 6. A nineteenth century drawing of fifteenth century houses which formerly stood by the old Water Gate leading to the quay

Plate 7. The Butcher Row as it was in 1831

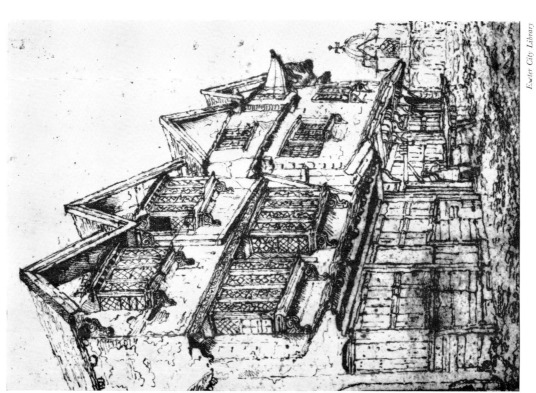

Plate 8. Another part of the Butcher Row

Plate 10.   No. 36 North Street (on the left) from the rear of No. 35, showing the modernized great window in the open hall

Plate 9.   A fifteenth century building, partly of cob, which formerly stood in Egypt Lane.   This photograph was taken soon after it was bombed in 1942

Plate 11. Nos. 45-47 High Street

Plate 12. One method of infilling between the studs shown on the top floor of No. 46 High Street

Plate 13.   The timber-framed Nos. 41-42 High Street, erected in 1564

P. J. Williams

Plate 14. The carved doorhead of No. 41 High Street, bearing the date 1564

Plate 15. Detail of external carving and plaster decoration at No. 226 High Street

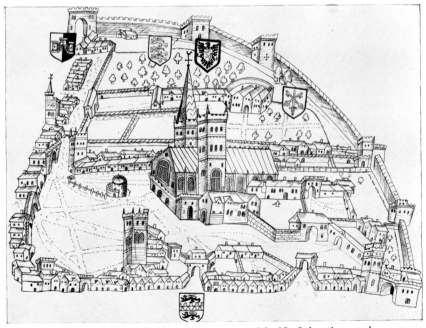

Plate 16. The Cathedral Close in the second half of the sixteenth century, from John Hooker's *The Description of the Citie of Excester*

Plate 18. No. 15 Frog Street, now demolished

Plate 17. An old view of Stepcote Hill showing the Tudor houses which once stood there

Plate 19. Nos. 1-4 The Close. The altered Nos. 1-2 Catherine Street can be seen on the left

Plate 20. Painted decoration of late sixteenth century date on the fifteenth century beam and joists above the first floor at No. 1 Catherine Street

Plate 21. Drawing by Crocker of an Elizabethan
fireplace formerly at No. 229 High Street

Plate 22. Part of a Jacobean plaster ceiling above the first floor at No. 38 North Street

Plate 23. A nineteenth century drawing of the former Nos. 19-20 North Street, a pair of merchants' houses erected *c.* 1600

Plate 24. No. 18 North Street from the rear, showing the enclosed galleries on the first and second floors. The rear block containing the kitchen stood in the foreground until it was bombed in 1942

Plate 25. A later gallery, an open one of seventeenth century date, behind the sixteenth century No. 47 High Street

Plate 26. Drawing by Crocker of an early seventeenth century plaster ceiling of the enriched rib type, formerly at No. 171 Fore Street

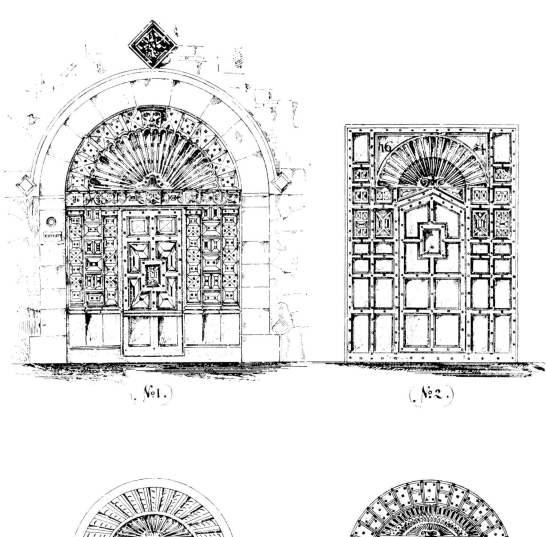

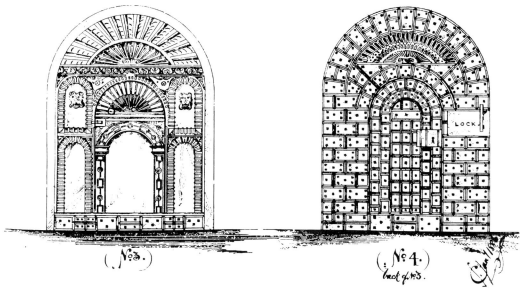

Plate 27. Late sixteenth and seventeenth century doors drawn by Crocker. The first is still at No. 10 The Close; the second, dated 1654, formerly stood opposite St. Sidwell's Church. Drawings Nos. 3 and 4 show the front and back of the door at the Guildhall (c. 1593)

Plate 28. No. 67 South Street, erected *c.* 1600

Plate 29. Original staircase at No. 67 South Street

Plate 30.   Nos. 78-79 Fore Street

Plate 31. The Tudor House, Tudor Street

Plate 32. Detail of the facade of the Tudor House

National Buildings Record

Plate 33. Nos. 36-37 High Street, now demolished

Plate 34. Houses dating from the second half of the seventeenth century outside the old South Gate

Plate 35. Late seventeenth century method of timber-framing. That shown in the bottom right-hand corner is of more recent date

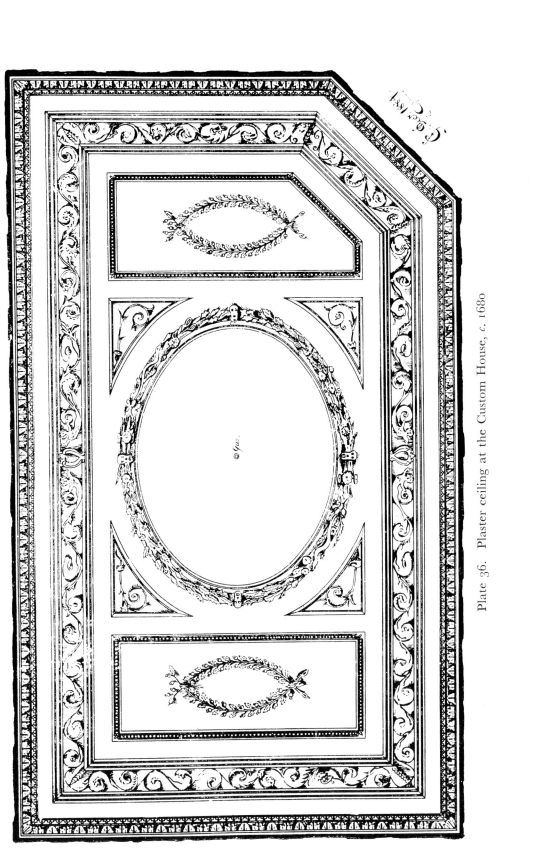

Plate 36. Plaster ceiling at the Custom House, c. 1680

Plate 37. John Abbott of Frithelstock (1640-1727), who made the ceiling shown in Plate 36.
Illustration from *DCNQ*, XIV (1927)

Plate 39. No. 40 High Street

Plate 38. No. 4 Cowick Street, now demolished

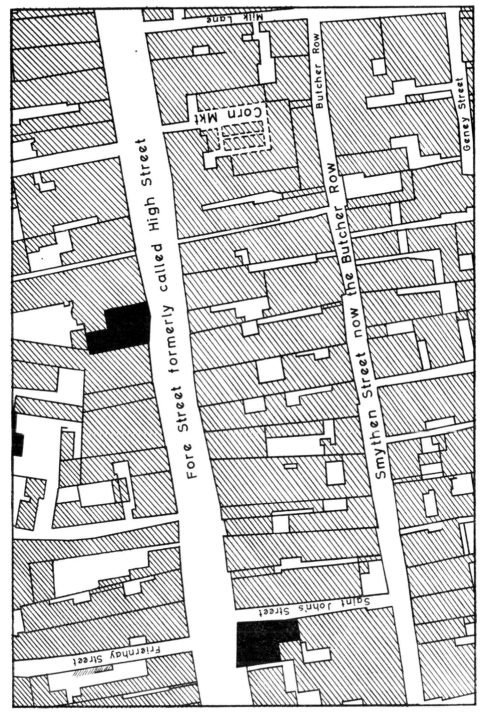

Fig. i. A part of Exeter, based on the plan made by I. Coldridge, Surveyor, in 1818-19 and now deposited in the City Muniment Room. The sites are characteristically long and narrow, and often run through from one street to another. Churches are shown in solid black.

(SCALE: I IN.=APPROX. 80 FT.)

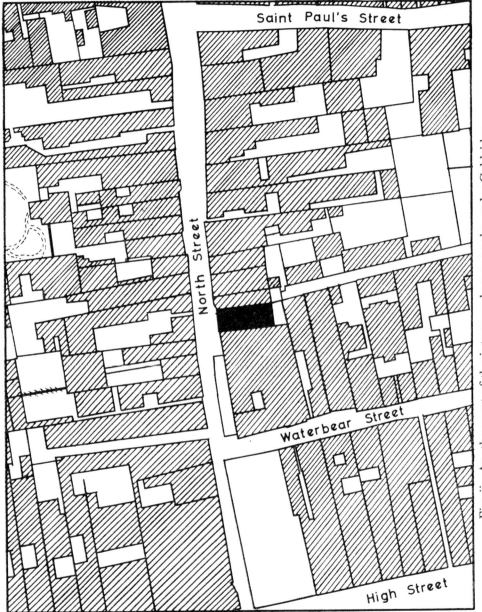

Fig. ii. Another part of the intramural area, as shown by Coldridge.

(SCALE: 1 IN. = APPROX. 80 FT.)

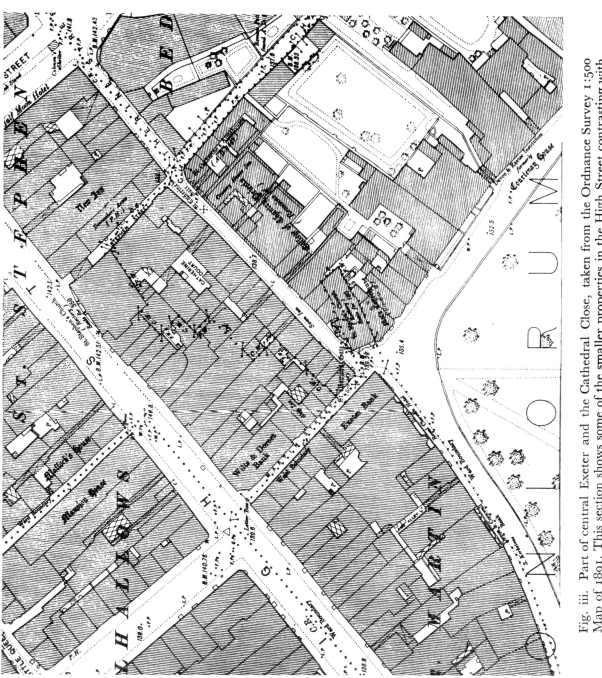

Fig. iii. Part of central Exeter and the Cathedral Close, taken from the Ordnance Survey 1:500 Map of 1891. This section shows some of the smaller properties in the High Street contrasting with the larger buildings in the Close.

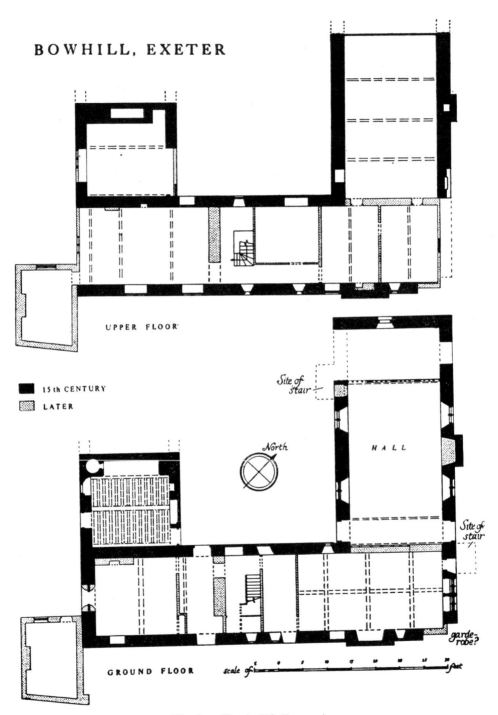

BOWHILL, EXETER

UPPER FLOOR

■ 15th CENTURY

▨ LATER

Site of
stair

HALL

North

Site of
stair

garde-
robe?

GROUND FLOOR   scale of   feet

Fig. iv. (By A. W. Everett)

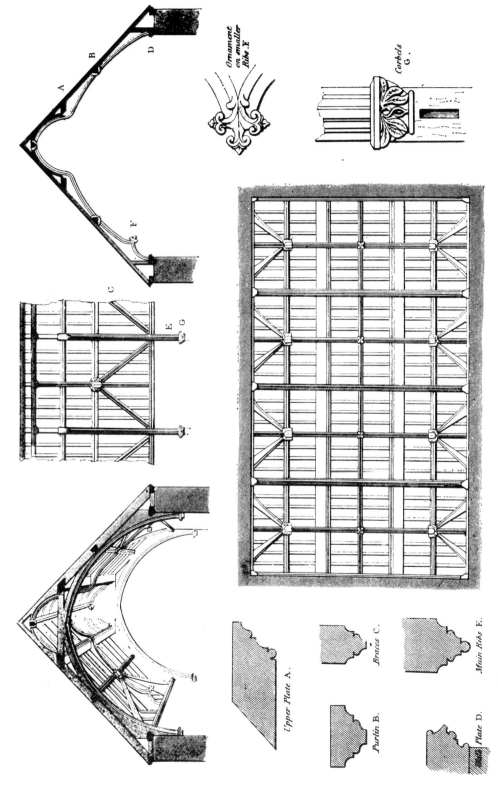

Ornament
on smaller
Rib. F.

Corbels
G.

Upper Plate A.

Purlin B.

Braces C.

Plate D.

Main Ribs E.

Fig. v.   The arch-braced roof at Bowhill, *c.* 1450—illustration from *Trans. Exeter Diocesan Soc.*, I (1843).

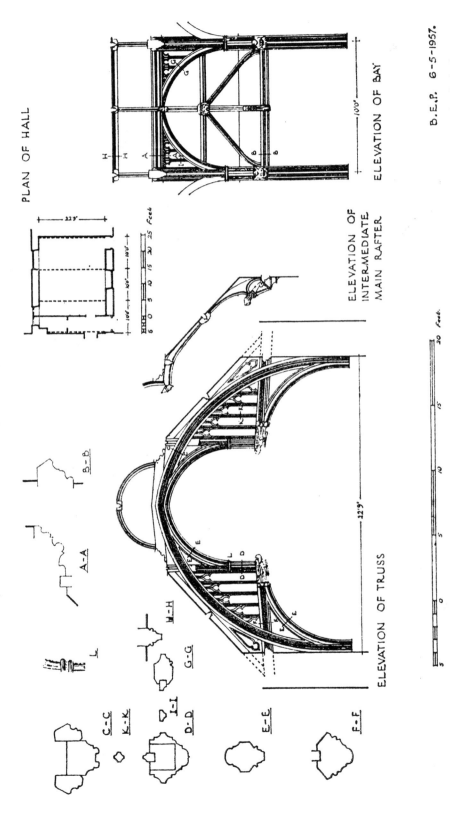

PLAN OF HALL

ELEVATION OF BAY

ELEVATION OF INTERMEDIATE MAIN RAFTER

ELEVATION OF TRUSS

B.E.P. 6-5-1957.

Fig. vi. The Law Library roof, c. 1450. (Plan published by permission of the Ministry of Public Building and Works.)

1 & 2 CATHERINE STREET

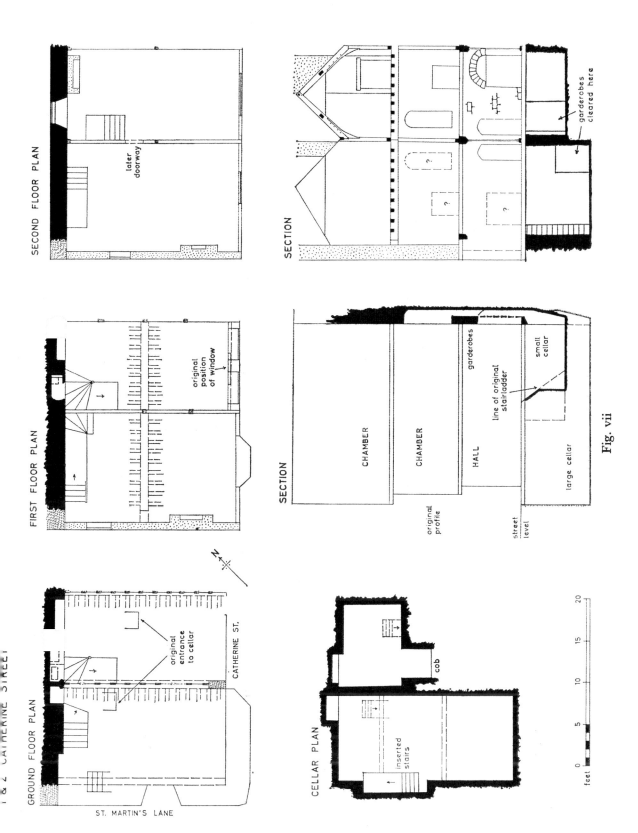

SECOND FLOOR PLAN

later
doorway

FIRST FLOOR PLAN

original position
of window

GROUND FLOOR PLAN

original
entrance
to cellar

CATHERINE ST.

N

ST. MARTIN'S LANE

SECTION

CHAMBER

CHAMBER

HALL

original
profile

garderobes

line of original
stairladder

small
cellar

street
level

large cellar

SECTION

garderobes
cleared here

CELLAR PLAN

inserted
stairs

cob

feet   0   5   10   15   20

Fig. vii

9, 9a & 10 THE CLOSE

GROUND FLOOR PLAN

18th century house

Law Library

Gateway

THE CLOSE

15th century
Kitchen, now in
No.11, originally
part of No.10.

Hall

Chapel
over

well

Gateway

N

feet

0   5   10   15   20

Fig. viii

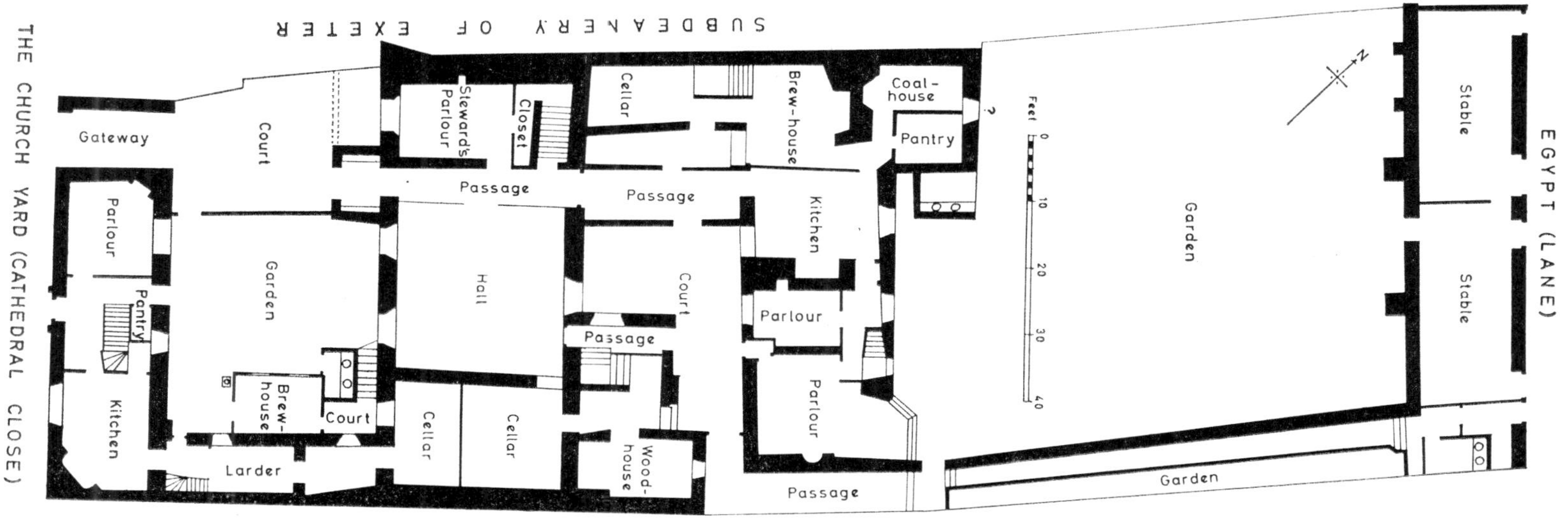

EGYPT (LANE)

Stable

Stable

N

Garden

Garden

Feet 0 10 20 30 40

Coal-house

Pantry

?

Brew-house

Kitchen

Parlour

Parlour

Passage

S U B D E A N E R Y   O F   E X E T E R

Cellar

Passage

Court

Wood-house

Passage

Closet

Steward's Parlour

Passage

Hall

Cellar

Cellar

Court

Court

Garden

Brew-house

Larder

Gateway

Parlour

Pantry

Kitchen

THE CHURCH YARD (CATHEDRAL CLOSE)

Fig. ix. No. 7 The Close. This is based on the plan made in 1764 by John Tothill, surveyor to the Dean and Chapter (see D & C, 6001/6/26). To avoid possible misrepresentation Tothill's method is reproduced here, i.e. solid black denotes not only the stone of which the greater part of the building is constructed, but also the timber-framed internal partitions.

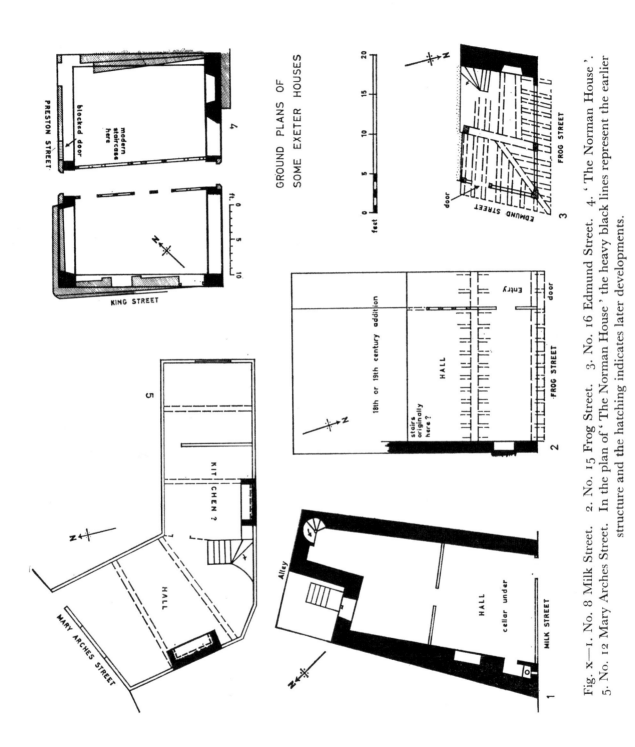

GROUND PLANS OF
SOME EXETER HOUSES

Fig. x—1. No. 8 Milk Street. 2. No. 15 Frog Street. 3. No. 16 Edmund Street. 4. ' The Norman House '.
5. No. 12 Mary Arches Street. In the plan of ' The Norman House ' the heavy black lines represent the earlier
structure and the hatching indicates later developments.

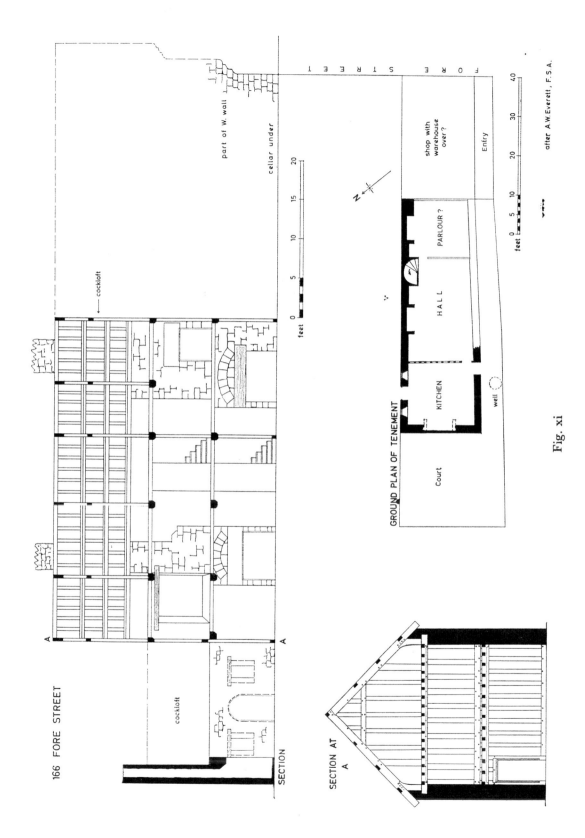

166 FORE STREET

cockloft

part of W. wall

cellar under

cockloft

SECTION

feet 0 5 10 15 20

SECTION AT
A

GROUND PLAN OF TENEMENT

Court

KITCHEN

well

HALL

PARLOUR ?

shop with
warehouse
over ?

Entry

FORE STREET

N

feet 0 5 10 20 30 40

after A.W.Everett, F.S.A.

Fig. xi

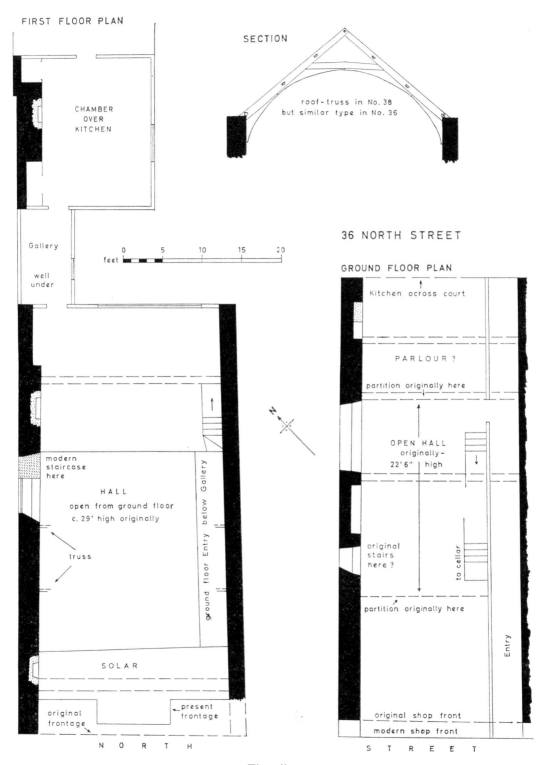

38 NORTH STREET

FIRST FLOOR PLAN

CHAMBER OVER KITCHEN

SECTION

roof-truss in No. 38 but similar type in No. 36

Gallery

well under

feet 0   5   10   15   20

36 NORTH STREET

GROUND FLOOR PLAN

Kitchen across court

PARLOUR ?

partition originally here

N

OPEN HALL originally— 22'6" high

modern staircase here

HALL

open from ground floor c. 29' high originally

ground floor Entry below Gallery

truss

original stairs here ?

to cellar

partition originally here

SOLAR

original frontage

present frontage

Entry

original shop front

modern shop front

N   O   R   T   H

S   T   R   E   E   T

Fig. xii

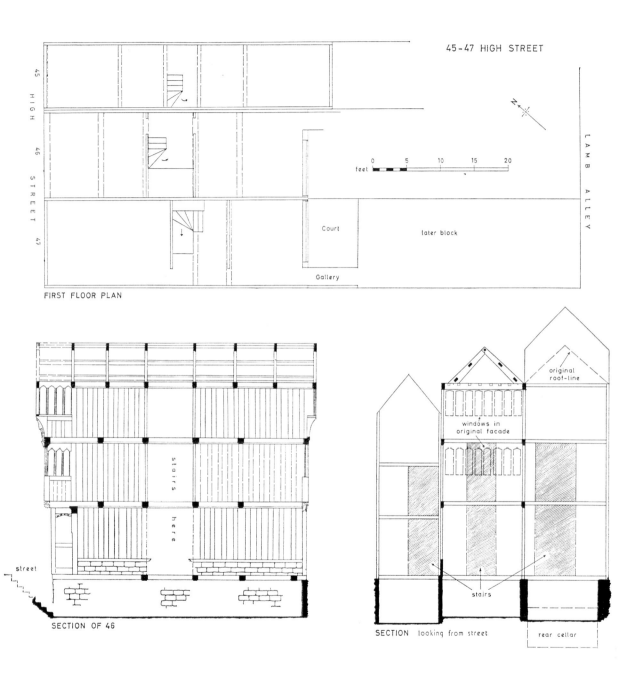

45-47 HIGH STREET

45 HIGH 46 STREET 47

LAMB ALLEY

Court

later block

Gallery

feet 0 5 10 15 20

FIRST FLOOR PLAN

stairs here

street

SECTION OF 46

original roof-line

windows in original facade

stairs

rear cellar

SECTION looking from street

Fig. xiii

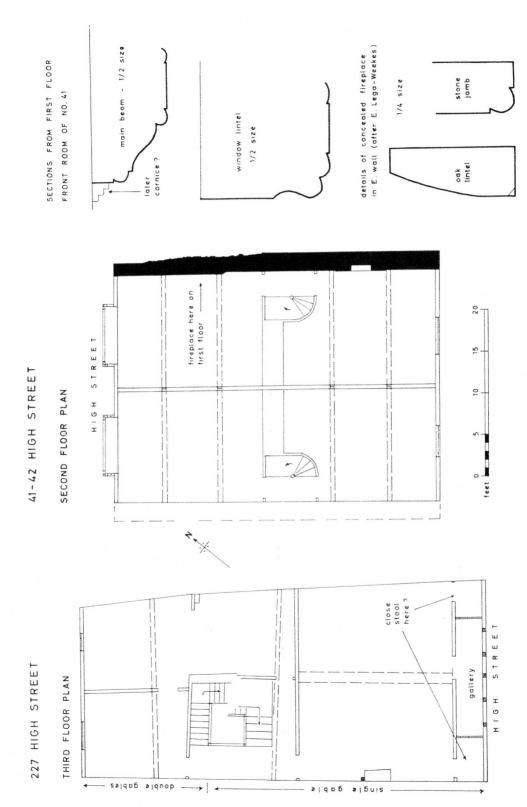

SECTIONS FROM FIRST FLOOR
FRONT ROOM OF NO. 41

main beam - 1/2 size

later cornice ?

window lintel
1/2 size

details of concealed fireplace
in E. wall (after E. Lega-Weekes)
1/4 size

stone jamb

oak lintel

41-42 HIGH STREET

SECOND FLOOR PLAN

HIGH STREET

fireplace here on
first floor

N

feet   0   5   10   15   20

227 HIGH STREET

THIRD FLOOR PLAN

close stool here ?

gallery

HIGH STREET

double gables   single gable

Fig. xiv

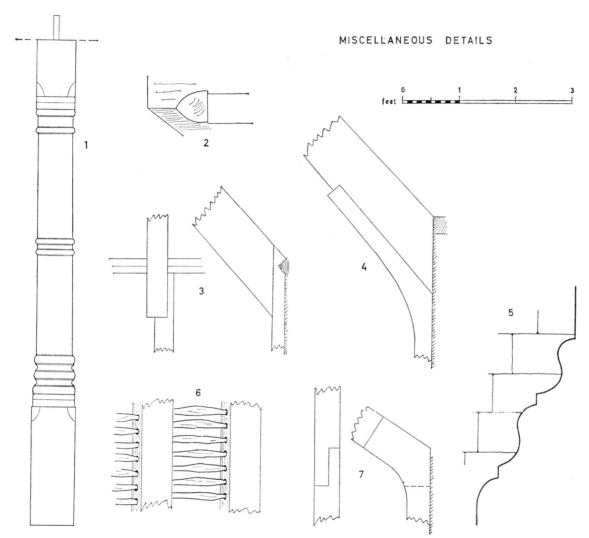

Fig. xv—1. Storey-post supporting gallery formerly at No. 229 High Street (*R.A.M. Museum*). 2. Raised hollow stop, not to scale. 3. Part of roof-truss, *c.* 1600, at No. 18 North Street. 4. Part of roof-truss at rear of No. 36 North Street and at Nos. 3-5 Cathedral Yard. 5.Corbelling of stone party wall at No. 41 High Street, approximately to scale. 6. Sixteenth century method of infilling from former No. 57 Preston Street (*R.A.M. Museum*). 7. Part of seventeenth century roof-truss at No. 40 High Street.

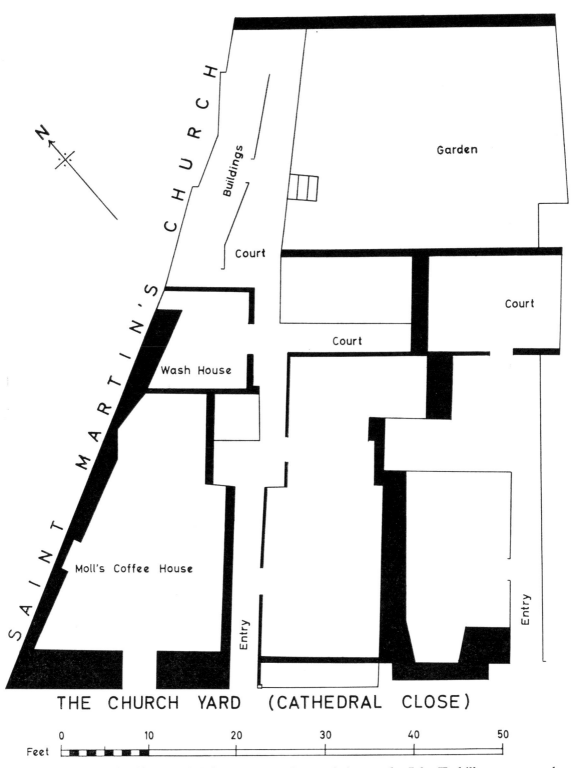

N

S A I N T   M A R T I N ' S   C H U R C H

Buildings

Garden

Court

Court

Court

Wash House

Moll's Coffee House

Entry

Entry

THE   CHURCH   YARD   (CATHEDRAL   CLOSE)

Feet
0   10   20   30   40   50

Fig. xvi. Nos. 1-3 The Close. This is based on the plan made in 1775 by John Tothill, surveyor to the Dean and Chapter (see D & C, 6004/13/35). Again, to avoid possible misrepresentation Tothill's method is reproduced here, i.e. solid black denotes both stone and timber-framed walling.

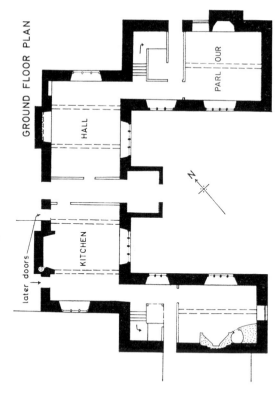

OLD MATFORD HOUSE, WONFORD ROAD

GROUND FLOOR PLAN

cob walls

PARLOUR ?

modern
addition

HALL

modern
insertion

KITCHEN ?

N

FRONT ELEVATION

Arms

original
mullions

later
buttress

feet 0 5 10 15 20

COWICK BARTON, COWICK LANE

GROUND FLOOR PLAN

HALL

KITCHEN

later doors

PARLOUR

N

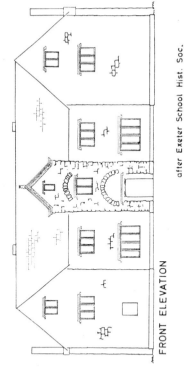

FRONT ELEVATION

after Exeter School Hist. Soc.

Fig. xvii

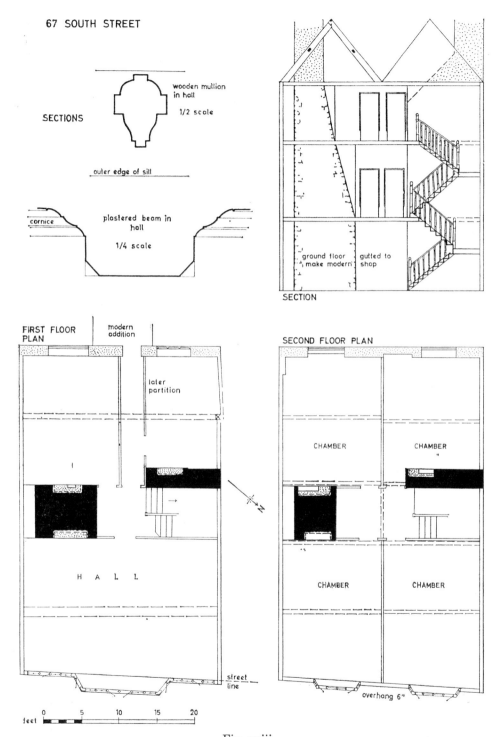

67 SOUTH STREET

SECTIONS

wooden mullion
in hall

1/2 scale

outer edge of sill

cornice

plastered beam in
hall

1/4 scale

SECTION

ground floor
make modern

gutted to
shop

FIRST FLOOR
PLAN

modern
addition

later
partition

HALL

street
line

SECOND FLOOR PLAN

CHAMBER

CHAMBER

CHAMBER

CHAMBER

overhang 6"

0   5   10   15   20

feet

Fig. xviii

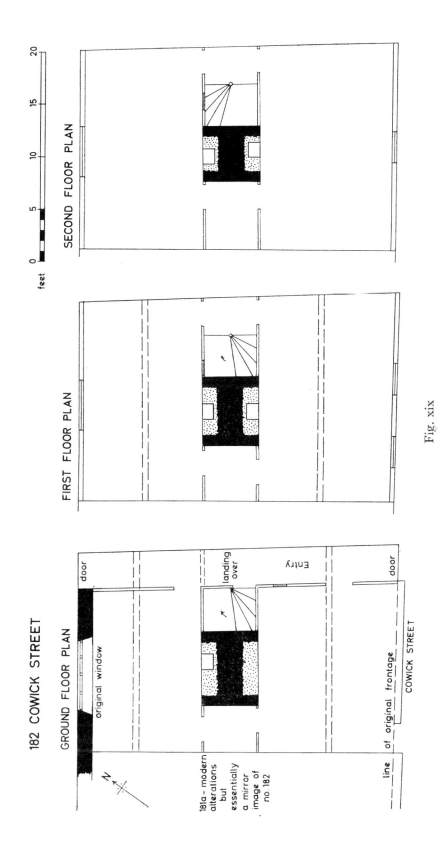

Fig. xix

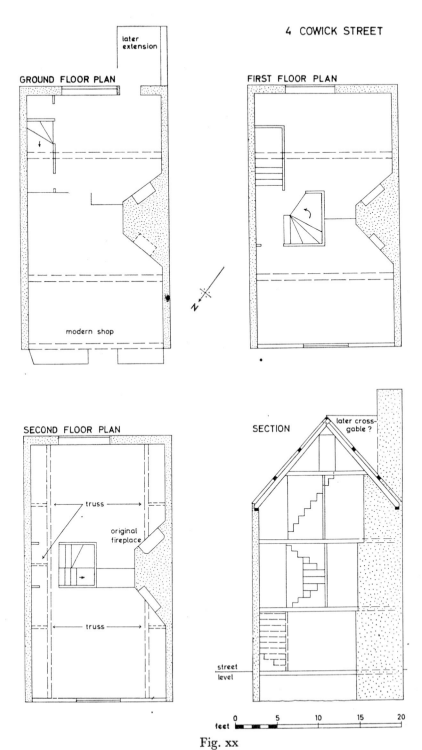

4 COWICK STREET

GROUND FLOOR PLAN

later extension

modern shop

FIRST FLOOR PLAN

N

SECOND FLOOR PLAN

truss

original fireplace

truss

SECTION

later cross-gable ?

street level

feet 0 5 10 15 20

Fig. xx